Gramps' Tales

E. Stanley Martin and His Stories

February 2008

To Annette —

Thanks for your interest in my first big book project — I think you'll really enjoy meeting my Gramps and especially reading the stories he wrote — Love from Kris Bush

Compiled with Commentary by

Kristin Harper Bush

Kristin Harper Bush

To order additional copies of this book, contact:
Xlibris Corporation
1-888-795-4274
www.Xlibris.com
Orders@Xlibris.com
42571

Contents

For Leland Bruce Turner,
Gramps' cousin and my dear friend.
Thanks for your wonderful memories
of Gramps' younger years, life along the Wabash,
and your Navy adventures in WWII.
We met up at Embarrass,
and you made them all dance with joy.
Rest in Peace.

Cousin Bruce Turner introduces Cousin Abner Wood at Embarrass Cemetery, Edgar County, IL.

Acknowledgements

At the beginning of 1997 my husband Robert and I purchased our first Personal Home Computer—a Compaq Presario with all the trimmings. My son James (Ball) seemed to have some genetic predisposition to an innate understanding of the inner workings of both this elusive machine and its vast internet partner. I am grateful to and proud of James for not only maintaining my equipment and constantly pushing me to update over the years, but also for his own brilliant ideas and technique as a writer, which have kept me either intensely thoughtful or hilariously laughing since he was about eight years old. Your book is next, James.

My sister Kelly had long since been following Gramps' (and Dad's) footsteps with the family history, and was way ahead of me in the world of technology, and she graciously loaded me up with discs of our genealogies as a starting place for further research. Since that time she has proven to be a great source of details for the genealogy, as well as family photo archives and any kind of software technical advice on formatting that I might need. Thanks Kel; partners, buddies and pals.

My dad, Jim Harper, was certainly susceptible to the thrill of family history research, and with some inspiration and guidance from his father-in-law, along with a trunk full of Harper and related memorabilia left him by his grandfather in 1965, he made and recorded many genealogical discoveries of his own. Our family vacation in 1966 took us through several states, east to Indiana, Ohio and Kentucky, with Dad calling distant relations and visiting old cemeteries all along the way.

Mom is the younger of E. Stanley Martin's two daughters, and reflects clearly his love of family and history, his attention to detail, and his love of adventure. Her exceptional talent in photography focuses on photo processing, restoring and retouching, as well as graphic arts, and she seems to have leapt the generation gap to an amazing ease with all of her computer tools. In addition, she is a wonderful story-teller, and both she and Dad have always demonstrated for us the importance of family ties, the creating of memorable family events and the detailed recording of those for posterity. I love you both for passing that forward.

My biggest thanks goes to Mom for handing me those boxes of Gramps' papers; for trusting me to process family details and his fabulous stories, and to move forward with this book. You have come through with so many stories, anecdotes, memories, and photographs, at a time of great transitions in your life, and with few complaints as I pressed you for more. You're a "keeper", and your delight in all the Martin history, the Photo Shop, and the Uncles and cousins has always been quite contagious and easily understood.

There are many people who support a project like this; Jim Gilson at the Vigo County Library; Dorothy Nicholson at the Indiana Historical Society; countless clerks and admins who generously look for and share needed information; family members and friends who share memories and kudos; and the added bonus of re-connecting with second and third Martin cousins, offspring of Gramps' brothers, who share the Martin Photo Shop legacy. From cousin Meredith's recent California wedding to our new partnership in the loving ministry[1] of cousins Tim and Dawn Patterson in Moscow, Russia, I am grateful for a large extended family that reflects Great Grandfather Frank J Martin's common saying, "Keep it sweet".

Finally, I am so blessed to have married my high school sweetheart, Robert Bush. He cheers me on, listens to infinite readings and ideas, and pulls me away to feed me or send me to bed when the book is "too much with me". Thank you for making such beautiful music for me and with me, you are my love. Allow me to proudly, and at long last, introduce you to my Gramps, E Stanley Martin.

Chapter 1

Remembering Gramps

This is a chronicle of the life of an extraordinary Midwestern man in plain clothes. One of the "Great Generation", my grandfather E. Stanley Martin was born fifth of eight children into a family of renowned Hoosier photographers at the dawn of the twentieth century.

Willard Martin and his father, Frank, in the back, and a young blonde Stanley in front, then Lawrence, Ray, Mother Ella, Esther and Kenneth; Stewart was not yet born. Abt.1915, Photo by Martin

His hunger for experiential and self-directed learning made him an insatiable reader, a cutting edge photographer, an avid horticulturalist, a meticulous federal IRS Inspector, and a "damn good" carpenter. He served two tours of duty in the United States Army, one in the late 1920's and again during WWII. But perhaps most revealing, and certainly reflecting a kaleidoscope of his life and accomplishments, are his stories and poems, which gave way in the last ten years of his life to an extensive genealogical study of his extended family and ancestors.

In his teens, and again as a young man and a middle-aged one, Mr. Martin dreamed of writing professionally, and took correspondence courses and college classes to that end. He made many submissions of poems and short stories to fine publications of the time—Colliers, Readers Digest, and Saturday Evening Post. Each time it would seem he was approaching success, family or federal work obligations would forge a detour, culminating finally with the death of his mother in 1956, when confused memories of ancestors now departed precipitated a sibling agreement that Stanley should spearhead an in-depth study of the Martin Progenitors. From that time until his death in 1969, his creative writing energy was poured into letters of inquiry to remote cousins all over the United States, and biographical sketches of his Irish, German, British and Scottish ancestors and their descending farmers, teachers, doctors and soldiers.

In 2004 my mother handed me two old file boxes, presumably of my grandfather's family history materials. To my surprise and pleasure, along with an astounding number of files filled with letters, Christmas Cards, and hand written or manually typed and "mimeographed" family trees and biographies, they contained a large stack of Grandpa's original stories and poetry. As I read his stories, I could see how powerfully they reflected and meshed with his autobiography, letters, and true life story. In this book I have transcribed the stories and woven them with narrative information to weave a portrait of my grandfather.

I was a twelve year old girl when Grandpa Martin died of complications from colon cancer. The important things I remember about him? He always had little packs of Chiclets gum in his pockets for us to find. He helped us plant seeds and bulbs, and grow radishes, zinnias, dahlias, and gladiolus. Once I helped him *sift* the soil of his entire backyard for better planting! He taught us card games and Scrabble and Cribbage. He took me to the Diving Bell at San Francisco's Playland, Golden Gate Park—the Arboretum and Aquarium, Fleischaker Zoo, and the Luther Burbank Gardens in Santa Rosa. He taught me to love Golden Delicious Apples, to core and cut them in quarters for evening snacks. He taught me to make a standard white sauce for Eggs a la Goldenrod—and insisted that I memorize the recipe[2].

Gramps and Gram helped me memorize "Little Orphan Annie" by the Hoosier poet James Whitcomb Riley, when I was three—and then when I recited it at the school where Gram taught, Gramps tugged his pants pockets out to the side daintily and showed me how to do a pretty *curtsey* when I was finished! He helped my brother put an amazing rock collection together, and he taught my sister to graft an apple tree, from a seed out of her lunch apple, in a wet napkin on the windowsill! That tree still stands behind his old home on West Third Street in Santa Rosa. He pushed us on swings and park-go-rounds, spun us like airplanes, and carried us high on his shoulders. In his grumbly-growly voice he sang us to sleep with "There is a Tavern in the Town" (much to Gram's amusement). And from the time he handed me my first Brownie box camera, he made it known that all family photographers, no matter their age, merited the respect and full cooperation of any subjects they chose to "shoot"[3].

Gramps sends granddaughter Kristy to deliver a Christmas package, 1959

I remember the story book Grandpa, and have come to know the man behind the story through his writing. And I've had to stop and consider how my own passions reflect his. On the side of contrast, perhaps I traded his interest in federal employment and workings for my own true musical talent and education—but give me a plot of land for a garden full of food, trees and flowers; a deluxe camera in my hand to record life's beauty; time (and a computer!) for genealogical research, and a good word processor where I can lay down my life stories and ideas, memories and philosophies.

Gramps joins the Harper grandkids, including Kristy, in Christmas cookie decorating, 1968

As a high school junior I read Kurt Vonnegut's new book, "Breakfast of Champions". I had been an insatiable reader since the age of 3 or 4, but this novel was so, as we say now, "outside the box". There I was, lost in the bizarre and dark humor of Kilgore Trout and Dwayne Hoover, when the narrative voice suddenly became a character in the book. He actually inserted himself into the novel, and in doing so, became an all-powerful character, a sort of cosmic director, with all characters and circumstances dancing to his tune. That's the moment I knew I had to write. I was compelled, to let the ink pour out of my heart and my thoughts; to preserve the poignancy of life and create it any way I chose. What a ride!

My grandfather was given his wings to fly, a long time ago. He would have reached his hundredth birthday in August of 2006. These collected stories and commentaries give him simple shoes out of time, to walk with you a while. Maybe he'll inspire you to take a picture, write a letter, smell the roses. Gramps probably would have said, "A picture is worth a thousand words . . . . and vice versa."[4]

Kristy and Gramps, both lost in thought, 1968. Merry Noel doll in the background belongs to Kristy's mother, Nancy Gene Martin Harper

Chapter 2

Autobiography
And Genealogy Years

September 21, 2001

At this writing I am looking at a stack of tissue paper carbon copies of letters written by Gramps Martin to so many of his friends and relatives. I suppose they almost qualify as genuine "antiques"—isn't it the fifty year mark which determines that? Well, all I know is that their beginning matches my own; that is to say that he began his quest for family history in 1956—the year his mother died, and I was born.

As I have gone through the huge file of correspondence and notes that Gramps saved over the years, I have had to make decisions about the massive files Gramps put together in just over a decade of research. One person's throw-aways can so easily be another person's treasures, and in many cases I have done data entry on my end and then searched for descendants who might like to have original copies of letters from their grandparents or great-grandparents in their hands. I suppose not everyone in the family got the "pack-rat" gene!

These letters did their job at the time of mailing. They bonded relationships, inspired closeness, exchanged information, expanded research, answered questions. Some were well written and entertaining; others were more perfunctory and dry. All were typed and carbon copied on a manual typewriter (1956-67). Oh, how I would love to pack up my PC and send it back a half-century to give Gramps a taste of how a word processor would change his life! And let's not even start with family history/genealogy software and online resources! His tools were his typewriter, a stack of 4-cent stamps, a station wagon, and pure determination and wit.

The files containing these letters also stored responses, most of them hand-written, from friends and relatives across these United States. The contents of those responses are entered to the family database both as historical data and as personal histories and tales of happy and sad times in the lives of our ancestors and cousins. Original copies of many of those letters have been sent to descendants of the folks who wrote them—making yet another lovely bond of family with the new generation, as well as putting personal family histories in the hands of those who would treasure them most, and who may not have been as meticulous as Gramps about preserving them.

With a large pile of these letters on my desk, I am attempting to piece together a picture of Gramps as he brought the family together with this work. I will include excerpts from the letters, sometimes paraphrased, and sometimes verbatim. Some pictures are formed by parts of several letters. Sometimes it is the responses that are telling. Genealogy is always a work in progress, and I always feel like I am starting in the middle . . . though I suppose that when the branches are filled in and the ancestry chart reads "Adam and Eve"—well, that's a "cut and print"—right?

—Kristin Joy Harper Bush

*   *   *

Let me start by saying this is in no way intended to be a complete history of my grandfather, Earl Stanley Martin. He was born August 1, 1906, the year of the San Francisco Earthquake.

This particular writing begins in the year of my birth, 1956. For Gramps, it was the year he lost his mother, and the year of his fiftieth birthday. Early in his research, (1960), he did write his own autobiographical information, as follows:[5]

> *"Stanley, fifth of the eight children born to Frank J and Ella Hockett Martin, was born at the family home on North Seventh Street Road, at Lee Avenue, half a mile north of the city limits of Terre Haute, Indiana, August 1, 1906.*
>
> *A precocious child, he began reading at the age of five, under the able tutelage of his paternal grandmother, and at the age of seven entered the Fort Harrison School near his home where he finished the third grade during his first year of school. The Fort Harrison school being a six-grade school, he attended the seventh and eighth grades at the Rankin School a mile east of his home, attended the Indiana*

State Normal Training High School for his freshman year, and then continued his high school education at Garfield High School in Terre Haute. Seized with wanderlust, he interrupted his schooling in 1923 for a trip around the country and a fling at various odd jobs, returned to Garfield for the spring and fall semesters in 1924, and then abandoned his efforts at education until he completed his high school by examination at the State Board of Regents in 1933.

Photo by Frank J Martin; Back steps of family home in Terre Haute, Indiana, the children are Ray, Lawrence, Stanley, and Kenneth is on Willard's lap, About 1910

Stanley worked at various jobs, including the sessions at the family photo studio at which he had worked at odd times since 1918, until he enlisted in the army in February 1927. In May 1929, while in Terre Haute on furlough before proceeding to the Panama Canal Zone as Department Photographer, he married Margaret Moore. In October 1929 he purchased discharge from the army because of a lack of suitable quarters for his wife at Corozal⁶, Canal Zone, where he was stationed, returned to Terre Haute to work for a while at the Columbian Stamping and Enameling Mill, and then took over the Albert Studio at Sullivan, Indiana. In the spring of 1931, with the Depression in full swing, this business and the marriage to Margaret went on the rocks coincidentally with the birth of their daughter, Kay Ann. Margaret instituted divorce proceedings and was granted sole custody of the child.

Stanley worked at home portraiture for a while in Milwaukee, and then returned home to help his father in the flower gardens he ran in his spare time as an avocation. In 1932 he met Mabel at the Breden Memorial United Baptist Church, where his sister Esther was a member, and in September (he and Mabel were married).

Mabel, second of three children of Elmer and Maude McKinney Thomson, was born while her parents were living at the "Parker Farm" about three miles west and two miles south of Fairbanks, Indiana, May 8, 1908. She attended first grade at Fairbanks School in 1914, second grade at the Wilson school southwest of Crawfordsville, Indiana, transferred to the Mills School in Crawfordsville during her third year, and continued there through sixth grade, and then attended Crawfordsville junior High School through the eighth grade. In the fall of 1921 she entered Wiley High School in Terre Haute, Indiana, as a freshman, and graduated in the spring of 1925. Three days after her graduation from high school she entered Indiana State Teacher's College at Terre Haute for the two year primary teacher's course, and attended continuously through the summer session of 1926. She then taught at Wallace, Indiana during the winter of 1926-27, returned to Indiana State for the summer session in 1927, taught at Elkhart, Indiana during the winter of 1927-28, attended the early summer session at Vincennes University, Vincennes, Indiana, in 1928, and the late summer session at Indiana State, to complete and receive her Primary Certificate.

In the fall of 1928 Mabel began teaching first grade at Greenwood School in Terre Haute, where she continued four years until June of 1932. In the summer of 1929 she attended Michigan State Normal at Ypsilanti, Michigan, where she took up the study of remedial teaching. During these years she taught a Sunday School class and sang in the choir at Breden memorial United Baptist Church, and it was here that Stanley found her in 1932.

At the time of their marriage Mabel was under contract to teach at the Mary Emma Jones School in Greencastle, Indiana, with the understanding that she was to remain unmarried. Stanley and Mabel, therefore, were married quietly in Marshall, Illinois, and she began teaching three days later at Greencastle, but found it necessary to resign her position in October when she developed a severe case of Erysipelas on her leg. They set up housekeeping for a while on South 19th Street in Terre Haute, and then moved to his parents' home on North Seventh Street, where Stanley helped with the gardening in the summers and did photographic work during the winter. In the fall of 1933 they went to Harrisburg, Pennsylvania, where Stanley was a department store photographer through the Christmas Season, and then returned to Terre Haute where he worked at the family studio. In the spring of 1934 Nancy was born, and in the fall of 1934 they moved to Amarillo, Texas, where Stanley was photographer for the McCormick Engraving Company, and remained there until the spring of 1935, when Stanley went to work for the Alcohol Tax Unit of the Internal Revenue Service with which he is still serving in 1960.

Stanley's initial work with the Alcohol Tax Unit was the inspection of taverns, which kept him moving and away from home, so in the fall of 1935 and spring of 1936 Mabel and Nancy joined him on the road, first in Hammond, Indiana, and later in East St Louis and Springfield, Illinois. In the fall of 1936 Stanley was sent to Terre Haute for storekeeper-gauger duty there, and the family set up housekeeping in the 1500 block on South 8th Street, and, after a few months, moved to Stanley's "home place" on North 7th Street Road, which he was purchasing from his mother. It was here that John was born July 6, 1937. In the winter of 1938-39 Stanley sold his interest in the home place to his brother, Kenneth, and moved the family to 1705 South 11th Street, where they shared an 11 room house with Mary Fuson and her two children, Jack and Nancy May, for whom Nancy Gene martin had been named. Because the house had been sold, they found it necessary to move just at the time Peter was expected to arrive in July 1939. For this event, Mabel went to the hospital from the house on South 11th Street, and returned to her home in the "Heidenreich" house in the 2500 block on South 8th Street. In February 1940 the family moved to 1708 North 8th Street.

In August 1940, at a convention in Louisville, Kentucky, Stanley was elected President of the National Association of Storekeeper-Gaugers, which office he held through the convention in New York in 1941 and until September 1942 when he resigned that office and his job as storekeeper-gauger with the Alcohol Tax Unit, to enlist in the Signal Corps at Fort Monmouth, New Jersey, under the command of Brigadier General George L VanDusen, in whose outfit he had served in 1927-29. Graduated from O.C.S. in March 1943, he served as a second lieutenant and first lieutenant, first at Ft Monmouth until April 1943, and then at Camp Pinedale, Fresno, California, until separated and placed in reserve status October 1, 1945.

E Stanley Martin in uniform, 1943, U.S. Army, WWII, Photo by Martin

His family had joined him in Fresno in May, 1943, to live at 331 Abby Street. It was here that Carl Frederick Martin was born March 27, 1944, with Thelma Hatfield, wife of Sgt Carl Hatfield for whom Carl was named, in attendance.

E. Stanley Martin in uniform, with children Nancy Gene, John Thomson, and Peter David in uniforms designed and made by their mother, Mabel Thomson Martin. Photo by Willard Martin at the Martin Photo Shop in 1943

From Fresno in October 1945 the family journeyed to Allens Park, Colorado, and remained into January, visiting with Mabel's sister, Elah, and her husband, Stuart Gore. The family then returned to Terre Haute, and Stanley returned to storekeeper-gauger duty at the Distilleries, but the family had been bit by the California bug, so Stanley requested and was granted transfer to duty in California. In May 1946 he reported for duty in California, and was given a post of duty at Napa, where his family soon joined him, living first at Vallejo, and then at Napa, in the government housing at Shipyard Acres. In 1948 Stanley was promoted to Inspector, with duty station at San Francisco, so the family again moved to Vallejo, within commuting distance of the city. Here, in 1949, Mabel returned to teaching school, first as a substitute and then under contract, with emergency and then provisional credentials, and began taking extension courses leading to her Bachelor of Education Degree, which she received in 1955, just 30 years after she graduated from high school.

Assigned to the Santa Rosa post of duty as resident inspector in 1953, Stanley moved the family there in August that year, living first at 720 Hurlbut Avenue, Sebastopol. Mabel transferred her teaching activities from Vallejo to Santa Rosa, and was assigned to teach the coaching class at Lincoln School, which she has since continued to teach with the exception of one year each at Burbank and Fremont Schools.

The house on Graton Rd that Stanley and his family lived in when they moved to Sebastopol in 1955

The house Stanley and Mabel purchased on Palomino Dr in Santa Rosa in 1956.

The family moved to 10945 Graton Rd, Sebastopol, in August 1955, where they lived for a year, and in August 1956 bought the house at 503 Palomino Drive, Santa Rosa, California, where they are currently (1960) living.

Stanley and Mabel are members of the First Baptist Church of Santa Rosa.

How It Started

In March of 1956, a couple of months after the death of his mother, and a couple of months before the birth of his granddaughter (me!), Gramps sent out the first of what was to become hundreds, maybe thousands, of inquiries to family members and "suspected" family members. This first letter was sent, wisely, to his Aunt Maude, sister to Frank James Martin, who became a wealth of information and support to Gramps through a decade of family research.

"Dear Aunt Maude;

I am a little tardy in writing to tell you how much I enjoyed seeing you again when I went through Chicago recently. I was delayed in writing because of a project that I am working on.

After mother's services the family gathered at Willard's and we sat around discussing this and that. We were chagrined to find that many things, which we thought were indelible in our memories, could not be recalled—facts about the family we thought we all knew. I decided right then that it was time that I seriously went to work on the project that I had worked on a time or two when I was younger—a history of the Martin family. And since I came home I have been working on it.

Mother Ella Hockett Martin with her grown children, Stanley, Willard, Esther, Ray, Lawrence, and Kenneth and Stewart, about 1954

All of the information I have concerning Alexander T Martin is that he was born June 12, 1815, married Sarah Darnall, had two sons, Moses W Martin and John James Martin, and died August 5, 1844. I have visited his grave in an abandoned cemetery not far from Embarrass. I would like to know more about Alexander T Martin but that is all of the information that seems to be available.

As to your Uncle Moses Martin I have no written information at all. Do you know what the W., his middle initial, stood for? I am under the impression that he was older than your father, that he worked for the government in some civil service capacity, and that he died a bachelor. I have a very faint recollection of having met him when I was quite small. Can you tell me anything about him at all?

As for your mother, my notes say that she was born Eliza Wood, the daughter of Theophilus Wood and Chloe Renfrowe Wood, in Scioto County, Ohio, September 26, 1842. I have no record of when she came to Terre Haute, but my notes say that she attended Coats College in Terre Haute, and that at one time she taught school at Seeleyville, near Terre Haute. Do you recall any stories of her early life or anything *concerning her fifteen brothers and sisters? Also, can you tell me the present name and address of Abner Wood's daughter, Jessie, who I understand lives near you? I understand that she has gathered some information about the Woods family.*

My notes say that your father, John James Martin, was born June 21, 1843 in either Edgar County or Coles County, Illinois; that he was teaching a rural school near Redmon, Illinois in 1865 and 1866, that he married your mother at Redmon, Illinois on September 27, 1866 and moved to Terre Haute. I understand that your mother and father built a house at 315 South 13ᵗʰ Street, Terre Haute, and that Aunt Clara, Dad, and Uncle Charley were born there July 20, 1868, July 6, 1870, and July 2, 1872 respectively. My notes say that Uncle Otto was born May 6ᵗʰ, 1875 near Redmon, and that you were born near Redmon October 21, 1877. I have no notes as to what your father did for a living in Terre Haute during 1866 to the time he moved back to Redmon, or when he moved back to Redmon. Can you tell me anything about how your folks made a living over the years? When they moved back to Redmon did they buy the farm which they still owned at the time of their death, or when did they acquire that? And when did they move back to Terre Haute?

John James Martin, father of Frank James. Photo by Martin.

If you feel up to it I would like any little stories that you may remember about your mother and father, and about your brothers and sisters at home. I particularly would like to know about Otto, since I have no information on him at all except the dates of his birth and death.

Eliza Ellen Wood Martin, Wife of John James, and grandmother to Stanley. Photo by Martin

(Here Gramps goes into a request for biographical info on Maude and her children . . . as well as childhood details about her brother—Gramps' father—Frank James Martin.)

I have asked you many questions. I have not asked them idly because the answers to them are of great interest to me and the rest of the family. We are a little late in getting this job done because the information was so much more readily available thirty years ago. Don't try to sit down and write all of the answers at once. It is too much of a chore. Don't bother with it at all if you find it too burdensome or boring.

My suggestion would be to jot down little things you remember as you remember them. Write them on the backs of old envelopes or old twenty dollar bills (☺!), and when you get a stack of information together, send it along. And then after you've sent it you'll think of lots more things that would be of interest to an informal family history. So—jot them down too and send them along the next time I remember to send you a Christmas Card or birthday card.

I did appreciate Maud and Hugo (Stanka) bringing me past your place when I was through Chicago. I enjoyed seeing you again and the chance to see your lovely home. Looking backwards, as I am now, I am reminded that you have always been my favorite aunt, and examining that thought more closely I am a little surprised to find that that is true not entirely because of your generosity and open-handedness towards me and my family, but just because you are one of those special people with a friendly heart.

I will be pleased to hear from you if you can find the strength and inclination to write.

Love, Stanley"

Maude Nell Martin Thompson. Maude is the sister of Stanley's father, Frank James Martin. Photo by Martin

Thus began a ten year dialog between Gramps and Aunt Maude about the Martin family history. The 1959 version of the mimeographed letter to general "Dear Cousin"—to request family info—went like this:

"Forgive me for mimeographing the first page of this letter. When writing to so many people it saves me a great deal of time. You will find that I have added personal messages, if any, following the general information.

I am forwarding you a copy of THE DESCENDANTS OF SARAH WHITE DARNALL, a partial compilation. It is a partial compilation for two reasons.

In the first place, I have not yet succeeded in getting in touch with all of the living descendants. That is my purpose in sending out this collection—to let you know the information I have, so that you can help me in getting the information I do not have.

*In the second place, no such compilation is ever complete—the scene is ever-changing—new descendants are being born, some are marrying, and the older of us are passing on to our rewards. But it is my hope to compile a report which will give the available data concerning **all** of the descendants of Sarah W. Darnall, as of the date of ultimate publication.*

Sarah W Darnall, as you can see by her picture, was a plain and homely daughter of the frontier. She was a hard-working, God-fearing pioneer, inured to hardship and sorrow, but with an inner spark that enabled her to raise eight children of her own and at least five of other parentage to useful and responsible adulthood. I am proud to be one of her descendants, as I hope you are.

Errors are inherent in this type of compilation. If you find mistakes in my compilation, please let me know. If you are an adult and there is no biographical sketch concerning you, please furnish me with a brief sketch on a FAMILY RECORD SHEET. If you are married, and data concerning your marriage is not shown, please furnish me with data on a FAMILY RECORD SHEET. If you have married children, please encourage them to furnish me with data on FAMILY RECORD SHEETS also. If I have not furnished enough record sheets for your use, let me know and I will send more."

At this point in his letter Gramps would add personal notes, referring to the recipient's specific situation or family, or recent events or visits.

In April of 1956, in a request for biographical information from cousins Ethel Foor and her sister Bessie, Gramps gives a quick "state of the family review". Apparently Gram had just had her teeth out, and was adjusting to dentures. (She would have been almost 49 years old). She was still teaching in Sonoma County. They were living at 10945 Graton Rd in Sebastopol. Oldest child, Nancy, was 22 years old and about to have her third child (that's me!) in June.[7]

Gramps (Stanley) feeding the turkey leg to little Kristy Harper in the high chair, 1957

Uncle John was employed as a dishwasher at a local restaurant. Uncle Pete was a junior in high school, and doing projects with the Future Farmers of America. Uncle Carl was only in sixth grade. Aunt Kay was also living with the family, along with her two little boys, Mike and Gary, and was in the process of a divorce.

Many of Gramps' notes make apologies for being less prompt than he had intended; these apologies are varied in wording. Actually, it's amusing how many ways one can ask forgiveness for their busy-ness and tardiness. Here's a fun one with lots of family "current events" written to Ethel Foor in December of 1959:

> *Dear Ethel;*
>
> *Christmas again and I find to my horror that I haven't written to thank you for your autobiography and nice letter of May 18ᵗʰ. I don't know how I get so far behind on my correspondence. My intentions are good!*
>
> *Of course, there have been a lot of things happen since I got your letter. Betty (Ethel's sister) was down to see us, and I think we showed*

her a good time. I got a nice picture to add to the archives, for which I am glad.

Then we moved. After years of threatening to do it, I bought a house. A modern flat-top, slab floor, four bedroom house about four blocks from my office in Santa Rosa. (This would be the house at 503 Palomino Drive). *It took us a while to get rid of the chickens and the rabbits and all of the junk we'd collected, but we finally got moved in August.*

As soon as we got moved, Kay got a job, of course, working in a dental office. She keeps the kiddies in Nursery School in the daytime. Doesn't make enough to pay her way, but it makes her feel better.

Then the boys went in the service. We sent Peter to Saint Louis to work for Ray this summer, to see if we couldn't get him enthused about engineering. When he came home, I thought we'd made it. But just after he started in school in September his old buddy came home from the Marines, and the stuff was all off. Pete enlisted in the Marines, and is now in boot camp in San Diego.

John couldn't stand Pete getting ahead of him, so he volunteered for the draft, and left for induction right after the first of November. He is now in Fort Carson, Colorado, in the Army.

Probably you haven't been told that Nancy has another little girl—Kristin Joy—Kristy—born June 5th. That makes three in her little family now, so we now have five grandchildren.

I think Peter said that you stopped by at Ray's on your way to Mexico City or somewhere during the summer. I haven't heard about that trip as yet. Or did Pete just think it was you?

My family history isn't progressing as fast as I would like. I have found that I have to write to people, and to answer their letters when they write to me, to get the information, and I haven't been very assiduous at it. But I am getting quite a little done at that.

At this point Gramps moves to the next page . . . .

Somehow I always manage to run over a page when I'm writing letters. Then I get the second page in the typewriter and sit staring at it, wondering what I'm going to do with all that paper.

Did you succeed in getting retired? I can't imagine you coasting to a stop. It just doesn't seem right somehow. So you must have found something to do with all of your spare time.

Does travel come with retirement? Or is that ruled out under conservation of funds? If travel is included, California is a nice place. Of course we have been having some pretty heavy frost this past week—something that we are not used to, but it's still a nice country. If you are planning on coming to the west coast at any time, be sure to include us on your itinerary.

*Have to get on to writing more letters, or I won't have anybody left to write me letters anymore. Forgive me for being so dilatory. (*Webster's alert!) *Thanks again for your very nice contribution to the family history. And have a happy holiday."*

By 1957, Gramps was beginning to contact more of the cousins, and more distant ones, to second and third generations. Each new contact and set of information led to more siblings and children and grandchildren, and his files grew. In January of 1957 he wrote to Betty (niece—Lawrence's daughter) and Norb LaVally, making reference to the fact that his last letter had to "chase" them to a new address, as they were on the move with the military service. He let them know his proximity to both Hamilton and Travis Air Force Bases, in case they could come and visit. One of his updates was that Pete had completed boot camp in the Marines at San Diego. In another letter to (niece) Mickey and Herb Patterson, he calls Pete a *"full-fledged Marine"*, and said he would go to Camp Pendleton, Oregon, for three weeks and then be able to come home for a few days. He also refers to Carl as *"big as a horse"*. As always, he was requesting further family information. When he asked about Ruth's married name and address, he said *"I asked your Dad (*brother Willard Martin*) for it, but he's as loquacious as a reluctant turtle when it comes to letter writing"*. Now doesn't that sound just like Gramps? (Get the dictionary!)

In May of the same year (1957) a letter to cousin Ethel makes yet another amusing apology: *"No matter how hard I try, if I get more than two letters a year written to you it seems like a miracle. I wrote to you last on December 9th and you fired right back on December 14th. I put your card and letter in the pending file for prompt reply, and it has been getting out-shuffled these past five months."* I'm thinking he could save time and space—a TREE, even—and just launch right into the letter knowing they understand that he's a busy man! This letter is long and detailed about tiny discrepancies he found in Ethel's autobiography, pointing them out and asking her permission to edit—details, details! He was a stickler . . . .

However, the same letter shows a kind of "progress report" on the research: *"This history becomes a larger project every time I sit down to the typewriter and start working. I have written literally hundreds of letters, but each new batch opens up new vistas, and it goes on and on. And while I'm thinking of it, do you by any chance know any of the Smith Descendants—offspring of John Martin's half-brothers and half-sisters? I am very weak in this side of the family and am looking for help. Aunt Rachel Weaver is the only one I remember, although I do recall a trip to Peter Chesrown's once. My latest phase is an effort to locate*

Alexander Martin's birthplace. I think I have located him in Roane County, Tennessee in 1837, but I'm still checking and trying to find his family.

The last of this letter describes plans for a visiting and research trip back east—God bless those government jobs with their generous vacation plans! *"While I am on the party line, I'd better tell you that we are planning on taking a vacation this summer and heading east. I have 6 weeks (!) of leave accumulated beginning the day school is out on June 14th. We plan to start the following day. We will have Carl and Kay and Kay's two boys with us, and because of the two little fellows, we probably will not make too many stops on the way east. Kay will probably come home on the train after a couple of weeks, bringing the kids with her, and we will then be more leisurely. I have not figured out the itinerary yet, although I have been making a long list of places I would like to go, or rather people I would like to see, graveyards to check, etc. If you are at home at the propitious (Webster's alert!) time, we definitely want to see you. However, if it is on the trip east, it will be a short stop. If we have to plan it for later, it may be more leisurely. If you aren't going to be at home, or some other place convenient for us to see you, I'll cross you off the list for this time, but I am trying to see as many relatives as possible in the time I have."*

Well, the trip back east in June was ill-fated, and a car accident put Gram in the hospital with a broken neck! Here is Gramps' telling of it—lengthy, but thorough and dramatic:

> *"When people ask about our accident I find that in telling the details I must again live through those horrible, agonizing seconds. My blood pressure goes up, my heart goes to pounding, my face takes on a haggard expression, and I almost literally die again! The strain is too much! So for those of you who may be interested, here is so much of the story as I can tell you.*
>
> *We left Santa Rosa on Friday evening, June 14th (1957) at about 7:15 PM in our 1957 Plymouth Savoy Custom Suburban station wagon on which we had taken delivery eight days before. The car had 1100 miles on it at the time we left Santa Rosa. In the car were Kay and her two children, Mike and Gary, my son Carl, my wife and me.*
>
> *After some road delay because of the blasting in the mountains we arrived at Reno about 2:AM and spent the rest of the night with Elah and Casey O'Brien, Mabel's sister and brother-in-law. We left Elah's about 9:30AM on Saturday, drove down to Carson City where we stopped for about an hour buying groceries and laying in a few more supplies for the trip. Then we took Highway 50 east to Ely, Nevada, where we arrived about suppertime. We had full camping equipment aboard but since the day had turned off cool and it was spitting snow we*

found a motel. After an early breakfast Sunday morning we continued east on 50, leaving at about 8. About 1PM we pulled in for a visit with Max and Leona Jones and their three attractive girls. After a sumptuous lunch and a very pleasant visit we again headed east on 50. An hour or so before sundown we pulled off the road and set up camp for the night about twenty miles east of Green River, Utah. Monday morning we ate breakfast, broke camp, and hit the road fairly early and without washing or shaving, since the air was pretty chilly. We would stop in Grand Junction and clean up.

About 8:15 AM some 23 miles west of Grand Junction, Colorado, we were coming up-grade on a long left curve, climbing one of the "benches" peculiar to the area. At the sharpest part of the curve a right rear tire blew out. At the sound of the report there was some comment in the back seat. I may have glanced over my shoulder. Then Kay was screaming and my next moment of full awareness I found myself partially in the left-hand lane with a Ford pickup approaching and nearing the point of a head-on collision. In a very small fraction of a second I decided that I could not make the left shoulder and give him clearance on my right. I had to get back into the right hand lane! I pulled the wheel. The car responded, but with only one wheel on the road, the back end started swinging around in a skid. The left rear fender of my car clipped the right rear fender of the Ford doing about $25.00 damage. My car continued skidding until it was going backward in the direction we had been moving, and headed for the shoulder of the road. The left front fender hit a boulder on the shoulder of the road and the car sailed through the air, turning over in flight to land upside-down on the car-top carrier, the greatest impact being on the roof immediately over Mabel's head, where she was sitting in the right front seat. The car then bounced over onto its right side, principal impact being along the top of the side.

Somewhere during the split seconds Carl must have pulled on the door latch. In any event, the right rear door was full open at the time the car hit on its right side. The car still had a very little forward momentum (going backwards, of course) so that the right rear door was crumpled flat back against the right front door. So far as we can determine, at the time the car landed on its right side, Carl and Mike were dumped out on the ground. The care still had enough momentum to roll it on over into an upright position, where it stopped, to the sound of fractured safety glass popping loose and falling around.

At the time the accident occurred, the sky was clear, the sun was shining, the road was dry, and it was a beautiful morning. The sandy loam ground where we landed was still wet from a shower the preceding night. The place where we landed was some ten or fifteen feet below the highway on a down-slope. Apparently when Mike was dumped out of the car, he landed running. Kay had to climb out the back and run him down. When she got him down, he passed out with a slight concussion. When I crawled out my door to survey the situation, Carl was lying in a mud puddle alongside the right front door. Out cold and bleeding like a stuck pig from holes in his forehead, neck, and right arm. The man in the Ford pickup helped me get Carl out of the mud and a little more comfortable. Other passersby were stopping and offering help, wrapping the kids to prevent shock, etc. When I got back to Mabel she complained of a severe pain in the shoulder and neck, which to me could mean only one thing, so I resisted all offers of help in getting her out of the car until the ambulance arrived. The Colorado Highway Patrol had arrived meantime and unsnarled traffic, and assisted in getting Mabel out of the car and into the ambulance. I intended to stay with the car to protect things until a tow-car could arrive, but Officer Bertogli assured me that he would stay and see everything safely into a garage, so I climbed into the ambulance with the rest; Mabel on wheel stretcher, Carl on hand stretcher, Kay and the two kiddies in the front seat, and me squatting at Mabel's head. At St Mary's Hospital, Grand Junction, after doctors were working on Mabel, Carl and Mike, they checked my pulse and pressure and found it going up while they watched so they tranquilized me and put me on a gurney.

Kay had a couple of nasty bruises and Gary got shook up a little, but neither were hospitalized or treated. Mike got three stitches under his chin, some vitamins and junk, spent two days in bed and then joined the family at the motel. I stayed overnight at the hospital, got five stitches in my upper lip and then joined Kay and Gary at the motel. Carl got sixty stitches that we could see and some internal stitches that stay in, but after two days in bed he was ready to start chasing the nurses, so we took him to the motel. They took his face stitches out on Thursday to prevent scars, and his other stitches out on Saturday.

Mabel's trouble was not too easy to diagnose, but in due time it was determined that she had suffered a cervical dislocation. Her head was shaved, two holes drilled in the skull and tongs applied to the skull to permit head traction to take the pressure off the spinal column at the point of injury. Dr Hall, a very capable orthopedist, tried four times in three days to reduce the dislocation by manipulation, but was unsuccessful. On Friday afternoon he informed me that it was his conclusion that it would be necessary to perform surgery to reduce the dislocation and might require three to six months of hospitalization for recovery. He informed me that he would be glad to perform the operation but suggested we might be happier in our home surroundings, and informed me that as long as she was immobilized in moving her, a few days' delay in the operation would not be material. At my request he called the Kaiser Health Plan, of which we are members, and where Mabel is entitled to several months of free hospitalization and treatment, to see which of their facilities would be best able to handle her case. They recommended the Oakland Kaiser Foundation Hospital. Dr Hall recommended that we fly her back because of the faster trip. Accordingly, Nancy made arrangements with Pacific States Aviation for a pilot friend of hers to fly a Cessna 172 to Grand Junction on Sunday to bring Mabel back on Monday. She made the trip east with the plane, expecting to come back in it with Mabel and me, but when we loaded Mabel aboard on the special stretcher there wasn't room for Nancy.

Elah had driven in from Reno in their new Plymouth station wagon, the mate to mine, to pick up Kay and Carl and the kiddies, so she squeezed Nancy in too and started back by car as Mabel and I started back by plane. After a fairly rough trip we landed at Buchanan Field about 8:20PM, where Jim Harper, Nancy's husband, met us with the ambulance and in due time we had Mabel in bed and back into traction. Nancy returned from Reno by plane on Wednesday evening. Kay and Mike and Gary went back to Santa Rosa from Reno in a friend's car on Wednesday. Carl is staying in Reno with Elah and Casey for a while.

After more X-rays it was determined that Mabel had a dislocation of the sixth over the seventh vertebrae with cervical fracture that would require a bone graft. In case you wonder, when you lean your head sharply forward, the knob that sticks out the farthest at the back of your neck, just between the shoulder blades, is the joint of the sixth and seventh vertebrae. On Friday, June 28, Dr Black of the Kaiser staff, assisted by other capable orthopedists, operated, corrected the dislocation, made the bone graft, and returned Mabel to head traction for the recovery period, which is expected to be some weeks yet. They had to return her to head traction because her neck is too short and of the wrong conformity to permit plaster cast.

I am writing on June 29th. We aren't out of the woods yet. When I saw Mabel this afternoon she said she hurt all over, which is to be expected and bears out the doctor's observation that there appeared to be no motor impairment or nerve injury, but she is glad the operation is over and she's on her way to recovery. We are praying that the good Lord who was standing by to keep us all from being killed in the crash will help her to a full recovery."

The following is a letter to cousin Ethel dated July 4, 1957, apparently after Gramps had mailed out some kind of letter to all concerned regarding Gram's accident and medical status.

Dear Ethel;

I have just checked off my "must" list, and apparently I did not include you in the mailing of an earlier report that I sent out. I'm sorry, but I have been a little confused. So many insurance forms to fill out and letters to write in between trips to the hospital to see Mabel. We appreciated your cards and good wishes. A thing like this makes you realize how many people love you.

Many of the details you will want to know are in the attached sheets. To bring that report up to date, Mabel had a special nurse in attendance through last night, but the doctor thought that she is now far enough on the road to recovery that we could dispense with the extra nurse. She has regained her color and has been feeling right spunky (yep, that's Gramps . . .) considering the fact that she is in head traction. I am still keeping my fingers crossed, however, and my little silent prayers continue. I will heave a big sigh of relief when I see Mabel on her feet again.

I have not told Mabel of Stewart's tragedy ** and would appreciate no mention of it in letters that Mabel likes me to read to her to brighten her day. Our troubles look pretty small compared to Stewart's, but my first thought for now must be for her.

I am staying at Nancy's, probably until Mabel is out of the hospital. If you want to drop her a cheery little note here I will see that she gets it, or you may write her at Room A-22, Kaiser Foundation Hospital, Broadway at MacArthur Blvd, Oakland, California[8]."

The reference here is explained in a letter from Gramps to sons John and Peter, who were away in the service at the time of Gram's accident and this simultaneous tragic event:

Dear John and Peter; (dated July 2, 1957)

I should have written you much sooner, but I have been very busy. We had an accident on the way home and didn't get there. See the report attached. Mother is much better now and on the way to recovery, but will probably be some weeks in the hospital. I DO NOT WANT YOU BOYS TO ASK FOR EMERGENCY LEAVE BECAUSE IT IS NOT NECESSARY, AND WE CANNOT AFFORD IT.

I am staying at Nancy's. Carl is at Aunt Elah's. Kay and the kids are staying at our house in Santa Rosa.

Now there is more bad news—family news. Mother has not been told about it and I don't want it mentioned in your letters. I will write to you about it, but I don't want you to write to me about it.

Mabel and Stanley Martin, showing good recovery several months after the 1957 auto accident that broke Mabel's neck.

You know Aunt Dot divorced Uncle Stewart Martin last fall, and married a man named Tom Whittaker. Whittaker's wife had divorced him. Her name was Alma. She had two children, a boy and a girl. After Aunt Dot divorced Uncle Stewart and married Whittaker, Uncle Stewart married Alma Whittaker and they had all four children, Don and Diane, and Mrs. Whittaker's two, living at Uncle Stewart's house. Last Monday night Tom Whittaker broke into Uncle Stewart's house and shot Alma (Stewart's wife) and her little boy dead with a shotgun, nearly killed the little girl, and shot Uncle Stewart in the foot while he was trying to get the gun away from Tom. Whittaker is now in jail, Uncle Stewart is out of the hospital, but I don't know if the little girl is still living.

Again, don't mention this in your letters. I haven't told Mother and don't want her to know for quite a while, but I thought you ought to know. Write to me here at Nancy's, and send Mother some cheerful get-well cards here. I hope you are both doing well.

Love, Dad

Mom—Nancy Harper—adds to this that *"The murder occurred at approximately 2-3AM, June 25, 1957. Alma and the son, Jackie, were killed outright. Regina, 9, pleaded with her Daddy not to shoot her. She was able to tell police "my daddy shot me", but died on July 15, 1957 in Union Hospital, Terre Haute, where I was born. Tom was, of course, convicted and sent to Indiana State Penitentiary. Aunt Dot, who stood up for Tom initially, divorced him, married someone named Cardinale, and kept up a scattered correspondence with Gram."*

The interesting continuation of this story is that Uncle Stewart went on to marry Charlotte Bonnett Stevens, who was his young nurse in the hospital; then after many years, when Uncle Stewart passed away, Charlotte married Uncle Stewart's son, Don Martin.

A later note to Ethel in October of 1957 tells of Gram getting out of the hospital but not being cleared to go back to work, so they got her a ticket on United Airlines to Chicago, and then had Maud Stanka pick her up at Midway Airport and take her to the train station to go to Terre Haute and visit her mom. The plan was for a week or ten days, but Gramps said no reservation had been made for a trip home. Many of the relatives—Willard and Peggy, and Maude and Hugo—had come to California to visit while Gram was under the weather. Gramps also made reference to the possibility of a visit from Stewart, although *"he still has two or three months of trials to look forward to, and it's a pretty gruesome prospect, especially since we understand the defense intends to defame his character."* What a difficult time for the Martin brothers!

Later, in the winter or spring of 1958, Gramps says *"Mabel is doing pretty well these days. She doesn't have her old pep—tires out much easier, but she manages to get an amazing amount of work done. She has been teaching regularly all winter. Has had to take a couple of days off when she got too wore down, but otherwise OK. I think a good summer vacation will brighten her up."* So she was beginning to recover . . . .

It was a bit more than a year later, as Gramps reflects in a April 1959 letter to Gertrude VanSickle Wood, that (brother Stewart) was married Christmas Day (1958). *"I haven't met his new wife, but I understand that she is a lovely girl."* He goes on with some commentary about picnics at Embarrass—a topic that he mentions often, in many letters—makes me want to go back to one of those lovely picnics . . . . *"In your Easter card you mention having a picnic at Embarrass the next time we get east, in case you aren't at Redmon. We hope to come back east again this summer, and we're looking forward to a picnic at Embarrass with you in person. And we're hoping there will be other picnics other years too."*

And in the same letter to Gertrude, an idea of the turn his research is taking . . . . *"This year I hope to explore the Wood family. I want to trace down all of the descendants of Theophalus Wood and Chloe Renfrew. Jessie has done a lot of work along that line, but this summer I will want to meet as many of the Wood family as I can. You might be remembering a few names and addresses for me. I'm sorry that I didn't get at this job while Abner could help me, as I know he could have."*

Stepping back in time for a moment, one of Gramps' info-seeking letters was to Ruth Wilson Cowsert, dated May 1959, and talks about the last time he had seen her, 36 years before: *"As a boy I was born and raised on the property adjoining my grandmother and grandfather Martin's place at Terre Haute, Indiana[9].*

Martin Farms, No 7th St, Terre Haute, IN. Looking northeast, Ella Martin with Ray, Willard is up ahead. John J Martin/Eliza Wood Martin home is in the center; Frank James Martin house is further back. Abt 1905, Photo by Martin

Of course they were also your mother's grandparents, and as kids we always looked forward to the visits of your grandmother Thompson and your mother and her sister. I regret that I have not seen you, so far as I can remember, since we visited at your house in 1933, during the Century of Progress." (The "Century of Progress"[10] was organized as an Illinois "not-for-profit" corporation in January of 1928, having for its charter purpose the holding of a World's Fair in Chicago in 1933. The theme of the exposition was to be the progress of civilization during the century of Chicago's corporate existence. The fair was opened on May 27, 1933, when the lights were turned on with energy from the rays of the star Arcturus. The rays were focused on photo-electric cells in a series of astronomical observatories and then transformed into electrical energy which was transmitted to Chicago. A Century of Progress drew 39,000,000 visitors (it was repeated in 1934) and for the first time in American History an international fair paid for itself.)

Another letter of the same month and year refers to his research along the Smith line . . .

> *"Alva E Smith turns out to be the president of the Merchants Van and Storage Company of Wichita. He sent me Ivy May's address and she tells me that she is invalid, but she still writes a pretty firm hand for a gal of 80.*
>
> *This history deal is a lot of fun, but at times it can get exasperating, like this Wichita deal. I knew these folks lived in Wichita, but I couldn't find an address, and it's too far for me to drive over for the weekend. Of course there are still some I'm trying to find and don't know where to look. They're the rough ones. I've been trying to find out for more than three years who my mother's father's people were, and so far I haven't found a trace. The next job is to search the census reports, but that gets expensive unless you are in Washington, and I don't like Washington.*
> (I bet there's a story there, too!)

Gramps goes on to tell about some weather and one of his greatest loves, gardening.

"Snow in the middle of April, as you mention in your letter, sounds like what we moved away from when we came to California. This winter it stayed just warm enough that we had to mow the grass at least once a week all winter. We picked a few strawberries Christmas Day (only in California!) *and have managed to find one or two on the vines each week all winter. These plants were protected from the wind by the fence, and I have now dug them out to put in flowers."* He then mentions plans to head east in the summer again, this time with a passenger to Arkansas (Bernyce Woods?) and a trip to New Orleans on the way to Terre Haute—hardly a direct line. But he was not clear on his vacation time, and refers to being very busy painting his house with *"2 coats radiant pink trim and exotic blue on the stucco"*. Guess that one will be easy to find!

A letter to Dorothy and Bud Roethe also in May of 1959 refers to a "contribution" of money they had sent to the research cause. He tells them it will go to the stamp fund, which although they were only 4 cents (and rising) in this decade, still his income matched the times, and the postage for hundreds of letters must have been a big investment. There's a great "Gramps-ism" in this letter . . . with all his playing with words, and the whole Webster's Dictionary routine (stop dinner and look it up!), we all learned the value of vocabulary—and the humor. In this paragraph he is making excuses for the lack of detail on the women in his history research—which is more difficult for all researchers, as the women take the married names of their husbands, and their birth families and names become obscured and left behind. Of course the insert to the paragraph is more word play:

> *"I'm sorry about the shortage of data on the distaff side in the history. (Incidentally, Doris Martin Nelson and Christine Martin Wahlberg are expert scrabble players and fond of acrostics, and they love to beat me at their games, to my chagrin. They asked me what the antonym of "distaff" was, and after searching all our lexicons and thesauri we have been unable to find one. As an English major, do you know an antonym for distaff? If so, please let me know.) I am trying to correct that situation in the re-write, but a lot of the girls still prefer to be coy, or else they have found it discreet to let the lord and master enjoy the limelight while they sit in the wings and pull the strings[11]."*

Gramps is heading up one of many family Scrabble games—a favorite for all of the Martins

A couple of other comments in this letter include Carl's frustration with the chore of mowing the big corner lawn at Palomino Street, and his desire for a *"San Francisco type row house with a handkerchief size lawn."* Also plans for an early summer visit to California by Stewart and Charlotte, and a later one from Kenneth and Margaret for the 1959 Photographers' Convention in Los Angeles. In another May '59 letter to cousin Marie Best Haggard, Gramps talks about the lengthy process of receiving information, re-typing it in his format, then sending it back to verify what he typed for spelling and dates and other details. This accounts for the hundreds of letters going back and forth. (Oh where is that time-travel PC—and some internet access—to help Gramps with this huge undertaking?!)

In October 1959 a letter to Aunt Maude tells of the many relatives Gramps had the opportunity to meet on his summer journey, including Alva and Phila in Wichita, then Grace Best and her family in Picher, Oklahoma, then Claude and Pricie Smith and Marie Best Haggard in Siloam Springs, Arkansas, and lastly to New Orleans to meet Marie Smith Baker, Homer and Margaret, Arthur and Irma, Orene and Harold, and Edgar Weaver and his family. He also talks of all the Smith clan in Embarrass, Illinois—O.K. Smith, Willard and Emily Weaver and their son Edgar and his wife Marjorie; Etta Mae and Frank Miller, Avis Chesrown's daughter Lois Redmon, and Santford Carrington's daughters Joyce Brown and Johanne Long, and more. Many of these heretofore unknown relatives hosted Gramps in their homes, and certainly brought the research to life and the family together.

The same letter tells about the family at home: "*All of our boys are at home again. Peter was discharged from the Marine Corps in August. He brought a buddy home with him* (this would be Jim Phelps); *they got jobs and are now attending the Santa Rosa Junior College. John worked for Mabel's niece and her husband in Estes Park, Colorado, driving a truck this summer, but the job was seasonal. He came home late in September and is now working on a construction crew. Carl is doing his sophomore year in high school. It's nice to have the boys home, but it's a little hectic at times with Mabel teaching. I suppose you have heard that Nancy added another girl to the tribe, Kelly Adele, on August 20th, bringing us up to six grandchildren. At that point we are up with Willard, but he tells us that Mickey will break the tie in the spring. We hope to rest on our laurels for a while, at least until the boys get married.*" A March 1960 letter to Mickey congratulates them on the birth of their son Chris—another blessing, and yes, another entry to the family tree[12]!

By 1960 Gramps was seriously pursuing the descendants of Cyrus Wood, including half-relatives and cousins in Illinois, such as the Abner Wood-Gertrude VanSickle family and those related. A letter to Jessie Esther Wood Polselli makes reference to summer plans for a visit east to Indiana/Illinois—which included Mom and all of "us kids"; Mom's first visit back there since 1949. A letter of May 3rd that year firms these plans—to Gertrude Wood: "*. . . Our daughter Nancy has decided to come east with us this summer with her four youngsters. We now plan to leave here June 24th and will probably see you folks sometime about the 4th of July weekend, or thereabouts. Nancy is interested in the family too and is looking forward to meeting some of the cousins. We are looking forward to seeing you in a couple of months. Hope the winter has not been too hard on you and that the spring sulphur and molasses has perked you right back to normal by now.* And from another letter to Gertrude . . . "*We hope to see you and your family, of course, and maybe have a little fried chicken and watermelon at the Embarrass picnic grounds or somewhere out that way. We think it's a real nice part of the family that we have out in the corner of Edgar County. Hope that the winter has not been too hard on you, and that spring is just around the corner in Redmon.*"

Four generations—Nancy Martin Harper and her dad Stanley Martin,
Ella (Hockett) Martin and Nancy's son Robbie Harper

In February of 1960 Gramps writes to Arthur and Irma Smith in New Orleans, reflecting on last year's visit, and presenting this informative apology for delay in correspondence: *"I know that I haven't written to express my sympathy for your power mower de-digitation.* (Arthur lost his big toe to the power mower . . .) *For my slowness in this regard I ask your forgiveness. I am still answering my Christmas mail. I can't seem to get caught up with the correspondence. Of course the five weeks that I spent in Idaho, Utah and Nevada right after Christmas didn't help any. We have three breweries and a number of other premises out in that area that have to be inspected quarterly, and we take turns making that circuit. Of course this year it fell to my lot to make the trip in mid-winter—and it was wintery, believe me!*

This makes me think of a story my brother Rob has told of going along with Gramps on his inspection routes through the Napa Valley to the wineries in 1955:

"What I remember is once, maybe more than once, being on the road with Gramps. I'm not imagining that I was over four years old, probably. From my earliest remembrances I was real sharp on cars, that sort of

thing, so I specifically remember that his government car was a Chevy, it seems like it might have been a '51. It was a government vehicle, black or very very dark blue, and I'm not sure that it had a back seat, like maybe it was a business (vehicle). There was something different about the car that was not normal. I'm thinking it didn't have a back seat—something like that.

Anyway, I remember going with him, and he was pretty good at talking. He would engage you in conversation and not just leave you sitting there staring out the window. I can't imagine why I was actually going to work with him. He was living up in Petaluma on that chicken farm on Graton Rd. They lived in the area; I have no idea why I would be with him on a particular day. But we would go to these various establishments, and it was real business-like. He's in a suit, wearing a hat, suit buttoned up, pretty formal. He was a real slow driver. I don't know why I think of that—we're puttin' along . . . and we would go in to a winery, and we would be talking to people. And it seemed like everybody knew him. Maybe he was introducing himself somewhere along the way, somebody he didn't know, but mostly I felt like people knew him.

Most of the day it was real business-like and we'd be walking around looking at stuff, and the men would be talking. It was basically a man or some men, or something—I don't recall women being involved. And there were times where there were kids maybe, or some diversion, something to look at, a pond, a tractor, some animals. I pretty much hung with him most of the time—I just remember these different elements being kind of a recurring theme. I was real curious, being a kid—and it was boring! I just seemed to feel like it was boring, and they were talking, and you know how you burn out on that pretty quick. I think I understood that he was working, and I wasn't the kind of kid that would be interrupting and asking questions and looking for attention and all of that. I kind of went on my own "cruise control" to some extent, for the most part. He carried a briefcase and papers—he was inspecting . . . I'm really not sure of what he was doing. We walked around, we definitely did a lot of walking, and pointing, and some sitting down . . . there were papers, but I'm thinking that wasn't the biggest part of it—it was mostly walking and talking. I didn't mind the walking around part of it near as much as, probably, the sitting and listening, because I had no idea what was going on. But in general it seems like most of the day it was pretty business-like.

And then all of a sudden we got somewhere, and it seemed like, almost like a park-like setting. It could have been Sebastiani. (Reflecting on Dad's comment that Gramps was a good friend of *theirs) I was just thinking about this today, because Gramps always had Christian Brothers Brandy, and he always had these big brandy decanters, with the thing you pour out, with the shot deal on it. You tilt this bottle over, it was on a special rack—and thinking about it, that doesn't seem like something he would necessarily **buy**. (So maybe it was a gift, another friendly connection . . .)*

But anyway, I remember the day being repetitive, and then all of a sudden it got really fun. And I think that's what sticks out in my mind and draws the difference between the bulk of the people, and then it was something really different. It was park-like, everyone was real friendly. I'm sure the winery doesn't look today like it did in 1954 ('55). Maybe it was later in the day, kids were home from school—I don't know what it was, but there were kids, they wanted to play, there was a dog or two, there was more than one woman. There were snacks. It was the same thing, there was some business stuff. But I just remember part of the fun about it was that at the end of this thing—first of all, I didn't have to go walk around, I just played. We were throwing sticks and rocks and making the dogs fetch, running around and doing stuff—me and the kids. There were older kids, a variety of kids. (Maybe the current Sebastiani owners?) But at the end of whatever the men were doing, I have this recollection that all of a sudden it got casual, like a line was drawn, business was over, and for the first time in the day Grandpa took off his coat and his hat. There was a table outside, and chairs, and a flurry of activity to get more chairs, snacks and food. I just figured all these people lived there, and this was their house, and we were playing—I didn't really think about it. I'd been to lots of Martin family things, so this was more like something I was familiar with, it was fun, and there was the lemonade and iced tea. I can't say they were drinking wine, I can't be positive—I just remember the difference between the general day and that part of the day. The men were off to the side a little bit—I'm sure they all smoked, and they were having fun conversation and being friends. I don't have any concept of how long that was; it was the end of the day. It didn't get dark; it was like the late afternoon."—Rob Harper

Dad (Jim Harper) adds to this that Gramps was a very fair inspector, and the vintners liked him, especially the Sebastianis. He came from a line of farmers back in the Midwest and seemed to be understanding of the agricultural lifestyle and its challenges.

In February 1960, Gramps says in a letter to Gertrude Wood, about the family: *"My daughter Kay was remarried on December 19th, an older man that she had met out here, and who we think will be good for her two boys and good to her. We had the family in for Christmas on Christmas Eve, of course, about 18 of them, and we had quite a time. Then Mabel and I visited around among our friends on the Christmas and New Years weekends."* And an interesting genealogy note: *"While I was out in Salt Lake City I visited with Willard Bergman and his wife, our Mormon cousins. Willard is a grandson of Dewitt Wood, brother of Cyrus and of Eliza Ellen. I found him and his wife to be very pleasant people, and quite busy in the affairs of the Mormon Church. He is or was a bishop in the Sandy Stake, just below Salt Lake City. He has done quite a little research on the Wood line and we were able to exchange some notes of help."* And here's one for the energy crisis: *"We were glad to hear you have half interest in a new gas well. It must be nice not to have a gas bill to pay, although our bill from Pacific Gas and Electric Company isn't too bad. (Yes—this is ancient history . . . .) How long have they been drilling gas wells in Redmon? And how much of a job is it?"*

In October 1960 in a letter to his Aunt Maude, Gramps gives an update on genealogy progress: *"It has been a busy and happy year for us. We have made some progress on the family history, although not as much as I might like. We have established that Alexander T Martin was, at the age of four, in Clark County Illinois in 1819 when his mother, Sarah Martin, married Moses Williams, on July 8th of that year, but we still have not established the name of his father or the place of his birth. Some day perhaps we will. In the meantime we continue working."*

In these December letters there are various references to the trip east earlier, in June, which included Mom and all four of "us kids". In a letter to Aunt Maude, *"We had a rather delightful vacation this summer. Nancy and her four children drove east with us for her first trip back since 1949. We didn't include Chicago on our itinerary because of the limited time available and because of the difficulty of keeping the youngsters corralled. We did get to go to Indianapolis one afternoon long enough to visit Nettie Taylor (Aunt Rachel's daughter) and Pat Armer (Christine's daughter) for a few minutes, and had a delightful picnic at Embarrass with Gertrude Wood and her children and grandchildren.* And in a letter to Gertrude, he says *"Nancy's children are still talking about their trip east with us this past summer. I think they like the Edgar County folks as much as we do. They did really have a good time and I think the family made a favorable impression on them. Mabel and I are getting so we struggle through the long, boring winter months, the working months, thinking "well, it won't be too long until we can get back to see the folks in Indiana and Illinois." And of course a picnic at Embarrass is always a bright spot.* And also in a note to Orene, Gramps says about the summer trip *"Carl was baby sitter for the 10 month old (Kelly) most of the time, and did very well at it. We had two nice visits with Avis Trimble and had a picnic at Embarrass picnic ground with the Abner Wood family. Grace Weaver Jones also was present, as a friendly neighbor.*

Stanley Martin barbecuing chicken for a family picnic at his home in Santa Rosa, late 1950's

And in every letter to the folks back there Gramps seems to include a very gracious invitation to visit in California, bragging about the nice weather, and offering lodgings and transportation and sight seeing services—and many of the folks took him up on it over the years, too!

In these same October-December notes of 1960 Gramps says *"Peter is still attending Santa Rosa Junior College and working at the local brewery to pay his way. John is working as an attendant at one of the local hospitals. Carl is a junior in high school this year and taking considerable interest in electronics. Nancy and her husband are both working too hard, but I guess while you are young is the time to do that."* He also mentions, as he often does, more visits with Doris and Johnny Nelson and Chris and Wally Wahlberg—they often had get-togethers or excursions with one couple or the other, or both.

In 1962 Gram and Gramps had moved to an apartment in San Francisco to cut back on commute time and hassles. Gramps finally resorted, in June, to a group letter as he owed letters to so many:

> *"Because I am so helplessly behind on my correspondence, I am resorting to the mimeograph to bring folks up to date.*

Since May 15, 1961 I have been working as a Program Analyst in the office of the Assistant Regional Commissioner, Alcohol and Tobacco Tax, in the San Francisco Internal Revenue regional office. Until the end of March this year I was commuting 56 miles each way daily between Santa Rosa and San Francisco, leaving the house about 5:45 each morning and returning about 7:15 each evening. That schedule didn't leave me much time for letter writing and family research.

Early this spring we sold our house at 503 Palomino Drive, Santa Rosa, to Kay and Ted May, my daughter and son-in-law, and on March 30ᵗʰ moved into this cozy "junior five" apartment under lease for a year. (375 27ᵗʰ Ave, Apt 3, San Francisco. We thought this move should allow us more time for letter writing and such like things, but so far it hasn't helped too much. Now I don't leave the house until 7AM and get back about 5:30 PM but without much enthusiasm left after a day of crash programs and impending crises at the office. Don't misunderstand me. I love it! But it does cut down on our correspondence.

Saturday afternoon, June 16, I will leave here by jet for Bemidji, Minnesota, where I will attend a two week management session for Internal Revenue supervisory personnel. Mabel will leave here the same day by car for Terre Haute, with stops at Reno, Nevada, and Estes Park, Colorado, to visit her brother and sister enroute. When I finish at Bemidji on June 29, I will fly down to Terre Haute, with a possible stopover in Chicago, to join Mabel and spend a couple of weeks with the family and the records of our antecedents, before returning to San Francisco.

In case you haven't heard, our son, Peter, took a trip to Reno a couple of weeks ago and on May 27ᵗʰ, married Nancy Eades of Santa Rosa. His Uncle "Bud" Thomson, deputy sheriff of Washoe County, was host and best man. We are pleased with Pete's choice and find Nancy a welcome addition to the family.

Many of the changes in job and residence are apparent in Gramps' letters of Oct-Dec 1962. He mentions that they and Mom had agreed it would be better to have the family to our house for more room (the SF apartment was too small), so Gram and Gramps decided not to have a tree at home that year. *"I guess that's one of the penalties of living in a junior 5, no matter how modern"* He continues to make reference to his new job duties interfering with his ability to focus on research and correspondence. He does refer to their summer trip, saying that on the way home he gathered quite a bit of information at the Mormon library in Salt Lake, but had yet to sit and sort through it—and was too busy with work to do it soon. *"I'm up to my ears in a new work program for our department right at the moment, and I have to take a tour of the region (Los Angeles, Fresno, and Lodi in California and then Seattle, Washington) right after New Years. My present job is cutting in on my family history time pretty much. After sitting at the desk doing creative thinking and writing all day I find it a little difficult to sit down at the desk again in the evening, but I still turn to it whenever I can. I am beginning to hope that I am at last on the trail of the Martin ancestors back of Alexander T Martin. Pieces of the puzzle are beginning to fit together in spots."*

He also talks a lot about Uncle Carl writing to them from the Philippines. *"A letter from Carl on Saturday said he was in the Philippine Islands and apparently enjoying his cruise on the Kitty Hawk, our biggest aircraft Carrier. Didn't say where he goes from there, but he did say that he was planning on re-enlisting for the submarine service. He thinks he would like to try one of the atomic subs."*

And this is one of my favorite letters, as it shows a lot of Gramps' sentimentality, and some of the rewards of his interest in this project. This is from December 10, 1962 to Donna and Dave Wilson. (Donna was the daughter of Gramps' Aunt Maude; so she was his first cousin)

"As I sit down to write, I am reminded that I didn't write to tell you how much I enjoyed the trip to the Museum of Science and Industry last July and the lunch following at the Surf and Surrey on South Shore Drive. That trip is a treasured page in my happy memory book. I enjoyed it very much, and I'm sorry I was so thoughtless as not to write. As a matter of fact, I'm not sure that I ever wrote to thank you for a very lovely visit to your place at Mamaroneck some thirty-five years ago when I was stationed at Ft Monmouth, New Jersey. I enjoyed that trip too. My happy memory book is full of times I like to look back and remember. Some of them are from a long time ago. Days on the old North Seventh Street Road in Terre Haute. Aunt Maude and Uncle Fred with Donna and Ruth down to visit Grandma and Grandpa Martin. The Chicago World's Fair and a visit with Willard and Peggy to Donna's.

Christmas is a time for remembering and I'm sure your happy memory book must be as full of happy memories as is mine. May all your memories at this Christmas Season be happy ones, and may you be filled with the peace of Love Everlasting.

Love, Stanley"

By 1963, Gram and Gramps were living in their apartment at 161 Karry Lane, #5 in Pleasant Hill. In an October letter to Aunt Maude, Gramps sends condolences regarding Don's passing. He mentions that they are watching "us kids" while Mom and Dad were gone to Long Beach. His "state of the family" news includes: *"Mabel is spending four days a week babysitting Nancy's children while Nancy is working (again) at Mare Island Naval Yard as a Naval draftsman. Jim makes a good salary but Nancy wanted to augment it so that they could make a substantial addition to their house to accommodate their growing family. The children wear Mabel out* (WHAT??? We were ANGELS . . . . !) *but she seems to like it.* (All right then . . . .) *Peter's new daughter, Linda Marie, is growing like a weed and at two months is beginning to look like her dad and her grandfather.* (Personally, I thought she was the spitting image of her beautiful mother . . .) *John is currently playing drums in a combo in Santa Rosa five nights a week, and Carl seems to be enjoying life in the navy aboard the Kitty Hawk. As for me, I am working too hard and enjoying every minute of it."*

In 1965 Gramps wrote to Uncle Stewart Martin and said he had sent the rough master of "Our Wood Family"—150 pages—under separate cover. He expressed concern that already the report was outdated, as the family continues to grow so rapidly. He says *"The family doesn't seem to hold still while I dig in the archives and put notes together"*. He has included the same information in a letter to Uncle Willard, talking about the vast number of pages still out to individuals to fill in their information. Also, a '60's technical note; he was very concerned about the reproduction of the work, as mimeograph was so cumbersome. He was having trouble finding a feasible reproduction technique. In May of this year (1965) he talks about their house in escrow in Santa Rosa. In his letter to Stewart earlier he had talked about the possibility of retiring, and going to Indiana to be with Mom Thomson during her final time. He was actually inquiring whether Stewart could give him a job at the Photo Studio. Stewart says *"I can't give you much to hope for in the way of a job. About the middle of November, we opened a little store up town at 7 South 7th and Don is running it. It's doing better all the time, but has not yet reached the break even point. We offered him $120 a week when he came back since he was making $115 at the newspaper. There is some question on my mind as to our being able to continue paying him that much. As it is now, we couldn't take on anyone else, but who knows what the situation will be then. Diane's husband was let out at Honeywell and would like to go to work for me, but there just isn't that much in our little operation. I will certainly put you on the list and who knows?* But Gramps was already debating the retirement question, as he notes that every two weeks he worked would add $20 per year to his retirement.

Guess they decided to postpone retirement and stay put for a while, because Gramps was talking in May about his plans for planting lawns and gardens when his new home in Santa Rosa passed FHA inspection, and also wanted to build in shelves and storage in the garage. He felt like his "book" of family history would have to wait some time to be "finished". Later, in December of the same year, several letters to various relatives talk about Gram and Gramps' Christmas plans, which included a six foot Colorado Green Spruce, live, in a planter tub. They planned to have 25-30 family and friends in for a Christmas celebration on Sunday Dec 26.

He does mention visiting Nellie Chapman, granddaughter of William Carter Darnall, in Seward, Nebraska in October earlier that year (1965). Nellie had a beautiful collection of photographs of her branch of the family, and filled in some of the blanks on that branch as well. Gramps makes so many references to the huge number of cousins he contacted and visited whenever he was out and about the country on work business or in his travels back east to see and research the family. It's no wonder he always felt behind in his correspondence!

It is interesting to note that a very large portion of the information—and the warmth—of this research is contained in many letters to and from Gramps' Aunt Maude. She was obviously a favorite, he wrote to her very faithfully each year in October at her birthday time, and talked so much about her wonderful talents as a hostess and her high energy level even in her late 80's. Because she wrote so often to him as well, I will take some other time in this research to make a record of some of the letters she exchanged with her nephew; she obviously had a big interest in the research, and added her efforts to the discovery of our ancestors.

In November of 1965 there are some interesting notes relating to a James T Guymon in Davis, California. He was a professor at the University there, and apparently Gramps went to see him and find out if he might have a connection through Hannah Martin, the sister of Alexander Tinen, who married a Guymon. Gramps said *"he looks enough like Ray to be his brother"*. But he was a bit distant; they found that the Isaiah Guymon that married Hannah Martin (Alexander's sister) was a brother of this guy's great-grandfather. Well, that's related, isn't it?? Anyway, he gave Gramps a complete list of Hannah's children, which furthered Gramps' clues in establishing the names back behind their generation, by showing confirmation of popular family names. It's a good example of how these histories are pieced together with many tiny clues and even some assumptions, though to be academic about it, we need to lean on fewer assumptions and more reliable documentation.

In June, 1966, Mom and Dad piled all of "us kids" into the station wagon and we headed east on a month long family visiting and research trek. Gram and Gramps were along, too, at least for part of the trip and certainly in Indiana, and because I was ten years old these are my strongest memories of actually meeting many of the aunts, uncles and cousins contained in this history, and seeing their home stompin' grounds. In addition to the many relatives who expected our visit and opened their homes to us, there were so many that Dad contacted along the way, (as he had begun searching for much of his own history—guess he had caught that genealogy bug from Gramps) and who were equally welcoming on the spur of the moment. The whole thing was quite and adventure and oh, what a testimony to the "blood is thicker than water" adage—not sure I've ever been treated so like royalty before or since!

Later in 1966, in another lovely birthday letter to Aunt Maude, we can enjoy more sweet memories and a clear picture of the busy life that led Gramps to retire by the next year:

> *Dear Aunt Maude;*
> *Sitting down to write your birthday letter, I am reminded of a fall day forty years ago (1926) when I rode a freight train into the western outskirts of Chicago with barely enough money in my pocket*

to pay the fare to 63rd and Stony Island Avenue. Then the walk down to 6906 Constance Avenue where I almost didn't have the nerve to ring the doorbell.

I can now imagine the sinking feeling you must have had when you saw the bum on your front porch, but I can also vividly recall the feeling of welcome that you emanated, and the quiet efficiency with which you went about seeing that I got bathed, dressed in clean clothes from the skin out, fed, and made to feel welcome and at home. And before you put me on the train for Terre Haute the next day, I recall that you saw to it that I was wearing the nicest sweater I had ever worn, to keep the chill out.

Recalling that one incident out of the many that give you a very special place in my memories, I wonder how I can be so un-feeling or forgetful as to go long without writing. I suppose that I could plead the pressures of the job and the work-a-day world, but I don't recall ever hearing of you making excuses when there was something that needed doing that was within your capability. So—I must plead guilty of neglect, and throw myself on your mercy. (Isn't he dramatic?? Clap him in chains . . . . a thousand lashes with a wet noodle . . . I'll tell you what; he really loved this old aunt . . . . ☺)

Mabel and I are really enjoying our new home. We are just now completing a patio so that we may better enjoy the outdoors and the view of our garden. I will be glad when I feel that I can afford to retire and enjoy more gardening and work on the family history full time.

Just now I am not doing any work on the history because of a shortage of free time. The schedule is like this—Up at 4:30, to the bus at 5:10, San Francisco at 6:50, coffee and roll and to work until 4:45, bus at 5:15, Santa Rosa at 6:50 and home at 7:10. Then to bed at 9:30-up at 4:30, etc. Weekends doing the lawn and yard work. I am seriously thinking of asking for reassignment to field work closer to home so I can have a little more time. Even with a little less money, I think it might be worth it.

The children are all doing well, as are the grandchildren—all 8 of them. Carl is the only one we don't see often now, since he is at Whidby Island, Washington. He expects to leave there about Christmas time, visit us here on his way to San Diego, and then board a carrier there for duty in the Far East again.

Out of Space, and time for bed. Do have a very happy 89th birthday.

Love, Stanley

The many letters, cards, etc contained in Gramps' research files taper off dramatically in 1966; it was a busy time of changes for him. Gramps actually did get around to retiring the next year, in 1967, at which time they moved back to Terre Haute to stay with Mom Thomson, Gram's mother. While there, he was working at the photo studio for Uncle Stewart. It was back there, in 1968, that he was diagnosed with cancer. He had some surgery in Indiana; Mom and Kim flew out to help out at Mom Thomson's at that time. He and Gram came back to California after the surgery so that he could be under the care of his regular doctor here. They lived with us on Viking Drive for a while, and then rented a house in Concord for a while. In 1969 Gramps passed away at John Muir Hospital in Walnut Creek. He was 63 years old. The wonderful family history work he began (but never *finished*, as he so often commented . . .) is continued (but still never *finished*, as that is the nature of the beast)—and enjoyed greatly—by his descendants. Gram outlived him by 26 years, most of those spent living at "The Old Harper Place" (Well, they *used* to say stuff like that, and after almost 50 years, it *deserves* a title!) in Pleasant Hill, corner of Viking and the old Contra Costa Highway.

Gramps (Stanley) in leisure, with his San Francisco Giants cap, and a nice striper from the Sacramento Delta in his hand

	Timeline of E. Stanley Martin
1897	Frank James Martin and Ella Alice Hockett were married on September 8th
1898	Willard Covert Martin, born August 26th
1899	
1900	Anna Maud Louise Martin, born 1900, died 1901.
1901	
1902	Fred Ray Martin, born February 6th
1903	
1904	Mark Lawrence Martin, born July 11th
1905	
1906	*Earl Stanley Martin, born August 1st*
1907	
1908	
1909	Kenneth Wood Martin, born March 14th
1910	
1911	Esther Ethelda Martin, born September 11th
1912	
1913	Stanley entered the Fort Harrison School, Terre Haute, Indiana
1914	
1915	
1916	Howard Stewart Martin, born November 22, last of the Martin children.
1917	
1918	Stanley began working with the family photo studio in Terre Haute
1919	
1920	
1921	
1922	
1923	Stanley "took a leave" from Garfield High School, (Terre Haute) to "ride freights" and travel.
1924	Stanley attended one more year of high school, exiting before receiving his certificate.*
1925	
1926	
1927	Stanley enlisted in the U.S. Army; Stationed at Ft Monmouth, New Jersey, Photo Instructor at the Signal School there.

1928	Department photographer in Panama Canal Zone, U.S. Army
1929	Stanley married Margaret Moore; purchased Army discharge (lack of family quarters in Panama zone)
1930	Worked at Columbia Stamping and Enamel Mill; Ran Albert Photo Studio in Sullivan, Indiana
1931	Stanley's marriage to Margaret Moore dissolved. Birth of daughter Kay Ann on May 11th.
1932	Stanley married school teacher Mabel Louella Thomson on September 3rd.
1933	*Stanley completed his high school certificate by examination at the State Board of Regents. He attended the "Century of Progress" exhibition in Chicago. Father Frank James Martin was killed by an automobile May 8th.
1934	Daughter Nancy Gene born to Mr. and Mrs. E.S. Martin on March 29th.
1935	Worked as photographer for McCormack Engraving Co, Amarillo, TX; then for *IRS Alcohol/Tax Unit.*
1936	
1937	Son, John Thomson, born July 6th to Mr. and Mrs. E.S. Martin.
1938	
1939	Son, Peter David, born July 27th to Mr. and Mrs. E.S. Martin.
1940	Elected President of the National Association of Storekeeper-Gaugers.
1941	New York National Convention of Storekeeper-Gaugers; Stanley enrolled in the *Modern Course in Syndicate Fiction Writing*, a correspondence course with Stuart Tynan, Newark, New Jersey
1942	Re-enlisted in the U.S. Army, Officer Candidate School.
1943	Second to First Lieutenant, Ft. Monmouth, New Jersey and then Camp Pinedale, Fresno, California.
1944	Son, Carl Frederick, born in California on March 27th to Mr. and Mrs. E.S. Martin, the last of Stanley's children.
1945	Stanley placed in reserve status of U.S. Army; moved from Fresno, California back to Colorado.
1946	Relocated to Napa, California; working again for the IRS Alcohol and Tax Board. Enrolled in second correspondence course, *Fundamentals of Fiction*, with Thomas and Camelia Uzzell in Stillwater, Oklahoma.
1947	
1948	IRS Alcohol Tax Inspector, office in San Francisco, CA; Relocated to Vallejo, CA.

1949	Wife Mabel returned to teaching, provisional credential
1950	First Grandchild—Nancy's son Robert Gene Harper
1951	
1952	
1953	Relocated to Santa Rosa, CA; assigned as a resident inspector (IRS Alcohol Tax Board)
1954	
1955	Wife Mabel Martin received her Bachelor of Education degree.
1956	Stanley purchased his first home, in Santa Rosa; His mother, Ella Alice Hockett Martin, passed away January 30th. Stanley enrolled in the Creative Writing class at the Santa Rosa Junior College, in California.
1957	Stanley began his "genealogy study" odyssey for his family. Wife Mabel broke her neck in an automobile accident.
1958	
1959	
1960	
1961	Stanley was reassigned to a regional IRS position in the San Francisco office.
1962	Stanley and Mabel moved to a San Francisco apartment on 27th Avenue, to eliminate his commute.
1963	
1964	
1965	
1966	
1967	E.S. Martin retired from the IRS; He and his wife Mabel moved to Terre Haute, Indiana, to be with Mabel's elderly mother, Maud McKinney Thomson.
1968	Stanley was diagnosed with cancer of the colon; he had surgery in Indiana.
1969	E. Stanley Martin passed away on September 24th in California.

Chapter 3

Aspiring Author

Among the many treasures in Gramps' genealogy and story files was a small yellowed and crumbling clipping from an early Terre Haute newspaper, circa 1922. The photo was of a young Stanley, sensitive and post-adolescent. The article read as follows:

> *"This is Stanley Martin, the young son of Frank Martin, photographer. Mr. Martin is a poet. He has been writing for some time, and just recently he has received payment for poems which have appeared in periodicals. A recent poem on "The Camp Fire Service" was published in the Epworth Herald, which publication has accepted several.*
>
> *Mr. Martin is a student at Garfield (High School, in Terre Haute, Indiana), and he shows great aptitude to being of a literary turn. He is studious and capable in his studies, and his grades mark splendid promise."*

By the next year Stanley's restlessness had him leaving high school, working a bit in Chicago, then freight-hopping with a friend all the way to Seattle, with little more than some extra socks and a razor in his pocket. This unique travel adventure, in turn, provided Stanley with unforgettable details and anecdotes for his passion to spin a tale. (see his story "Handout" in Chapter 7)

People who write journals and diaries, those who pursue frequent correspondence, who are avid readers and thrill in a clever turn of phrase, and who go beyond that as storycrafters, leave the legacy of their written words as a reflection and a revelation of their inner selves. Their thoughts, feelings, ideas, philosophies, observations, opinions and adventures—all their experiences—are the things that feed the flow of words. Captured on paper, or these days, on file, they can become the most personal and revealing elements of history, bringing life to otherwise dry and statistical volumes we use as reference to our past.

A good example of this is the diary kept by Mary Boykin Miller Chestnut during the Civil War. She was not a published author, nor an aspiring one, simply the wife of James Chestnut, Jr, a senator and eventual governor in South Carolina. Mrs. Chestnut kept a personal daily diary as a habit, and during the Civil War Years recorded events and impressions happening all around her. Although she passed away in 1886, her diary did not come to the public eye until 1905, published as "A Diary From Dixie", with a new edition garnering the Pulitzer Prize in 1982, as a definitive personal glimpse of the Civil War period from a southern freewoman's point of view.[13] And who has not heard of (and read) the private diary of young Annelies Marie Frank, a holocaust victim who died at the young age of fifteen, yet whose "Diary of Anne Frank" was translated to languages all over the world, and in fact became one of the world's most widely read novels.[14] This woman and this teenage girl had a commonality; not that they were "authors", at least not deliberately, but that they had both talent and a compulsion to express themselves in written words.

Gramps was blessed with many exceptional God-given talents; an eye for a good photo and facility with the tools of said trade; a strong sense of integrity and responsibility; a magic hand in the garden; and certainly a love of all aspects of literacy, with a passion for authoring and the skills and humor to go along with it. Let's be honest and say he was certainly standing behind the door when they passed out singing voices; one cannot expect to excel on every avenue. But all in all he was a highly talented man, with just enough restlessness and angst to inspire him to a host of fascinating pursuits in his lifetime. His stories paint a panorama of that life. They reflect the language, morals, artifacts and adventures of his Hoosier heritage and the early twentieth century—"vintage", as we say. His classes and correspondence courses may have been a vehicle for inspiration and expression, but the experiences, ideas, feelings, dry wit and humor, and "Hoosier-isms" are all Gramps.

Stanley in a sling-back chair with coffee and cigarette, Abt 1950

1940's Suggested Reading List for Aspiring Authors
(from one of Stanley's author courses)

Baron, Salo W.	A Social and Religious History of the Jews
Briffault, Robert	The Mothers
Buckle, H.T.	The History of Civilization in England
Carpenter, Edward	Pagan and Christian Creeds
Case, Shirley J	The Supernatural in Early Christian Times
Castiglione, A.	A History of Medicine
Coulton, C.G.	Life in the Middle Ages
Coulton, C.G.	The Medieval Scene
Crawley, E.	The Mystic Rose
Cumont, F	Oriental Religions in Roman Paganism

Cumont, F	Afterlife in Roman Paganism
Davenport, FM	Primitive Traits in Religious Revivals
Davids, T.W.R.	Sacred Books of the Buddhists
Ellis, Havelock	Studies in the Psychology of Sex
Ellis, Havelock	Man and Woman
Farbridge, M.H.	Studies in Biblical and Semitic Symbolism
Faure, Elie	History of Art
Ferrero, G	The Greatness and Decline of Rome
Fowler, W	Religious Experience of the Roman People
Frazer, James G	Folklore in the Old Testament
Frazer, James G	Totemism and Exogamy
Frazer, James G	The Magical Origin of Kings
Freud, S	Totem and Taboo
Friedlander, L	Life and Manners Under the Roman Empire
Gardiner, E.N.	Athletics of the Ancient World
Glueck, Nelson	The River Jordan
Goodenough, E.R.	The Mystic Gospel of Hellenistic Judaism
Gray, G.B.	Sacrifice in the Old Testament
Guignebert, Charles	Jesus
Hall, G Stanley	Jesus in the Light of Psychology
Hannay, J.B.	Sex Symbolism in Religion
Harnack, Adolf	History of Dogma
Harnack, Adolf	Mission and Expansion of Christianity
Harrison, Jane	Prolegomena to the Study of Greek Religion
Hartland, E. S.	Primitive Paternity
Himes, N.E.	Medical History of Contraception
Hocking, W.E.	The Meaning of God in Human Experience
Huntington, Ellsworth	Civilization and Climate
Huntington, Ellsworth	The Character of Races
Jackson and Lake	The Beginnings of Christianity
Jastrow, Morris Jr.	The Civilization of Babylonia and Assyria
Kiefer, Otto	Sexual Life in Ancient Rome
Kohler, Karl	History of Costume
Latourette, K.S.	The Chinese: Their History and Culture
Laubscher, J.F.	Sex Custom and Psychopathology
Lea, H.C.	History of Auricular Confession and Indulgences

Lea, H.C.	Historical Sketch of Sacerdotal Celibacy
Lea, H.C.	History of the Inquisition
Lecky, W	History of European Morals
Legge, F	Forerunners and Rivals of Christianity
Leuba, J.H.	The Belief in God and Immortality
Leuba, J.H.	The Psychology of Religious Mysticism
Lewis, Joseph	The Ten Commandments
Licht, Hans	Sexual Life in Ancient Greece
Lippert, J	The Evolution of Culture
Loisy, Alfred	The Birth of the Christian Religion
Lorquet, P	The Art of the Middle Ages
Maine, Henry	Ancient Law
Mantzius, K	History of Theatrical Art
Mahaffy, J	The Silver Age of the Greek World
Malinowsky, B	The Sexual Life of Savages
May, G	Social Control of Sex Expression
Mommsen, T	History of Rome
Montefiore, C.G.	The Synoptic Gospels
Moore, G.F.	Judaism in the First Centuries
Muller-Lyer, F	Evolution of Modern Marriage
Murray, M.A.	The Witch Cult of Western Europe
Oesterly and Robinson	The Hebrew Religion
Payne, G.H.	The Child in Human Progress
Petrie, W.F.	The Revolutions of Civilization
Pfeiffer, R.H.	Introduction to the Old Testament
Porteus, S.D.	The Psychology of a Primitive People
Prentice, E.P.	Hunger and History
Prestage, E.	Chivalry: Its History, Significance and Influence
Rey and Boutroux	Science in the Middle Ages
Robertson, J.M.	Pagan Christs
Robertson, J.M.	History of Freethought
Rostovtzeff, M.	History of the Ancient World
Schweitzer, A.	Quest of the Historical Jesus
Scott, George, R	The History of Torture
Sheldon, W.H.	The Varieties of Temperament
Shotwell, J.T.	The Religious Revolution of Today

Smith, G.A.	Jerusalem
Smith, G.A.	Historical Geography of the Holy Land
Stephen, J.F.	History of Criminal Law of England
Strzygowski, J.	Origins of Christian Church Art
Summers, M.	History of Witchcraft and Demonology
Sumner and Keller	Science of Society
Taylor, H.O.	The Medieval Mind
Tennant, F.R.	The Doctrine of the Fall and Original Sin
Thorndyke, Lynn	History of Magic and Experimental Science
Toynbee, A.J.	A Study of History
Trachtenberg, J	Jewish Magic and Superstition
Venkateswara, S.V.	Indian Culture Through the Ages
Vinogradoff, P.	Outlines of Historical Jurisprudence
Westermarch, E	Origin and Development of Moral Ideas
Weigall, A	The Paganism in our Christianity
Wheless, Joseph	Forgery in Christianity
Yerkes, R.M.	The Great Apes

Narrative Technique—Why do *You* Want to Write Fiction?

The written word has fascinated me for as long as I can remember. I learned to read while I was very young, and if I remember correctly my ability was the cause of much, to me, desirable praise and comment. I was the middle of seven children, and the ability to read, and later to write and rhyme brought food for my suffering ego from my family and friends, which was probably a contributing factor in the development of exhibitionist tendencies in me.

When, at the age of twelve or thirteen I sent for Pitkin's Pamphlet Course in Fiction Writing and sat down to the typewriter and began writing in earnest, my older brothers began pointing out how silly I was, and after the Curtis Publishing Company had confirmed their opinions I began to get discouraged. And there was no one to give me encouragement except Aunt Clara. Aunt Clara's encouragement, was, I think now, actually an additional discouragement, for she had been writing for years and never sold a line, her house was a mess, and so was she.

So I began writing poetry. My poetry was an excellent outlet, fed my ego and my exhibitionist tendencies. I even sold a couple of religious poems. But the sale brought me neither fame nor fortune, and I had become (or always had been) definitely an introvert, so I thereupon confined my poetry to love poetry for my girlfriend, of which I had but one. When that affair broke up I was through writing. I do not mean that I quit writing, for periodically, like the sap rising in the trees in the spring, the old urge would return, but never with sufficient force to throw off the memory of earlier failures or the ingrown conviction that I would fail.

So, I wish to write fiction first of all to gain fame and feed the inward exhibitionist tendencies within me. Secondly, I wish to write fiction as a means of livelihood—to serve as a means of escape from my present public service job. I can envision myself pounding away at my typewriter turning out my annual best seller, taking a long vacation tour each summer, and scraping the bottom of the barrel to pay my income tax each year. Yeah, man!

—E.S. Martin (undated)

1941 Letters Between E.S. Martin and Stuart Tynan
Modern Course in Syndicate Fiction Writing
2010 Raymond Commerce Building
Newark, N.J.

July 28, 1941

Dear Mr. Martin;

Thank you for your enrollment in the Modern Course in Syndicate Fiction Writing. This is my first mailing to you of the information, instructions, the first lessons etc.—it is the form mailing merely to acquaint you with my working processes and start you on the road toward the production I'm to get for you. Aside from occasional "mimeograph" spot messages sent to all students in your section of skill or quality who may be level with your own particular talent later on—it will be my long dictated personal letters and the scribbled pencil notations on your lesson scripts which I intend shall make a competent selling writer out of you.

Enclosed you will find the duplicated copies of the first batch of lessons in the Course. Be sure and save these "newsprint" lesson sheets after you are well into the course work. Do not destroy them. At times they will augment my letters and penciled notes and revision outlines very much.

So that I can know you as intimately as possible from the beginning of our work together, rather than wait until I have become familiar with you through your handling of assignments, I wonder if you would care to forward to me IMMEDIATELY two full pages, say, of information regarding your intimate friends, the types they are, the few spots of major experiences in your life which have influenced you greatly, what sort of material you read both serious and professional and for entertainment (but especially professional) and what sort of prose fiction you have always admired the most. This is important. Please consider this additional personal information as strictly confidential—the purpose is to better chart your progress-to-be in advance, and principally the better to understand your own individual case and the planning of how much time, effort, etc., you have to spare me in handling our work accurately. Please favor me promptly with this information requested. Thank you very much.

Sincerely Yours,
Stuart Tynan

Mr. Stuart Tynan
Madeira, Ohio
August 3, 1941

Dear Mr. Tynan,

Your letter and first two lessons arrived Wednesday following my return from New York on Monday. In New York last week I presided at the Annual Assembly of the National Association of Storekeeper-Gaugers, and organization with a membership of six hundred of the thirteen hundred total storekeeper-gaugers in the Federal Civil Service. I was not permitted to lay aside my toga, but must serve another year as president. However, during the coming year I anticipate having more time free for writing than during the past year.

What the hell is a storekeeper-gauger, did I hear you ask? The S-G is the boy who supervises the manufacture, storage, bottling, labeling, and ultimate sale of all alcoholic beverages and gauges and assesses the Federal Tax on the same. It sounds easy but it takes two thousand pages of fine print regulations for Uncle Sam to put it all down in black and white. He is a Civil Service employee, and the good ones (like me) got the job by taking an exam that some PhD's I know weren't even able to complete.

Who are my intimate friends? I have many friends and acquaintances, but of intimate friends I have but three. One is a long legged, double jointed, pointed beaked Polack artist photographer in Chicago. He is so much an artist and such a capable photographer that he preferred working on a W.P.A. artists' project to degrading his art by making photographs at a price people would pay. His stuff has been hung in every major salon in five countries, and he has as many medals and ribbons as Goering. I am myself a photographer by birth and education, although not now working at it, and I met this boy in the army back in '27. In fact he was my assistant instructor when I was chief enlisted instructor of the Photographic section of the Signal School at Ft Monmouth, New Jersey, in '27-'29.

Another intimate friend is a local boy with moronic or at least childish parents, a brother confined in a state asylum, and a normal sister. He has an unusually keen mind but lives in silent horror that his own mind will be affected or that if he married his children would be simple-minded. He has an amazing capacity for responsibility, and has maintained his entire able-bodied family for the past ten or fifteen years. While we were in . . . (last line of page cut off) . . . . newspapers, and he has been with them ever since, through three changes in ownership. High school reporter, cub, court house, city desk, and now telegraph editor. He a bachelor, and me with my three kids, we now have little in common, but I still drop in on him at the paper, or have him out for a shot on Saturday night, and he still rates as one of my three intimates.

My third intimate friend is also a newspaper man. In high school I loaned him the clothes he wore on his first date. In fact I even made the date for him. Of destitute parentage and an ingrown inferiority complex, he's come a long way since then. We worked on roustabouts together, and on one occasion hopped freights from Chicago to Portland, Oregon, together. While I was in the army, my second friend above got this friend a job on the local paper as a cub. In '30 he handled the news angle of the local Congressional candidate, and after the battle was won, went to Washington as the congressman's secretary. After two years the congressman was out and my friend hit the west coast in the early Depression days, landed him a job in the L.A. area, and has been there since. He was a pioneer in the journalistic C.I.O. movement, and has been fired from a couple of good jobs on that account, but he is now building his own home in a L.A. suburb, and acts like he might be expecting to hold on for a long time.

Among my friends are a stationary boiler fireman and his corn-fed wife, a rural letter carrier and his minister's-daughter wife, a traveling drug salesman and his part-Indian wife, and a host of others representing a pretty fair cross-section of corn-belt society.

How did I get this way? The fourth of seven children, all of whom have done better than average for themselves. In our family, since we attended a rural school, we didn't start to school until we were seven. I finished the third grade at seven, the eighth at twelve, and spent parts of seven years trying to finish four years of high school and getting around to see the country. I finally gave up high school, and completed my work a few years ago by state examination when I needed a H.S. diploma. I wasn't much hand to stay at anything. In '27

I joined the army, and I had to stay. In six months I was a corporal, and in another year a sergeant. I married while in the army, took a job as a Department Photographer in the Canal Zone, left my wife in the states, bought out and came back in October '29. With my wife I set up a little studio in a small town near here in '30, went broke in '31, and my wife divorced me early in '32. Broke and without a job I married my present wife, a dentist's daughter, in the fall of '32. Since then I've traveled as an itinerant photographer, worked as production manager for an engraving company, inspected saloons for Uncle Sam, and for five years have been at my present job.

I've never yet seen the book I wouldn't like to read, and I've read lots of them, no subject barred. I love popular history and biography. For relaxation I read Wild West stories aloud to my wife in bed. For current reading I read Colliers and Coronet regularly, and most of the other popular slicks at intervals. Professionally I read the Writers Digest, The Writer, Writer's Monthly, fairly regularly. I have a copy of Uzzell's Narrative Technique and a Roget's Thesaurus on my desk, and have read every book in our library on writing that is recent enough to be authoritative. If I had to choose what type of fiction I wanted to read it would lie between Damon Runyan and Clarence Buddington Kelland, with Runyan having the edge. For years I read and preferred the Post stories, but now I decidedly favor the Colliers story.

And there I stop, right at the top of a new page, so you can go on to the two assignments of lesson one not too groggy from the maze of words.

A second money order will be headed your way as further payment on my course in a day or two.

Does this give you the information you want? I hope.

Sincerely,
E.S. Martin

8-20-41

Dear Mr. Martin;

I had lunch in Manhattan yesterday with a prolific modern writer who, while she isn't one of the best slick bets of the year as yet, I suspect she will be before long. The item I want to pass along to you and the three other students of the month I have placed in the grouping lead by you, is a tip she mentioned that certainly could have much bearing on your own work later regarding the revision process of writing—so much so that I'm having this mimeo'd for your files and the files of the other three in your group.

It is: tackling a revision isn't the hardest part of writing—getting the fundamental idea into a plot plan is that—but revision work is (to quote her) "the surest way I know to reduce my typewriter into a mangled heap of twisted steel". The lady in reference went on to complain that revision would be the only possible excuse she would ever have to give up her thriving profession! But she knew, and I knew, that she hadn't the slightest idea of giving it up—and that revision after revision had worked the charm that is putting her right up on top. To a beginning writer, revision is practically ALL there is to writing when small or large checks begin floating in. DO remember this word I am passing along to you. Thanks. I'll try to make an additional note or two in my regular criticism notes on your assignments regarding this if I think you are slipping on understanding its importance.

Sincerely,
S. Tynan

Mr. Stuart Tynan
Madeira, Ohio
August 27, 1941

Dear Mr. Tynan;

Yesterday I received Lesson Number 6. Although I have not yet completed lessons four and five, I sat down at once to go through the new lesson.

I read through the story and started into the discussion of it at the bottom of page three. With mounting interest I turned to page four.

Imagine my surprise and chagrin to find that there wasn't any page four. After page three there just wasn't any more. There I was, right in the middle of the discussion and searching eagerly for the explanation of the side notes on the story, and the assignment—and there I am yet!

What the hell?

Sincerely,
E.S. Martin

P.S. Don't fire the girl. Just fire the rest of the lesson at me. I made a mistake once myself.—E.S.M.

Madeira, Ohio
November 28, 1941

Dear Mr. Martin

It is a trying experience on your part perhaps having your professional understanding of "climax" dragged out in the open to be deflated so many times in succession. But you have got to learn, and there is nothing left but to cram your writing stomach with mental food on this subject until you're writing effective climax twists in your sleep!

I like the style of your short-short story titled "BOX SUPPER" ; but you have added too many unnecessary details. See if you can't change this by taking out some of the details, and inserting some incidents and situations that will really have a direct bearing on the outcome of the main plot. Try to build up your climax—make it more outstanding to the reader. Do you see what I mean?

You've proven you understand my instructions. You've proven you assimilate them. I am hoping with several more illustrations you'll feel the click inside and have the applicable ability with this irritable element forevermore secure. I am sorry it is being so difficult.

Sincerely,
S. Tynan

Dear Mr. Martin;

You have followed my outline in re-casting the character situation's effect on the reader as I suggested. But you have lost something else which disappoints me. When you re-write, do you revise the good lines as well as the bad?

Now please do not be disappointed. You have a long steep hillside row to hoe in this commercial fiction-production-for-profit game and regardless of the amount of work it is going to entail you've got to remain enthused. That is the main thing in pounding through this course.

Before you tackle my second series of suggestions let me give you just one more word of advice about re-writing. When you receive criticism suggestions back on a script, regardless of how fatal or how complimentary, please USE YOUR OWN NATIVE JUDGMENT IN APPLYING THEM. One excellent way I have noticed authors successfully apply constructive script re-building notes is by the following method:

a. Read the notes over carefully 3 or 4 times if need be to thoroughly digest their meaning. Read them over with your finger on that part of the script to which they apply.
b. Then file them AWAY, place a new sheet of paper in your machine, AND START THE WHOLE STORY OVER FROM BEGINNING TO END.
c. DO NOT RECOPY A SINGLE LINE, REWRITE IT.

That is as graphic a remedy as I can offer you for keeping your original flare of creative-emotion (enthusiasm) present in re-writing a story which needs revision.

Here are the weak points now, most of them brought out by the revision you've given this, exposed, rather than removed or left acceptable. Please stand by me, won't you?

1. Watch this closely: Your story doesn't "feel" plotted. You've got to make the reader semi-conscious of your plan of plot as he reads the story. When you build a new script from a NEW plot plan be sure and KEEP THE PLOT PLAN IN YOUR MIND ON EVERY PAGE to give the reader the ability to follow.

(. . . at this point there is no more of the letter, presumably a last missing page . . . . KHB)

1946 Letters Between E.S. Martin and Thomas and Cornelia Uzzel Narrative Technique Correspondence Course Stillwater, Oklahoma

Thomas H Uzzell was a writer, editor and teacher, living and working in New York City in his early years and then in Oklahoma by the 1940's. He was a fiction editor at Collier's Magazine for some time, and his books on Narrative Technique, Writing as a Career, and The Technique of the Novel continue to be utilized in college level writing classes as definitive and specific blueprints for aspiring authors. The format of this course, as well as the precious one with Mr. Stuart Tynan, was one of teacher-produced texts accompanied by regular manually typed overland mail correspondences directly from the teacher to student, and vice versa.

240 E Lane, Apt 959
Vallejo, California
Sept. 6, 1946

Mr. Thomas H. Uzzell
Stillwater, Oklahoma

Dear Mr. Uzzell;

Can you make an author out of me?

I am one of those hopeless individuals who has always wanted to be an author, who has done some writing, but didn't stick with it. I'm old enough to know better (40), have a family, a good job, and might be able to find enough time to put in an average of two to four hours a day. We can go into other gory details later, I trust.

I have both enlisted and commissioned service in World War II behind me and can qualify for instruction under the GI Bill, and would like to do so.

I have seen enough of your Narrative Technique to feel that if you can make me follow it you might make something out of it or me or us. Want to try?

Very Truly Yours,
Earl S. Martin

Thomas H Uzzell
Camelia W. Uzzell
Stillwater, Oklahoma
September 12, 1946

Dear Mr. Martin;

Thank you for your letter of September 6 which has come to my desk in Mr. Uzzell's absence. I'm answering, since he'll not return for another month.

As to making an author out of you, you know the answer. We can be pretty sure, however, that our course in Fundamentals will be a good prescription for any weak spots in your technique, and that it will also be a good test of your gifts. If you are familiar with Mr. Uzzell's book NARRATIVE TECHNIQUE, you know our method generally, and the enclosed pamphlet and General Directions for Fundamentals may answer all your questions. If not, we'll be glad to have you write.

The one disadvantage in Fundamentals is that it doesn't put much pressure on the writer. The fee is low, $50.00 for the full course, and the time limit is six months. If you were to enroll for personal direction, the fee for which is $50.00 a month, the pressure on your pocketbook would be greater, and we could push you harder to produce copy. I can't help feeling, however, that if you buckle down to a series of assignments, the purpose of which you could see clearly, you'll not need any pushing from your instructor.

You write a good letter. Just possibly this may mean that you have it in you to write some good fiction. We'll be very much interested to explore that question further if you so decide.

Yours Sincerely,
Camelia W. Uzzell

---

240 East Lane, Apt 959
Vallejo, California
September 19, 1946

Mrs. Camelia Uzzell
Stillwater, Oklahoma

Dear Mrs. Uzzell;

Referring to my inquiry of September 6, 1946, and your reply of September 12th, we didn't get together.

Paragraph three of my request was, for me, the pertinent one. The one dealing with instruction under the GI Bill. I supposed that you would automatically send me the necessary forms to close the deal under the GI Bill.

I had and have no doubt of your qualifications and ability to make an author out of me. The point was that I am entitled to instruction at Uncle Sam's expense, and although I could pay for the instruction myself, I don't want to deprive dear old Uncle the privilege of sharing with you the distinction of having made an author out of me.

I understand that there are some necessary forms furnished by you, aside from those furnished by the Veteran's Administration that are pertinent to the deal. Am I right? And if so would you care to send me same so we can get going?

Very Truly Yours,
Earl S. Martin

Thomas H Uzzell
Camelia W Uzzell
Stillwater, Oklahoma
September 24, 1946

Dear Mr. Martin;

Thank you for your letter. I'm sorry we didn't give you the details you wished about our instruction under the GI Bill. We can enroll you in our Fundamentals of Fiction. All you have to do is to fill out and send us forms 1953 and 7-1950b which you can get from your VA Office. As soon as we receive these forms we will mail you the material you will need for the course. Let us know whether or not you have the textbook, Narrative Technique. If not, we'll send one.

Yours Sincerely,
Mary Jo Holmes
Secretary

Napa, California
November 15, 1946

Mrs. Camelia W. Uzzell
Stillwater, Oklahoma

Dear Mrs. Uzzell;

Sorry it took me so long to getting around to completing the details of enrollment in your course of Fundamentals of Fiction. Since writing to you from Vallejo, California in September, I have been about the business of getting the necessary forms 1953 and 7-1950B from the V.A. I finally have the forms and here they are.

You will note that the form 1953 needs to have inserted (in my portion) the name of your institution and the date of enrollment. I have left all of the form 7-1950B to you excepting the signature and the C number. Perhaps I shouldn't be such a sucker on a business deal, but I have a feeling that you can get the right information on there easier than I can without writing an extra letter or two.

So now I am enrolled and we set about the gruesome business of making me do it right instead of just doing it. I do not now have a copy of "Narrative Technique". I had one before the war but it and several hundred other volumes of my library and I hate to think how many tons of other impediments lies somewhere in the wake of the last few hectic years. You say you will send me a copy. Please do.

Please note that the address shown on form 1953 is incorrect. The address below is currently correct, and the VA has been notified of the change.

I am looking forward with pleasure to our work together on this interesting project.

Very truly yours,
Earl S. Martin
288 Wake Street
Shipyard Acres,
Napa, California

Thomas H Uzzell
Camelia W Uzzell
Stillwater, Oklahoma
November 20, 1946

Dear Mr. Martin;
WELCOME TO FUNDAMENTALS OF FICTION! Mrs. Uzzell has asked me to write and thank you for your application. She will write you when your assignment #1 comes in.

The material you will need is enclosed with this letter. The book is being mailed to you today. Your term will be dated from the time we receive your copy on the first assignment.

Yours Sincerely,
Mary Jo Holmes
Secretary

288 Wake Street
Napa, California
Jan. 5, 1947

Camelia W. Uzzell
Stillwater, Oklahoma

Dear Mrs. Uzzell;

Here is Assignment one. I have purposely delayed sending it because of a recent change in assignment which always keeps me busy for a couple of weeks. And then of course the holidays are always hectic with four kids (from 2-1/2 to 12) around to pester Santa Claus.

Don't know how this assignment will strike you. Down to page four it's strictly fiction by way of introduction. From the middle of page four to the bottom of page twenty I will testify as to the basic accuracy of the text. The name of the character and the name of the town are fictitious. In our business we are forbidden to name names or state details without a special dispensation from the great white father.

This may not be what you are after. I selected this item at random from a list of six incidents with sufficient emotional interest (I thought) to qualify. For instance there was the time I was lost in the mountains on a deer-hunting expedition and unable to make it out because I had just been out of bed three weeks after a hernia operation and my stamina ran out.

Or there was the time down in Louisville, KY, in '40 when I attended the convention of the National Association of Storekeeper-Gaugers as an alternate delegate because the elected delegate's twins came down with Scarlet Fever—and I came home as national president of the outfit—elected by delegates not one of whom had ever seen me before.

Or maybe you would rather have heard about the time when I was the party of the first part in a kangaroo court held in the middle of the street in a little town down below Paducah, KY, because I had made the mistake of making some photographs for profit in the town without asking the permission of the local yokels. The fine on that deal cost me all the cash I had on me and my Parker pen that I had cherished for ten years.

Probably there would be too much red tape involved in the telling of the story of a riot that resulted when some of the prisoners in the post stockade at Camp Pinedale got tight on some brew made from raisins and hominy grits stolen from the kitchen, which occurred about taps one night when I was Officer of the Day. You see, I still hold my Army Reserve commission.

The other was an isolated incident, a few minutes when I was caught out in a car on the highway in the most terrific wind and rain storm I ever saw. I died a thousand times in those tense three or four minutes.

I don't know how much if any you want to know about me other than the poop sheet attached. I was born into the photographic profession back in Central Indiana forty years ago. I rode the freights to the west coast and to the gulf coast before I finished high school. I did a hitch in the regular Army, including a little time in Panama, in the late twenties. I went bust and lost my first wife running a studio in Indiana in '32. I was production manager and new photographer for an engraving plant in the Texas Panhandle in '34. I went to work for the Alcohol Tax Unit in 1935 and have been with them since as a Junior Inspector and Storekeeper-Gauger, except for my 3-1/2 years in the Army during the late war. This spring I transferred from the Chicago District to the San Francisco District and am now an Officer-in-Charge of Storekeeper-Gaugers here in the Napa area, alternating between two little Rube Goldberg Distilleries both of which I could drop in one fermenting tub in some of the plants I've worked in back in the corn belt. But it's a job, and it only takes forty hours a week of my time, so it leaves me a little to get seriously at this job of writing.

I sent my first contribution to the Saturday Evening Post in 1920. By 1930 I had a pretty fair collection of rejection slips. Up to them, of course, I had nothing to write about. Or at least the things I wrote about were not the things I could have written about authentically. Since then I have devoted myself to accumulating a rather weird assortment of experiences and a little knowledge, and now I think maybe I have something to write about, and maybe with your help I can be about writing it.

What do you think?

Sincerely,
Earl S. Martin

Thomas H Uzzell
Camelia W Uzzell
Stillwater, Oklahoma
January 14, 1947

Dear Mr. Martin;

In your letter of the fifth which accompanied your Assignment 1 you mention a number of experiences that you might have used instead of the experience with Rasmoses. Some of these, I suspect, might have given you better practice with emotional writing, specifically, but the sketch you've sent will do. The one objection to it for our present purpose is that the complication itself is so interesting (the concealed moonshining) *(*refers to OLD UNCLE JOE)* as to prevent any strong response to the emotion.

The emotion, as I've indicated with blue pencil, is due to the clash between desire to do the job, (which seems to be the main or decisive desire) and the desire to be safe. This second desire is blocked, apparently, by Joe, the external obstacle, and thus the internal conflict (emotion) is created.

I think my blue penciling in connection with the answer sheet will be sufficient comment. This exercise is intended as a bridge between what you know about real life, and your story plotting. If you were to handle a story as you've handled this exercise, omitting any detailed development of the main desires involved in the conflict, you would leave your reader cold. Only when the desire (trait) is developed until the reader understands and responds to the character, and sympathizes with him in his troubles, can there be any suspense even in a story about such an exciting complication as this one.

You may have some questions about my notations. If so, hold them until you do the work on Assignment 6, which calls for further practice with the same problem.

I'm rather glad that you attempted this formal opening, setting the stage, for you've given me an opportunity to warn you against such devices, which are always artificial. This introduction undoubtedly is a hangover from your boyhood reading, when such elaborate stagings were much used. Today's taste prefers a story that plunges into the action with no apology. Your story could begin very effectively and with equal clearness at X on page 4.

I can congratulate you on your writing. This account is simple and direct, with the colloquial quality that readers today prefer. If in your fiction you can write with equal directness, the practice period that you're now entering upon will not be too long, I predict.

You're to be congratulated too, upon your range of experiences, most of which will certainly supply you with story stuff. We'll discuss your ideas with you as you submit them together with future assignments. I'm sure that you realize that any story idea suggesting the Volstead[15] era will seem dated. Even if some adventures similar to those of that period are still current, they will seem dated. There must, however, be current complications in your present business in which there will be human interest and popular appeal. The experience that you've used for Assignment 1 has too much of the gangster flavor, but the problems of the Napa Valley Industries must surely provide some useable story stuff. Watch your step, of course. Remember that the Saturday Evening Post, and some other publications, carry no liquor ads. That means something to all editors. You'll have some nice editorial questions to solve, and on this we'll try to help you.

And now a word on business. First of all, there is the fact that we've had to resubmit our contract to the Veterans Administration, in order to make some changes, among others an increase in the fee. We haven't yet had the final OK on this point, and until it comes through, we'll hold your papers. If there are any questions on the part of your local office, this explanation will account for our not at the moment being listed.

A copy of NARRATIVE TECHNIQUE was mailed immediately on receipt of your letter of November 15, and it must surely be in your hands by this time.

In accordance with our secretary's note of November 20 we are dating your term from the arrival here of Assignment 1, which came in on January 10. This means that your deadline will be July 10, 1947. This looks like plenty of time, but better budget the work carefully, putting a little pressure on the first ten assignments, in order to have a little extra time for the final five.

You've made a good start, and now let's have assignment 2.

Yours Sincerely,
Camelia W. Uzzell

February 12, 1947

Dear Uzzells;

In Mrs. Uzzell's letter of January 14th she mentioned having to resubmit your contract to the Veteran's Administration, etc. May I ask, is the tuition angle of my course taken care of or will it be in due time, when the contract is renegotiated?

Then there's the matter of the copy of NARRATIVE TECHNIQUE you sent me. Do I owe you for it, or is the cost, as I supposed, included in your fee?

The above two questions are just by way of keeping the record straight. We haven't spoken much of such mundane matters.

Both of you mention the possibility of using Alcohol Tax problems in my writing. Unfortunately there is a law which prohibits us from disclosing in any manner whatever the manner or style of business of any permittee, and the Bureau therefore holds that we can publish nothing that has even the faintest breath of spiritus frumenti about it without first submitting it through them. They also have a prohibition against outside employment without permission, so I figure it's none of their business that I'm taking up a new career until such time as I have to start splitting the profits with the Income Tax Division. After I've sold my third or fourth best seller then I'll write an eye-opener on the evils of the "hair-off-the-dog",—or—"How many cockroaches can there be in the distiller's beer before he has to call it roach whiskey instead of Bourbon", which is a problem that has troubled me at times.

So for the present I prefer to write of other things—and I've done other things. I have cut timber in Colorado, done trucking, worked every photographic angle there is, have ridden the freights without paying fare, have been a gandy-dancer[16] (RR extra crew), stevedored, etc. I've been a scoutmaster. I've been president of a Sunday School class. Right now I'm just learning the ropes of 4-H work, having recently been inveigled into accepting the job of herding some 30 junior farmers. All of those things will yield stories in due time. Right now what I'm after is just learning how to write the same kind of crap the other guys are selling from whatever angle is easiest to me—confessions—slicks—pulp love—Wild West—I don't care. When I acquire facility and flow then I'll do the stuff that knocks the editors' eye out. Of course if you insist that I have to dig up some of that stuff now for the fresh angle to make the sale or something I'll do it, but right now I prefer to do what Woodford[17], if I remember correctly, called Formula stuff. Or should I mention Woodford in your presence? He shocks me at times too and I'm mounted on rubber.

I must apologize for my second story idea at this time. I flouted your instructions. I went too long on you and left you no space for comment. After all, my theme is in the first line, but how could you tell what I was thinking if I just wrote down a theme and didn't produce my complications. Besides which, I copied the thing right out of my notebook with as much squeezing as I could do, and I swear I had tears in my eyes and a lump in my throat when I dreamed up my part of it. Maybe I'm just a sob-sister tabloid reporter at heart.

And now, about you. I find that your blue pencil notations are just the ticket for me. And I am still a little surprised that I do not resent them, however accurate and just, as I have in times past resented criticism. Maybe I have grown up or broadened or something in the interim, but I definitely have the feeling that if you can put up with me long enough you may make something out of me.

Sincerely,
Earl S. Martin
288 Wake St.
Napa, California

Thomas H Uzzell
Camelia W Uzzell
Stillwater, Oklahoma
June 12, 1947

Dear Mr. Martin;
We have had no copy from you since February 24. This means that under instructions from the Veterans Administration, we must cancel your enrollment unless you begin regular work immediately.
Please let us know what we can count on.

Yours Sincerely,
Camelia W Uzzell

1956 Creative Writing, Interest Inventory of E. Stanley Martin

Creative Writing, English 555
Santa Rosa Junior College
E. Stanley Martin
September 18, 1956

I. You ask for a list of the ten most important books I have ever read. In my lifetime I have read many books. I have also read lists of books—lists of the world's most important books—lists of the world's great literature—lists of what other people would like me to believe that they believe are the best in their class—and I have read at least parts of the recommended fare. But if you really want to know, I find Plutarch and Plato pretty dull reading. I will admit that Boccacio is much easier to read, although you don't find him on many of the "Best" lists, unless it would be "The Best of the World's Worst Literature".

Here are ten books that have been important to me, more or less in the order in which they assumed importance in my life:

1. *The Bible*. The first book of which I had knowledge.
2. *Laddie*, by Gene Stratton Porter. My mother read it aloud to us at the supper table.
3. *The Boy Mechanic*, and its companion, *The Boy Electrician*, by Popular Mechanics Magazine. It opened up the magic of the world around me.
4. *Short Story Writing*, by Walter Pitkin. At the age of 13 it caught my interest, and I have a definite goal of writing a saleable story by the time I'm 60. That should allow a reasonable scope of experience as a basis for writing. (My eldest grandchild will then be 16).
5. *The Oxford Book of Verse*, or a similar Title. I had written doggerel and verse, but here was some good stuff to stir my blood.
6. *The Saga of Andy Burnett*, by Stewart Edward White. A group of books, appearing first as serial short stories and novels in the Saturday Evening Post, *The Long Rifle, Mountain Man, Californio, Ranchero, and Folded Hills*.
7. *Across the Wide Missouri*, by Bernard DeVoto. A living history of the trans-Mississippi, gathered together by a capable historian.
8. *The Rivers Ran East*, by Leonard Clark. Breathtaking modern adventure by a well-informed adventurer.

Having reached that point, I find that I have omitted two in order of progression. At about Number 4 should be "The Boy Scout Handbook", and between 5 and 6 should be "Military Photography" written by Corporal E.S. Martin. The latter was a text for the photographic section of the Signal School at Fort Monmouth, New Jersey, of which I was the chief enlisted instructor. I believe I learned more from writing that text in 1927-28 than my students ever learned from reading it.

II. You ask for a list of the magazines I most frequently read. Here is the list, with comments.

1. The Saturday Evening Post. I have listened to stories from the Post, and later read it myself for the past 40 years with persistent regularity, although there have been lapses.
2. Colliers. I have read the short-shorts in Colliers for the past 25 years, and such other items in it as I have found of interest.
3. Popular Science Monthly
4. Popular Mechanics. 3 & 4 are a pair that I have been reading consistently for 40 years.

5. Readers Digest. Cover to cover for twenty years, although I now find myself skipping a few, articles, that is.
6. Sunset. Since 1943—the conversion of a Hoosier to a Prune-picker.
7. Holiday. I have a complete file from Volume 1, number 1, March, 1946.
8. National Geographic. An avid reader for many years, when I could find it to read. A subscriber (member, that is) for the past five years.
9. Life. One picture tells more than 1000 words, but the scheduled articles are surprisingly authentic and informative. Painless culture for the masses.
10. The Writer. A capably written trade magazine slanted to the feminine would-be writer, but worth the reading.

That is my regular magazine fare, with the exception of "The Western Stamp Collector", a strictly philatelist's news sheet. The occasional fare—for those odd moments when I haven't a thing to read—there would be True, Argosy, Saga, New Yorker, Playboy, and an occasional Coronet, although at one time I read Coronet and Esquire (the Varga era) consistently.

III. I scan two newspapers a day on weekdays—The San Francisco Examiner, and the Santa Rosa Press-Democrat. In addition to scanning, I read the second editorial page of the Examiner, Herb Caen when I have time, and always work out the crossword puzzle.

IV. I am interested in writing the short story. Particularly I am interested in writing the light and airy story with firm undertones of reality.

V. When the sweat runs down through your eyebrows and sets your eyes to smarting, when the dust clogs your nose and throat and grits between your teeth and turns your shirt to a muddy rag, when your hands are so sweaty they can't hold the hoe handle and your back aches till it feels like it would never straighten, it's time to head for the cool shade of the back porch and a tall, cold, dew-covered glass of lemonade.

The knobby nosed barkeep with the velvet jacket, and the trowel-tailed eager beavers from the land of the sky-blue waters, that are forever interrupting the programs on TV would blow a tube to hear me say it, but to my way of thinking there is no finer drink on a hot day than lemonade.

And when I say lemonade, I don't mean just lemon juice and sugar and water. I mean lemonade like my mother used to make it. Ripe, golden lemons rolled back and forth under the palm of your hand with gentle pressure, and then sliced thin into a three-gallon milk crock, sugar sprinkled on frugally, and mashed with a wire potato masher. Then chunks of ice chipped from the block hauled from the ice house wrapped in burlap in a coaster wagon, carefully washed and placed in the crock, and clear cold spring water added while stirring with a long-handled spoon between sips to get just the right dilution, preferably to the chanted accompaniment of a group of kids singing

"Fresh Lemonade
Made in the shade
Stirred with a spade
By an old maid".

Ladled out with the long-handled dipper into a tall glass, with a chip or two of ice and a slice or two of lemon, your mouth waters to see it and watch the little drops of dew forming on the outside of the glass. The first delicious sip, fragrant with the oil of lemon from the peel, and sweetly tart from the sugared juice, cleanses the dust from the throat and brings you eagerly alive again. You sigh with contentment and settle back against the porch post and watch a bumble-bee busily buzzing in and out of the red cups of the Hollyhocks seeking nectar. You tinkle the ice in your glass, take another sip, and think to yourself that the nectar he is seeking, or even the nectar of the Gods, cannot compare with your glass of lemonade.

Setting
(The Casino)

By Earl S. Martin
September 25, 1956

Everywhere was noise and movement. Wheels whirred, bells rang, voices chattered or shrieked, arms jerked convulsively, heads bobbed and threaded their way through the jungle of machinery and people, lights flashed on and off about the room, the loud speaker droned above the babble.

A man shook his hand and tossed a pair of cubes toward the green bank-board at the opposite end of the table, snapping his fingers as he peered at the cubes under the bright light. The game-keeper called a number, pulled the dice to him with his little hook, collected silver dollars from the table and racked them before him, after stacking five in front of one player and two in front of another.

A black-jack dealer intoned steadily and laid cards on the table. Dollars jingled and slid across the green felt.

A handle came down with a jerk. Wheels whirred and clicked into place, followed by the sound of a flood of nickels dropping into the catch pan. A light flashed on the big board over the cashier's cage. "Jack-pot on 73", the loud-speaker blared. The white haired woman in front of the slot machine that had just paid off was dancing up and down and shrieking "I hit it! I hit it!"

Intent white faces peered at her for a moment in the area around her, then the handles of the machines nearby came down with renewed vigor, and the whirring, clicking, jingling, ringing, and babbling continued as before.

Chapter 4

Poetry and Sonnets

The wonderful thing about poetry is that it has form, rhythm, meter—structure, which can provide a certain security for the author of less experience or intrepidity. With a multitude of formats, from limerick to sonnet, cinquain to haiku, one has the opportunity to focus on a predictable form, a framework within which to express feelings and ideas. Add the rhyming game in there, and most of the breathless fear of staring at a blank screen or paper with an empty head is vanquished.

A poem is something of a puzzle to solve, really. Gramps was a great puzzler, regularly working crosswords and other word games, and often setting up intricate jigsaw puzzles which became the focus of many family gatherings. Of course his unique brand of humor was to tuck away one piece in his coat pocket until we all realized with chagrin at near-completion that there was a missing piece. At this opportune moment Gramps would produce the vanished item with a flourish and a chuckle, and triumphantly complete the puzzle!

Stanley Martin was a fan of the classic American poets: Longfellow, Poe, Emerson, Frost, Cummings and especially Walt Whitman. But I think Ogden Nash, a contemporary of Gramps', was a particular favorite with his witty humor and wordcrafting in light verse. Many of Gramps' poems reflect playfulness akin to Nash's style, while his sonnets show his truly romantic nature.

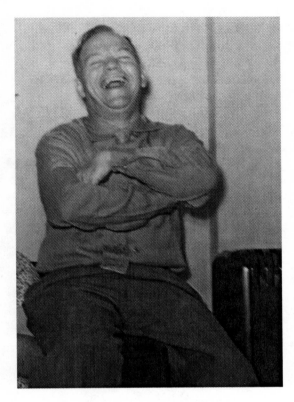

Stanley (Gramps) with a big belly laugh, early 50's

E.S. Martin, Collected Poems, 1954-55
These contained rejection responses from the Saturday Evening Post, American Legion Magazine, and Good Housekeeping, so he presumably was submitting them for publication at various times.—KHB

WRITING
Words must be written in a smoothly flowing way
With gentle swells and verdant swales between,
With evanescent thoughts like butterflies
To flutter up a path and lead us on
Up steeper slopes and deeper glens until
They lead us to a mountaintop
Ablaze with sun—
Sharp swept with wind—
And holding for us
Mental ecstasy.
8/10/54

ELECTION RECOLLECTION
I don't begrudge to Uncle Sam
The pay I do not see—
That part they call withholding tax
The boss holds out on me.

But when the Ides of March roll round
And June, and then September,
That out-of-pocket estimate
I pay, I long remember.

I think of it election day
And mutter, "By the Prophet,
Republicans and Democrats
All must go to Tophet".

MY TACTFUL SPOUSE
My handsome handywork I show
And ask her what she thinks,
And with her brightest smile and glow
She says, "It stinks".

DELAYED REACTION
Why is it that my apt cliché
Fits what we talked of yesterday,
And while we're speaking, to my sorrow,
I am dumb until tomorrow?

MATHEMATICAL DAZE
My son is short on long division,
Addition and subtraction.
He sees no point to decimals
And simply cannot fraction.

The things he doesn't know in Math
Defy enumeration,
But since I bought him rabbits he
Knows all about multiplication.

PARENTAL FRUSTRATION

In stern reproof I tell my child,
"This thing you must not do!"
She frowns, then smiles as if beguiled
And says, "Don't you?"

IT'S FOR THE BIRDS

A bird in the hand
Is worth two in the bush
Or three in the air flying yonder,
And fruit that's been canned
Beats fruit on the bush
To thrifty folks pausing to ponder.

But the bird on the wing
Is a sight to behold—
Unfettered and gloriously free!
Let it fly! Let it sing! And when hungry and cold
Eat the apples I left on the tree.

COMING AND GOING

The man who dreamed up income tax
To fill the treasury with dough
Furnished endless jokes for hacks
And brought the world a world of woe.

But woe is you! And woe is me!
If that same joker checks the facts,
And finds, to fill the treasury
They also need an outgo tax.

LOOK MA! NO HANDS!

I have never envied Washington
Napoleon or Lee,
I have never ever wanted to
Be anyone but me.

I don't want to be a hero, and
For gold I have no lust,
I don't want a name, acclaim or fame—
I don't want to be a bust!

TOUCHE

My mind has neatly filed away
An apt remark, a neat cliché,
For every situation.
But I can never think of one
That someone hasn't just begun
In any conversation.

1926 article clipping from a Terre Haute newspaper:
SOLDIER WRITES MOTHER POEM

Private Earl S. Martin (*according to my mother, Gramps' daughter and eldest child, he hated the name Earl, and always used only the initial E, with the name Stanley*)
An unusual Mother's Day greeting was received by Mrs. Frank J. Martin of North Seventh Street Road, in the form of a letter in verse from her soldier son, Private Earl S. (Stanley) Martin, who is stationed at Ft. Monmouth, New Jersey. Private Martin, who has been in the army since the first of the year, is in the photo section of the signal corps and is a laboratory instructor in photography.
His Mother's Day letter to his mother follows:

Mother's Day

(A Soldier's letter to his mother)
In this one day of all the year
Inadequate as it may be,
We turn away from toil and care
And fill our hearts with thoughts of thee.

We have not reached the mountain top,
We are not rich as riches go,
But we can all find time to stop
And think of you as on we go.

We know your pain; we know your tears,
In our small way, as all men do,
And as we journey down the years
Our sweetest thoughts are all of you.

We are not pure as you are pure,
We have not lived without a stain,
But in this day of all the year
We're being pure for you again.

Dear Mother, may you always be
Beside us on our battle line
And keep our hearts as pure and free
And full of simple Faith as thine.

Even Gramps' brothers got into the act-Some June Ditties by brother **F. Ray Martin** for E. Stanley Martin(stapled together on mimeographed cut paper copies, manually typed)

6/4/1969
Pleasin' Season

Snow
For an Eskimo.
Sticky hot
For a Hottentot.
Rainy? Shucks,
Ideal for ducks.
Indian Summer?
I like it wummer.
Balmy May?
Hey hey hey!

6/4/1969
The Verse I Hope To Write Sometime

I'd start it out just fine
With six words and a dash;
And end up with a long last line of twenty-nine words without foot
or meter but which rhymes, like Ogden Nash.

6/5/1969
Magna Cum Lawdy

If you want a Bon Voyage
With champagne and swell fromage
And have a really bang-up party,
Ya gotta go furder away than Sparty.
So, to make our hearts grow fonder

Y'oughta pick a longer wander;
But don't feel blue and shed a tear—
We love to have ya stay right here!

6/7/1969
*A Verse I'd Like to Write Sometime In
Emulation of One of My Favorite Poets*

I'd start it off conventionally
With six words and a comma;
Then wind it up eventually
With a long last line of twenty-eight words without foot meter break or punctuation
which would leave the reader gasping as if he had Emphysomma.
(*Did I spell it right? I can't find my dictionary!*)

6/7/1969
Naughty??

When a teacher who taught
Met a preacher who praught,
The teacher taught the preacher
Things she hadn't ought.

Love Poems and Sonnets
By Earl Stanley Martin
For his dear wife,
Mabel Louella Thomson Martin
Evansville, Indiana 1935

Life's a kaleidoscope—
Swift changing patterns—
Heartaches and springing hope—
Crowned heads and tatterns.

Tuesdays are made for love—
Fridays for sorrow—
Nights are for stars above—
Love me tomorrow!

Swiftly the color schemes
Waver and sever—
Object of all my dreams,
Love me forever!

Mabel and Stanley Martin, 1960's

(For my darling wife,
Done at Evansville, September 24, 1935.
E Stanley Martin)

Sonnet

When I have held you in my arms at night
And kissed your breasts, your eyes, your cheeks, your hair,
Your parted lips—to me you are more fair
Than sunset on a tropic sea, than light
At morn when storm-tossed nights are past and gone
And heaven is blue and in its place again;
And your caress is like sweet music when
The morning thrush sings joyous in the dawn.

All heaven and earth are mine when you are in
The cradle of my arms. When you're away
I am alone and friendless in the din
And furor on a dismal cloudy day.
I love you, darling—hold me to your breast
Where all is quietude and love and rest.

(To my wife, at Evansville, September 24, 1935
E. Stanley Martin)

Sonnet

My very dearest darling, you must know
How difficult it is at times to write
The things that lie within our hearts; to show
Our love in hieroglyphics—black on white.

"A thing of beauty is a joy forever"
As Keats once said, but beauty told in words
Lies not within the symbols, but is rather
Within the heart of him who reads:

                                              The herds

Of kine that wander slowly o'er the lea
Are things of beauty to the poet, still
The farmer checks the butter-fat—and me—
I order loin of beef and eat my fill.
And so it goes. I love you, sweetest one,
Beyond a doubt you've heard that line before,
But let me tell you, moon and stars and sun
Of mine, I love you, and little more.

Love, Stanley
Indicted at Evansville, September 24, 1935

Sonnet: "Dream"

Down the velvet treaded stairs of night
A dream soft clad in silken negligee
Steps softly, proudly in the silver light
Of twinkling stars—a wanton thing, and gay
With laughter of a thousand nights repressed
Behind the budding of her virgin breasts.

Straight-limbed and contoured for an artist's eye
With black silk hair, and diamonds set in jade
For eyes, and lips that like a butterfly
Steal sweets and go. A dreamer's fairy maid
Who comes with eager step across the dew
To nestle in my arms—My dream of you.

(To my wife, at Evansville, September 25, 1935
E Stanley Martin)

Sonnet

These things are beautiful: The stars at night,
Pure silver set in lapis; Wind at dawn;
A singing brook; the patient mellow light
Of candles lighted for a one who's gone.

These things are beautiful, but all of these
Are pale cold replicas without compare
Beside the radiance—the warming breeze
Of your sweet smile, my fairest of the fair.

(To my wife, 10-1-35
E Stanley Martin)

Sonnet

When our two hearts have worn themselves at last
With wounding each the other, and with pride
And never-ending conflict, and with love,
And heed the shining silver stars above
And in our parquet sit quiet, side by side,
As lovers should, and hold each other fast
The winds of chance will belly out the sail
And blow us where they will, some distant port
Sun-drenched perchance and filled with riotous bloom
Of fragrant flowers; and there will be a room
Whose walls are horizons where we may sport
In hearts ease, and where love will never fail.

(To my wife 10-1-35
E Stanley Martin)

Chapter 5

On The Job

This is the wording of the Eighteenth Amendment to the Constitution.[18]

Section 1. After one year from the ratification of this article the manufacture, sale, or transportation of intoxicating liquors within, the importation thereof into, or the exportation thereof from the United States and all territory subject to the jurisdiction thereof for beverage purposes is hereby prohibited.

Section 2. The Congress and the several States shall have concurrent power to enforce this article by appropriate legislation.

Prohibition went into effect in the United States in 1920 and was repealed by the twenty-first amendment in 1933, which gave the power of alcohol regulation to the individual states. Interestingly the hub of anti-Prohibitionist sentiment was the city of Chicago, where organized crime and gang violence was thriving in the 1920's—exactly the time Stanley Martin was pulled like a magnet to that city and away from his high school education. Of course he left Chicago to hop freights to Seattle, so perhaps the call of the "frontier" and the more open spaces of the Pacific Northwest had more hold on him.

Stanley Martin was blessed with some inherited job opportunities in his youth, between the family Photo Studio, and the family farm, where there was always useful work to be done, in particular with the flower growing projects of his father, Frank J Martin. In addition, Stanley served twice in the U.S. Army in his young life, so was suitably employed during those times. And as this book demonstrates, there was always a dream career lingering in his future, one of being a published author, a rainbow he chased all his life. However, in 1935 he began his lifetime career in government service, an agent of the

Alcohol Tax section of the Internal Revenue Service, at that time called a "Storekeeper-Gauger".

With the repeal of the Prohibition Act in 1933, and the new ruling for state regulation of alcohol sales, the federal government kept a hand in by increasing control and regulation of taxation, for which enforcement agents would be required. Shortly after his marriage to Mabel Thomson, Stanley rode in on this need for agents, probably a shoe-in with his veteran status. He continued in this career, which included a period of time when he made regulatory visits in official capacity to many wineries across California's beautiful Napa Valley, until his retirement in 1967. With a combination of a great sense of responsibility, a facility with writing, and attention to detail, he had all the makings of a fine federal agent[19].

The polished professional and conservative look of Stanley Martin, ready for work. Photo by Martin

The stories in Chapter five reflect Gramps' experiences in federal work, showing the serious side as well as some humor. The last two, *Notorious Lil* and *Feature Story*, reflect his association and fascination with newspaper reporting and journalism, with which he had a bit of experience as well as close friends who were career reporters.

Caught By a Thread, with Critiques

Stuart Tynan
Madeira, Ohio
August 28, 1941

Dear Mr. Martin;

Why, in your script CAUGHT BY A THREAD, don't you have the stranger really be a counterfeiter? There could be a reward out for him, and Janet and Bill could use the money to get married with. In this way, both Bill and Janet would be the main characters in the story. Make Janet seem more interesting, so that the reader will want her as a heroine. You could make your story more mysterious, by using the stranger as the biggest incident in your story. Play up your romance between Bill and Janet so that the reader will want them to get married in the end. These changes will definitely improve your script.

Sincerely,
S. Tynan

Dear Mr. Martin;

In your short-short story titled CAUGHT BY A THREAD, I want you to change the incident of the stranger stealing the thread to make counterfeit money with. This hardly seems probable, for a counterfeiter would hardly go to the trouble of stealing his thread when he could buy it so cheaply and not have to run the risk of being caught. Do you see what I mean? In other words, simply have the man to buy several spools of thread and hand Janet the counterfeit money. Then, when she sees Bill go to the manager's office, she can connect the counterfeit money with the thread that the stranger always buys at her counter, and can follow him. I suggest that you leave out the incident of the girl entirely. Your ending is much better since you have revised your story. See if you can't make these changes just as well.

Sincerely,
Stuart Tynan

MODERN COURSE IN SYNDICATE FICTION WRITING
2010 Raymond Commerce Building
Newark, N.J.
October 28, 1941

Dear Mr. Martin;

We are certainly having a hard time with this script.

You have diligently approached each revision suggestion I have made, and I am satisfied that you understand them competently on this script's letters sent you—but it doesn't click. I could put it out on the markets with the others for a month or two of traveling the complete rounds, but it would hurt the chances for better ones. And I do not feel that it would sell as it stands.

Your script has definitely improved since you have revised it, and yet, there is still something lacking. I want you to insert some more conversation into the first half of your script, for I feel sure that this is what is holding your story back. Have Janet say something else to the stranger besides "I'm sorry, that's the smallest I have", etc. Have her suspect him from the very beginning, and have her immediately start up a conversation with him in order that she might stumble on to some clue.

One more lecture is necessary for you; I'm having a brief illustration duplicated for you herewith attached, to bring out the way a story should be built up.

Sincerely,
Stuart Tynan

E.S. Martin
1708 N. 8th St
Terre Haute, Ind.
Third Revision, Lesson #1
November 25, 1941

CAUGHT BY A THREAD

By
E.S. Martin

"I'm sorry; that's the smallest I have." He handed me a ten dollar bill.

Right then I knew it was counterfeit. Not because of the bill, for, except for the fact that it was new, it felt all right and it looked all right.

Not that I looked at it! Not me! I was too smart for that. I was looking at his eyes. They were the give-away.

The minute he had walked in the front door I had known he was a wrong number. How? Well, I don't know exactly, but by the way he was dressed, and by the look on his pan.

I shouldn't have been looking towards the front door, but Bill Benson, the floor manager, was my boyfriend and I was looking around for him. It was almost lunch time and Bill hadn't been around to ask me to have lunch with him. So I saw this fellow walk in.

He was middle height, but he was well built and well dressed, and he was good looking. He was in his early thirties, and he wasn't the ten-cent-store-type, and if I hadn't been engaged to Bill my heart would have fluttered when I saw him. Until I saw his eyes.

He walked in the front door like he owned the place, and then he stopped and looked all around the store. And it was the look on his pan that was the first tip-off. I was three counters away, but that was close enough that one look at his face told me he wasn't the ten-cent-store-type.

You work in a dime store a while . . . . And I've been at Woodruff's for five years . . . you learn to type your customers. If it's a man he's a hen-pecked husband running an errand for his wife, a mortgage-ridden home owner buying a plug for the bathtub, or a papa with a kind heart and an empty purse trying to find something nice for the kids. And whichever type he is, he'll be wearing his worries on his face.

But this guy wasn't wearing any worries. He had a *confident* look. After he'd looked all around he started down my aisle. When he stopped at my counter you could have blown me over with a breath . . . without garlic, please,—I get enough of that on my job. I turned on my best smile . . . you never know when a smile will pay dividends, and it doesn't cost anything . . . . And I said, "Good morning, Sir! May I help you?"

I'm at notions and there isn't much on my counter a man would want. He picked out two spools of silk thread, a bright red one and a bright blue one, and he said, "Can you give me ten of each of these?" I thought, "What on earth . . . ," but I said, "Just a moment, please," and dived under the counter and came up with his twenty spools of thread, and showed him as I dropped them in a bag.

"That's fine," he said, and he smiled real nice. But when he made that, "I'm sorry; that's the smallest I have," crack I was looking at his eyes and I knew the ten he handed me was a phony.

His eyes didn't match his smile. They were narrow and hard and cold, and when he looked at me as he handed me the ten I felt like I didn't have any clothes on. So I smiled and went to my register and rung up the sale, but I was cold inside. "Don't let the customer know you suspect him," were our instructions on counterfeit passers, so I made a play of making change out of my register before I called my counter number for change.

Standing by the register after I called my counter number, I hoped Bill would come instead of one of the floor ladies. Bill knows all about counterfeiters and phony money. He's worked his way through a night law school, and he's passed the examination for a job as a secret service agent, and he's only waiting for his appointment to quit his job at Woodruff's and marry me. Maybe if he caught this counterfeit passer he'd get his appointment sooner, because that's what secret service agents do.

Sure enough, Bill came. He nearly always answers my call if he can. I handed him the bill with my hand upside down, "thumbs down," but in case he missed that I said, "Can you get me some change from six?" The change drawer at twenty was closer, but the drawer at six had the counterfeit check charts.

Bill had his back to the customer and he winked one eye. "How about lunch?" he asked. "It's a date," I said, and he was gone, headed towards six.

"Engage the customer in conversation while the floor-walker goes for the police," our instructions were, so I went back to talk to this guy. "I'll have your change in a minute," I told him. He sort of relaxed. But his eyes were still sharp, looking around the store and at me.

"This is a tough racket for a pretty thing like you, isn't it?" he said. I'm not pretty, and I know it. I'm five foot three when I wear my high heels, and I'm wider across the hips than I used to be. That's from standing on my feet all day every day for five years. And my face has never been used in any cosmetic ads; but I have to keep the customer talking.

"Working in a dime store has its compensations," I said, and I gave him what Bill calls my "exclusive" smile, with my chin down and sort of peeking up from under my lashes and eyebrows. I could see him begin to be really interested. Then all of a sudden his eyes got frosty and he said, "Excuse me! I'll be right back!" and I knew by the way he turned quick and headed for the door he wouldn't ever be back if he could help it.

I turned around quick to see what he'd seen, and there was Bill just going in the back office door where the phone was. This fellow had been watching Bill all the time. When Bill didn't come back with his change he knew the play and was ducking out the front door. And there went Bill's chance of catching him and my chance of getting married any time soon. So I ducked out too.

When I got on the walk, I thought I'd lost him. I can't see over people so I have to look around. Then I caught sight of him and away I went.

When I called the store and asked for Bill, he answered quick like he'd been standing right there. I was all out of breath. "Janet, honey, are you all right?" he asked quick. "Sure, I'm all right," I said, "except my breath is in short pants. But come quick! This counterfeiter is in a flat right across from this drug store I'm calling from, and I couldn't follow him another step if he decides to leave." Bill said, "We'll be right there," and hung up.

I didn't know who "we" was until Bill showed up with the secret service he'd called. This S.S. agent says to Bill, "Give me three minutes to get around to the back door, and then you try the front door. When he hears you, he'll duck out the back and I'll nab him." Bill nodded and this agent crossed the street and went down the alley.

"You stay here," Bill told me, but when he walked up the three steps fo that flat I was right behind him. Bill pulled a gun out of his pocket, and it was the first time I knew he owned a gun. Then he reached over and turned the knob to rattle the door, and at the first push the door swung open.

There was the counterfeiter, right in the middle of the room throwing things in a suitcase on the floor. When the door came open he turned quick and reached under his arm, but when he saw Bill's gun he let his arms drop.

Bill stepped into the room but as I started in behind him, out of the corner of my eye I saw something through the crack between the door and the jamb . . . and the door was slowly moving shut. I'm not very big but I put all I had into the shove I gave that door. A gun clattered across the floor and a little rat-eyed guy came out from behind that door holding his wrist and swearing a blue streak. Bill turned quick to cover both those men with his gun, and he told Rat-eye, "Shut up. There's a lady present."

Then the secret service agent came in from the back door where he'd been waiting for them to come out, and in a minute he had them frisked and handcuffed. "The Treasury Department thinks enough of this pair that it's been offering a thousand apiece for them for a long time. How did you happen to get wise to them?"

"The little silk threads in that ten he passed at the store weren't the right color," Bill said.

"Yeah! I was buying some the right color so I could make some new paper," this fellow that had been in the store snarled. "I never raise a bill. I always do it the hard way."

"Then the papers can say, 'TWO MEN CAUGHT BY A THREAD', can't they?" the secret service man said.

Bill had his gun back in his pocket and both arms around me and a look in his eye I'd been waiting a long time to see.

"Make it three," he said.

THE END

Old Uncle Joe

By
E.S. Martin

"Humph," I grunted to myself. The test set showed the whiskey to be 100 proof. The bottle was "Old Uncle Joe" bourbon and the label said 90 proof.

I reached up and took the bottle of "Stag Horn" from its spot on the shelf between the canned peas and the spinach. I poured a sample of the whiskey into the tube of my Williams test set, filled the tube with reagent, shook them together and took a reading, 100 proof again.

That stumped me. Usually when a bartender refills a bottle he uses cheaper whiskey of the same or a lower proof. His purpose of course is to make a few more pennies out of the customer who will pay extra for a favorite brand. And it was to prevent just such consumer deception, and to prevent the even worse deception of refilling with tax-unpaid whiskey, that the prohibition against the refilling of bottles was included in the Internal Revenue Code that I work under. In my experience I had never run into a bottle refilled with liquor of higher proof.

I leaned back against the counter and looked along the grocery shelves. Altogether there were seven quart bottles of whiskey shelved among the canned goods. Not much of a stock. All of them had been opened, and since the first two had evidently been refilled I had to test the rest of them.

All but one of the bottles was labeled as containing 90 proof whiskey. The other was labeled 100 proof. They all tested 100 proof. That meant I had six refills on my hands.

The dumpy, talkative woman that the storekeeper had been waiting on took her little bag of groceries under her arm and the bell on the front door tinkled her departure.

"Where do you keep the rest of your whiskey, Joe?" I asked the storekeeper.

"Joe Lamonsky, dba Joe's Grocery" the special tax stamp, or federal license, as some called it, had read when I copied it onto my report form which I always did first thing on one of these inspections.

Joe moved down the aisle between the shelves and stood looking at me, his ham-sized hands hanging loosely. He filled the aisle and I had to lift my chin to look him in the eye.

"I ain't got any other whiskey. I don't sell by the bottle. I just pour a shot for the people when they pay the bill. Sometimes the men have me put one on the bill when they come by after work."

"Okay Joe," I said, and took my flashlight and walked over to check the beer stamp on the quarter barrel of beer he had on tap in the dinky little cooler. I wanted to get his mind off the whiskey while I looked around some more.

I had already made one tour of the place. It was a typical edge-of-town grocery on the working man side of the tracks in the town of Auburn, about seventeen miles southwest of Springfield, Illinois. The people of the neighborhood were mostly of lover European stock to judge by the goats and geese and garden patches in the fenced-in yards I had passed.

There were canned goods on the shelves along one side of the store, with the whiskey bottles set among the cans. The counter in front of the shelves had pull-out bins underneath, filled with beans, rice, oatmeal, polenta and such like. Along the other side of the store were a few bales of hay, feed in sacks, and some hardware.

While I was checking the beer a truck backed up to the door and Joe and the truck driver started unloading feed. The feed was in hundred pound bags. The driver would drag them to the tail gate. Joe would them pick them up and toss them the ten feet across to the stack, each bag falling into exact position.

"I wouldn't want him mad at me," I thought. I'm not very big and Joe was well over six feet, about 220 pounds I judged, and by the looks of him all of it was muscle. From his name and appearance I guessed him to be Lithuanian.

While the feed was being unloaded I pulled out the dry grocery bins, felt to the bottom of each bin, and then peered in behind it. Somewhere Joe must have a gallon jug of cheap whiskey he was using to refill his bottles, and I knew from experience that these boys could think up some weird places to hide such things. If Joe had a jug I wanted to find it.

Of course I could seal the six refilled bottles as evidence and suggest to Joe that he make a sixty dollar offer in compromise in lieu of criminal prosecution. Ten dollars a bottle was the minimum offer that the Bureau would accept on refills in those days right after repeal. But as a matter of pride I wanted to find the bottle of whiskey he was refilling from so that I could name it in my report and state that it was taxpaid goods. Otherwise there was always the suspicion that he was using moonshine for refilling, and that was a violation to be handled in court rather than by an offer in compromise.

While I was poking through the stock I kept taking the place apart in my mind. I had a feeling that there was something peculiar about the layout. Of course there was the door at the back of the store that led into the living quarters. I couldn't go in there without a search warrant, and so far I had no basis for asking the Commissioner for a search warrant. Besides, search warrants were a job for our enforcement personnel, not for us "permissive" boys who inspected the legal or tax-paying premises. No, it was something else. A glance around the store told me that it wasn't the storeroom that was bothering me, so it must be the basement.

Of course! That was it! The basement! The store was square on the first floor, but the basement wasn't, and they don't build buildings that way in Illinois. They dig a hole the size of the building, put in the basement walls and set the building on top.

I walked over to the stairway, flipped the switch and walked down. Joe was busy with a customer. In the basement the single small bulb in front of the furnace showed the coal bin, a collection of empty cartons and chicken crates and the usual miscellany of other junk. The area I could see here was only half the width of the store. I walked forward into the gloom and found that this direction the basement ran to the front of the building, and that beyond the half-width of the furnace room it widened to the full width of the building. That left one fourth of the basement area next to the furnace room unaccounted for, closed off solidly with a concrete block wall the same as the outside basement walls. So—maybe they had only put a basement under three-fourths of the store area.

To my sorrow at times, I don't give up easy when I'm on the trail of something. I took my flashlight and started searching that wall that shouldn't be there. I had worked my way along the wall facing the furnace and halfway down the other wall in the gloom and spider webs when I noticed a tag end of black covered wire sticking through the rafter at the top of a wall and hanging down about a foot. It didn't belong there. I noticed that there weren't any spider webs along the rafter here. I reached up and pulled on the wire cautiously.

I got a funny feeling in my stomach when a section of that concrete wall swung out towards me just like a door, which it turned out to be. Cleverest arrangement I had ever seen, and no sign on the wall to give it away.

The beam from my flashlight showed a light bulb on a drop cord beyond the door in the wall. I edged cautiously in, sort of holding my breath, and turned on the light.

One quick look told me that here was what I'd been looking for. On top of an up-ended barrel was a five gallon demijohn full of what looked like whiskey. But I also saw a three burner gas plate, a wash-boiler still, a copper condenser coil and a barrel rigged to cool it in, a couple of hogsheads for setting mash in—even a hydrometer for testing proof. I was standing in the middle of a bootleg distilling outfit, and that was out of my line.

My job was that of inspecting legal, taxpaying, licensed premises, looking for infractions of the federal Internal Revenue Regulations pertaining to Alcohol Tax. I worked alone and unarmed. Stills and bootleggers were the job of our investigators or enforcement personnel. They work two or more in a team and are always armed.

My chest was tight, and I noticed that I wasn't breathing good. Obviously I had stumbled onto more than I had bargained for. And now that I had found this layout something had to be done about it—but what? I didn't hanker after the job of arresting Joe, alone and unarmed as I was. Probably the best thing I could do under the circumstances would be to get back upstairs and not let on that I had found anything. I could tell Joe that everything was okay, then hop into my car and scoot into Springfield and get a crew of enforcement boys and let them take this layout over.

I didn't have much choice. That was the only smart thing to do. I reached up for the light to turn it off and turned to locate the door.

My heart seemed to stop beating, and I couldn't draw breath at all. There stood Joe, filling the doorway and lapping over the edges. I hadn't heard him come down stairs. He didn't say anything.

So it was my baby now, whether I wanted it or not. It was my move. I couldn't just stand there. I hoped Joe couldn't hear my knees knocking. "Nice little layout you have here, Joe," I said.

"Yeah," he said. "Works good. How'd you find it?"

"Oh, I just figured it had to be here so I came here and here it was."

I hadn't any more than said it until I liked to choke, remembering the story I had just paraphrased. That's the shape I was in. I recalled that that was one of Dad's favorite stories about the half-wit farmhand. The farmer's favorite horse had gotten out of the pasture and was lost. He put his whole family out looking for it and enlisted the help of the neighbors, but none of them found the horse. When they had all failed, the half-wit asked if he could go look. The farmer said, "If we can't find him, I'm sure you can't, but you can try if you're back in time to do the chores." In a little while the half-wit was back with the horse. The farmer of course wanted to know how he had found him and the half-wit explained, "I just thought, if I was a horse where would I go, and I went there, and there he was."

"You're smarter than them prohibition agents," Joe told me. "I bet there's been a dozen of them in here in the last ten years and none of them never found nothing. What you going to do now?"

That was the question I was trying to find the answer to myself. Looking at Joe it came to me all at once that for all his size he was about as nervous about this deal as I was. I took a deep breath and brought my hand down from the light where it had sort of frozen when I saw Joe in the door.

"Well, Joe," I said, "I guess you and I are goind to have to take a little trip into Springfield to the United States Commissioner. You know those bottles of whiskey upstairs have been refilled. That's a violation of Internal Revenue regulations. From the looks of this layout my guess is that you have been filling those bottles with moonshine. How about it?"

"That's right," Joe agreed. "Good stuff, too. Aged it myself. Will I have to stay in Springfield?"

"Probably not," I assured him. "Know anybody that will go your bail?"

"I can put up cash," he said. "Or I can hire a lawyer."

"You're all set then," I said. "Do you have a sack or something we can put this bottle in? I don't want to carry it out like this."

"I'll get something," he said, and disappeared in the gloom beyond the door.

I didn't try to stop him. "He'll probably keep right on going," I thought to myself. Then I realized that I was only hoping that he would. In a minute he was back with a feed bag.

"This do?" he asked, and picked up the demijohn by the neck and slipped it in the bag. I had visions of him dropping the bottle and destroying the evidence against him in the best bootlegger tradition, but he didn't. He set the bottle in as gently as if it was a baby, then picked up the bag and headed for the stairway.

"I got to tell Mama," he said as we got to the top of the stairway. He set down the bag and went into the living quarters at the back of the store.

I put my test set back in my briefcase and started putting evidence labels on the six refilled bottles and the five gallon jug.

Joe was gone so long that I was about to conclude that he had ducked out on me. Then he came into the store with a beset look about him, a little bit of a woman following him, crying and wringing her hands and fussing at him by turns.

"You going to take my Joe?" she said to me, her black eyes snapping.

"He's going with me to Springfield," I said. "He ought to be back home tonight, if he's lucky."

"He'd better be," she snapped. Then she grabbed Joe's arm and shook it. "Go ahead, ask him!" she said.

Joe shrugged and rubbed his chin. Then he nodded me over into the corner behind the counter. He pulled a roll of bills out of his coat pocket that was almost too big for his ham of a hand. The bills on the outside were twenties. Biggest roll I'd ever seen outside of a bank. Must have been a couple of thousand bucks at least in that roll.

"Can't we fix this up?" he asked. "Just you and me. Nobody else would know." He wasn't looking at me and he didn't sound very convinced or convincing.

I was stunned. Nobody had ever offered me anything more valuable than a cigar or a drink before, and the sight of all that money scared me. I had been raised to believe that honesty was the best policy, and the Internal Revenue Service had imbued me with its tradition of integrity.

"No, Joe," I said rather harshly. "This is a case for the Commissioner. Quit stalling and let's get going."

The woman overheard me. She grabbed a broom that was leaning against the wall and started to swing at me. "You can't take my Joe," she shrieked. "I'll kill you!"

I jerked up a shoulder to ward off the blow, but Joe caught the broom, jerked it from her hand, and then pushed her towards the door to the living quarters.

"Stop it!" he told her. "I told you it wouldn't work. I got to go. You take care of the store. I'll be back."

He picked up the sack with the jug in it. "Come on," he said, and walked out to my car.

"This is too easy," I thought, as Joe set the jug on the floor in the back of my car and then climbed into the front seat. And I hadn't gotten a mile out of town before I saw a car tailing me in my rear view mirror.

I stepped on the gas. The car behind speeded up too. I was almost sorry I had ever gone to work for the Internal Revenue Service. This was a lonely road in spots, and not too much traffic. I kept goosing the gas. Out of the corner of my eye I saw Joe eyeing me and holding on to the door with a death grip. The car was giving me all it had. The needle was up to seventy, which was twenty miles an hour too fast for this cracked up slab of road. The car behind was still gaining and I was wondering if they intended to crowd me into the ditch, when I heard the siren.

I slapped on the brakes and pulled onto the shoulder. I pulled out my handkerchief to wipe the sweat off my brow as I hopped out and walked back to the car behind.

"Boy am I glad to see you," I said to the stern-visaged state policeman.

"That's a switch," he growled.

I pulled out my credentials, identified myself, and told him my story. He caught on fast, and was kind enough to tail me clear into Springfield, just in case.

When I got in sight of the big office building where the investigators had their office, I gave the trooper the high sign; he beeped his horn and then went on about his business.

The enforcement office was in the biggest office building in town and the entrance to the building was at the busiest corner in town. I drove around the block looking for a parking place, but there weren't any. Then I pulled into the no-parking zone in front of the entrance to the building. I hadn't even braked to a full stop when the police whistle scolded at me, and here came a red-faced Irishman with fire in his eye. I'd had trouble enough. I had to get the jump on this one.

"Say," I greeted him, before he could get going on me. "Will you keep an eye on my car for a little bit? I got a prisoner on the front seat and five gallons of moonshine in the back and I can't take both upstairs at once." I flashed my credentials.

"Sure! Take him up; I'll keep my eye on the car."

He did, too. I took Joe upstairs to the Investigator's office. It took a little bit to give them the details so they could start writing up the jacket before taking Joe to the Commissioner for arraignment. They were also rounding up a crew to dash back to Auburn and pick up the still, when I remembered the jug in the back of my car. One of the Investigators went down with me to bring it up, and we hadn't any more than gotten the car door open when there was that big Irishman breathing down our necks.

"Oh, it's you!" he said.

"Say, thanks a lot for watching the car," I told him. "I'll move it out of here as soon as I get rid of this."

By the time we got back up to the office the crew was ready to go back to Auburn to pick up the still. Naturally they wanted me to go along. The office crew would take care of Joe. So I moved my car over to a quiet spot, climbed into their car, and took off.

When we pulled up in front of Joe's Grocery I looked at my watch. I had been gone less than an hour and a half. When we walked in the front door Joe's "Mama" greeted me very civilly, if coolly. The three Investigators followed me into the basement and to Joe's little hideaway.

The place was bare. No still! No condenser! No Hogsheads! Not even any cobwebs or dust. The room was completely empty.

I must have had a silly look on my face. Tom Conner, the oldest of the Investigators, burst out laughing.

"Don't take it so hard," he said. "In this business it happens all the time. Might as well go back to Springfield."

And we did, but it was hard for me to believe that in the short time I had been gone the stuff that I had seen in that room could disappear so completely.

What became of that still has always bothered me since. But what really bothers me is the thought of all that money Joe offered me.

At the time Joe offered me that bribe, I couldn't accept it even for the purpose of turning it over to the government, because I had no witnesses to protect me. I have since learned that what I should have done was stalled Joe off, tell him I'd think it over and be back. Then get an Investigator to search me before I went back to collect and pick me up as I came out with the money. That way we would have set Joe up for a long stretch for bribery.

That would have been better than the way it wound up. Joe got off for twenty-five bucks. The Grand Jury wouldn't indict him. Seems he convinced someone that he hadn't run his still since repeal and the five gallons I picked up were the last of his bootleg, so they let him off with a twenty-five dollar offer in compromise for refilling the whiskey bottles.

If I just hadn't found that five gallon jug I'm sure that I could have gotten a sixty dollar offer in compromise on the refilling of bottles. And when I think of that roll of bills Joe offered me, that could have gone into the Treasury if I'd played it right, it makes me a little sick.

The End

"Picture of a Man Hung on the Horns of a Dilemma"

A short story with verse, written by Earl Stanley Martin in 1954-55, when he was taking a writing correspondence course, and submitting various

manuscripts for publication to an assortment of periodicals. The difference?
True story—absolutely happened just like this—almost!—KHB

*Stanley Martin in his San Francisco IRS office, with a statistical
chart of his own design, for which he won an award. 1960's*

We who constitute the field force of the Internal Revenue Service store our
government-owned automobiles in garages which have been awarded contracts
as lowest competitive bidders for the furnishing of storage and repair facilities.
When a car is in need of repairs the operator of the car has the contract garage
manager write up, in quadruplicate, an estimate of the cost of repair, and if the
estimate appears to be reasonable to him, and if the cost is under fifty dollars, he
signs all four copies of the estimate as an authorization to the garage to perform
the work. If the work is not to be completed on the same day, he then sends the
fourth copy of the authorization to his administrative office to let them know
that he has authorized the expenditure of the amount indicated on the form.
Usually, however, we don't bother with the fourth copy. We just have the form
written up to indicate that the work is done on the date it is signed, and thus
save ourselves the bother of sending in the fourth copy. In our area the form
used for this purpose is RC-SF-27.

Operation and maintenance of government cars is paid for from contingent funds, allocated quarterly. In the middle of march we were instructed to cut down operating expenses because we had run out of funds for the quarter, so I refrained from having my car washed and greased when due.

I was authorized to take a week of leave beginning April first. April first begins a new quarter and, so I thought, we would have plenty of funds in the kitty for a while. So when I drove into the garage on Friday evening April first, I asked the manager to wash and lubricate the car, change the oil and the filter cartridge, pull and pack the front wheels, drain and refill the transmission and differential, and tune up the motor. I told him he would have all week to do it, to keep the cost under fifty dollars, and that I would sign the authorization and work order when I came back from leave.

On Monday morning April eleventh, I stopped at the garage to get my car. They fixed up the work order and authorization, Form 27, dated it April eleventh, as usual under such circumstances, and I signed it and went merrily on my way. The bill came to twenty-nine dollars.

I drove past the Post Office and picked up the mail that had accumulated for me in my absence. There were two important letters. One was from my top boss and one was from my supervisor. They each said that we had exceeded our contingent fund allowance the previous quarter by four thousand dollars, which had to come out of the funds allocated for this quarter. Therefore we were to spend nothing on our cars without prior written approval from them. One of these letters was dated March 30 and the other April first.

And there I sat with a completed work order, dated April eleventh, in the amount of twenty-nine dollars.

I can talk fast on occasion, but nobody can talk fast enough to beat a situation like that. I had put myself out on a limb and they had just sawed the limb out from under me.

So—what to do? Any explanation I could offer would only put me farther in the hole. If I had forwarded an estimate April first, as I should have, the office could have called and cancelled authorization and saved my neck. I could, of course, go back to the garage and get them to re-write the work order dated April first and I could tell the office that I had forgotten to send it in. But that would be a pretty lame excuse—and after all, I had authorized the expenditure from our diminished funds.

After a lot of brain wracking and a waste basket full of discarded explanations, I remembered that my supervisor had a sense of humor and fancied himself as being pretty handy with a dactyl or a trochee. Also, he had no idea that I knew an iambic pentameter from a frosted hoe handle. So I sharpened up a dozen pencils and went to work.

The following is what I came up with, and attached to it is his carefully considered reply.

Pax vobiscum

Santa Rosa, California
April 11, 1955

M E M O R A N D U M
To: A.F. Bullfinch, Supervisor, Inspector Unit
From: E.S. Martin, Inspector (Doghouse)
Subject : Stupration of contingent funds

Attached hereto is S.F. twenty-seven
      In duplicate, for whom it may concern,
            (Like you and me, and J.A.P.
            And maybe old friend Albert Lee
      And any others who may give a dern),
To mark the end of all my hopes of Heaven.

To send these forms without an explanation
      Would bring a cacophony 'round my ears.
            But though I try to tell you why
            It happened; It won't get me by,
      For well I know a jury of my peers
Would, justly, tan my hide for expiation.

In March I heard our funds had been depleted
      So I postponed the washing and the greasing
            'Til April one. And then the fun,
            As here reported, was begun,
      For Betsy had developed grunts and wheezing
And it was time to get the job completed.

As luck would have it I had leave beginning
      At close of business April first, and so,
            I said to Bob[20], "Please do this job",
            And that is when I sure played hob
      By not demanding estimate to go
To you. Alas! I knew that I was sinning.

When I came back from leave on four-eleven
      The job was done—and nicely, I might add.
            Old Betsy gleamed and, so it seemed
            To me, she also purred and beamed,
      And in my heart I knew that she was glad,
So we fixed up attached forms twenty-seven.

Now picture my discomfiture when I
   Drove past the old P.O. to get my mail,
     With notes from P. and A.F.B.
    Addressed especially to me
   "No dough! And absolutely, without fail
Spend nothing on your car!" I thought I'd die.

So what do I do now? The deed is done!
   The die is cast! The fat is in the fire!
     The dough is spent! My head is bent!
    And for my sins I must repent!
   And so, with fear and trembling, I enquire,
What is my penance? Better load your gun!
BOTH BARRELS

        —E.S. Martin, Inspector

       San Francisco, California
         April 13, 1955

Mr. Martin

Now Stupration's a word
That I hadn't heard
But it aptly described what you dood.
First you robbed our slim purse
Then you explained it all in verse (?)
And that makes *twice* we was screwed.

Spending dough at this time
Was a serious crime
Which your verses did little towards easing;
But the Versemaker's Guild
Should have the guy killed
That tries to rhyme "greasing" with "wheezing".

—A.F.B.

E.S. Martin
681-1/2 Wabash Ave
Terre Haute, Ind.
975 words
Usual rate.
(1941)

NOTORIOUS LIL

By
E.S. Martin

"Who's that boy?" I asked.

"Which one?"

He knew darned well which one.

We were sitting at a table close to the door in an orderly and well-behaved club in the west forties a few doors off Broadway. I had just come to town to work on one of the tabloids, and Dick Thomas, who had cubbed with me on the Indianapolis Arrow four years ago, was showing me around. Dick hadn't cubbed long. After a year on the Arrow he came to New York to work on the biggest sheet in town. He had it coming to him. Graduated from Columbia, he could write a good story and he was the friendliest cuss alive. That's why I was interested when this boy gave him the cold shoulder.

"The boy that passed you up like a dirty shirt when you spoke to him just now," I reminded him.

"Listen, Ned," he said, in his earnest friendly way. "If you're going to work for a big-time sheet, particularly a tabloid, you're going to have to learn some big-time similes," and he smiled.

"All right, school ma'am," I accepted the linguistic rebuke. "But who is he, and why, when, where and what, as required by chapter one of the reporters' guide book?"

I knew he was catching my interest for one of his stories and I was ready to listen.

"That's Tim Jewell. Worked on our sheet when I came to town, but went over to the Journal right afterwards."

He lit a cigarette and turned to watch the little girl doing an indifferent sort of dance in the middle of the floor. When I saw he wasn't going ahead with his story my curiosity got the best of me. I wanted to know why a man would pass Dick Thomas up without speaking to him, when he was spoken to.

"Why didn't he speak to you?" I pursued.

"Who?" he queried, turning. "Oh, Tim? Have another gin and I'll tell you."

I had another gin.

"It's not much of a story," he began. "I suppose you know that Jean's folks live up at Mamaroneck?"

I did. Jean was his wife.

"I met Jean while I was at Columbia, and I married her while I was on the Arrow."

I remembered. I had been his best man at a parsonage wedding.

"When I came to New York to work, Jean came on ahead to visit her folks. I stopped at a hotel just off Times Square, and dashed around to the paper to line up my job. The next couple of days I spent getting straightened out. Then I called up Jean and told her to come on in and we'd find us a place and start settling down."

He lit a new cigarette from the butt of the old one, and took a sip from the glass at his elbow.

"Tim was doing sports. He was a wise-guy, just a year out of the corn belt, and he thought he knew the town like a book. Offered to show me the town, and I was willing. After all, I hadn't been to the city for more than a year, and a lot can happen in that time."

"Tim assumed that I was a hick, and I let him. I got a real kick out of it. The evening I called Jean he suggested we have dinner at one of the clubs, and take in a show later. So we left word with the girl at the switch-board where to reach us, and went over to the 'Monties'. On the way, he pointed out this and that celebrity, and such landmarks, already familiar to me, that he thought would interest a country reporter come to town."

"At Monties we ordered, and Tim started pointing out folks as people of interest. Among others he pointed out the mistress of a famous producer, a bootleg baron, an ex-prize-fight-champ, and Clara Bow's sister, if she has a sister. He had a good line, so I let him rave and kept my laughs to myself."

"He was eulogizing an actor with a wooden leg when he suddenly leaned over and gripped my arm. 'Say', he said. 'Do you see that tall blonde just coming in?' I saw her. She was a good looking kid standing just inside the door waiting for the head waiter who was then escorting a party to their table."

"'That girl', he said, 'has started more hell than anybody else on Manhattan.' It was hard to believe. She didn't look the part."

"Yes?", I said, and he went on. 'Yes. That's Lil White. She's Big Tony Cabino's moll. When Rod Gaffney tried to kidnap her last winter, Big Tony's mob finished off nine of Gaffney's gang before he got wise and pulled out. Then when Slink Cellini got fresh with her over at Mack's one night when two or three of Cabino's torpedoes were around, Slink got nineteen holes in him, and when the police got there, there wasn't enough left of Mack's to tell whether it was a joint or a kindling pile.'"

"I looked at the girl again. The head waiter was escorting her up the room. 'Those are real pearls she's wearing,' Tim went on. 'Big Tony paid a "fence" ten grand for 'em and had 'em re-strung.'"

"'Yes sir,' he said. 'The wildest moll on Manhattan, and suicide to monkey with. I'd sure hate to get caught out with her.'"

"The head waiter with the girl in tow, stopped at our table. I rose. Tim jerked around, and you could have knocked his eyes off with a feather.

"I pulled out a chair. Jean, I said, I want you to meet Tim Jewell. Tim's been showing me the town. Tim, meet my wife.

"Tim suddenly remembered an important engagement. He hasn't spoken to me since."

THE END

Feature Story

Modern Course in Syndicate Fiction Writing
2010 Raymond Commerce Building
Newark, New Jersey

October 28, 1941

Dear Mr. Martin;

I was very glad about this script from when I met the last line. The freedom of your character-situation development, particularly the ease in swinging right to the end of your story without a fumbling, that dialog seems to give your writing, is heartening.

This story seems to need but one small change. That is:

In your short-short story titled FEATURE STORY, don't have Martha give the coon back to the game warden, but make her keep it. Your last sentence is particularly good—don't change it at all. In your first paragraph, your sentence is too long. Try breaking it up into two or three sentences. As it stands now, it is too hard to read.

Do that, then let me have this revision right back. I am still waiting for you to come through, as I expect you are waiting. Perhaps it will do it on this one.

Please rush this!

Sincerely,
Stuart Tynan

October 31, 1941

Mr. Stuart Tynan
Madeira, Ohio

Dear Mr. Tynan,

Here is FEATURE STORY back again.

In your revision suggestion you say "Don't have Martha give the coon back to the game warden, but make her keep it." Then you say, "Your last sentence is particularly good—don't change it at all."

The last sentence ("Girl forsakes coon for Cub", Jerry read.) hangs on Matha giving the coon back.

Therefore I have followed your revision suggestions but I have re-written the last line to read ("Girl keeps coon and catches cub," Jerry read.)

Does the story hang together now?

Or do I hang?

Sincerely,
E.S. Martin
1708 N. 8th St.
Terre Haute, Ind.

E.S. Martin
1708 N. 8th St.
Terre Haute, Ind.
Firs Revision, Lesson #4
October 31, 1941

FEATURE STORY

By E.S. Martin

"Green, come here!"

Jerry jumped half out of his chair when Tom O'Connor, the editor, roared at him. He wondered if he would ever get over being apprehensive when thus summoned to the throne of authority.

"Coming right away, boss," he sighed, and pushed himself back from the typewriter where he had been laboriously pecking away with two fingers. The green celluloid eyeshade which he wore for no other reason than that the older men all wore them he laid across his sheaf of notes. He crossed the fingers on both hands as he shoved them in his hip pockets and faced O'Connor.

Tom O'Connor was really a pretty nice sort of a guy and the outstanding editor of the state, as testified by his yearly selection for that honor by the state editorial association. At heart he was a mild mannered fellow, but he had seen so many movies in which the editor was a blustering tyrant that he had finally adopted that pose himself in self defense. Now he leaned back in his chair, wreathed his head in a cloud of smoke from his stubby pipe, and poked the stem accusingly at the cowering hulk before him.

"How about this girl with the pet coon?" he roared.

Jerry Green was twenty and just out of college. The college had not honored him with a degree but he was definitely out. His rotund face, the little wrinkles at the corners of his mouth, gave him the look of a playful overgrown cub—which as a matter of fact, he was. He was cub reporter on the Newcastle Tribune by virtue of his father's long acquaintance with Tom O'Connor. He shifted his weight uneasily under the editor's piercing gaze.

"Wh-what about her," he countered.

"That's what I want to know," O'Connor thundered. "What about her? First you come along with a story about how her old man brings in a baby coon from the woods where he cuts up firewood because he's too proud to go on W.P.A., and how she raises it on a bottle and makes a pet out of it. You tell how it gets to be a neighborhood pet and how all the kids miss their supper watching it do tricks. It makes a pretty good feature story, for you, so we run it in the local and we put it on the wire.

Then you come along with a story that your first story had made coons sound so good as pets that half the people in the state had besieged the state department of conservation to find out how they could get one. Then the state department suddenly comes to and remembers that this girl or anyone else can't have a coon for a pet because it's a protected wild animal and the law don't let people keep protected wild animals for pets."

"So what do they do, according to your story, but send a game warden to go and get the coon and take it back to the woods and turn it loose? Again we run the story in the local and put it on the wire. It makes everybody sorry for the girl and mad at the department of conservation, but we can't help that. All we can do is print the news.

But we have to print all the news, and our public is waiting for the rest of the story. Does it end there, the girl with no coon, or does she adopt the game warden or a stray dog for a pet?"

"Well, no sir," Jerry managed.

"What do you mean, 'well, no sir?'"

Jerry gulped, scratched the back of his neck, leaned one big paw on O'Connor's desk, and stared out the window.

"That day you bawled me out," he began, "because I was just working my beat and not bringing in any feature stories or anything, you made me feel pretty bad. So here I was walking down the street past this Martha Petersen's house and she's sitting on the porch playing with her pet coon. I stop to watch the coon and she says 'Jerry, you look sad,' and so I tell her the story. 'Don't they write features about people's pets?' she asked. 'Sure, but who's got any pets worth writing about?' I asked her. Then she told me the story about her coon and I wrote it up."

"Then when I was out to her house for a date about a week later she told me about the game warden being there just that afternoon to get the coon. That made me sort of mad, because this Martha is an awful pretty girl when she cries and looks at you through the tears on her lashes, so I went right over to this game warden's house and talked to him. He said he couldn't help it about the coon. He had a letter from the department to get it and turn it loose, and he had to do it." Jerry scratched his leg with the top of his shoe.

"I thought about it for a minute and then I said, 'Look. A woods is made up of trees, and there's trees all along her street. Couldn't you mistake the trees on her street for the woods, and turn it loose pretty close to her house?' and he said, 'Maybe you've got something there.' So I wrote the second story, but I didn't say anything about the game warden turning the coon loose so close to her house or maybe he'd get fired."

"Next morning the coon was back at Martha's, and she kissed me and called me her hero, but I knew if the department of conservation heard about it they still wouldn't let her keep the coon. So I went to the library and read a book and then I wrote them a letter. The conservation department I mean. And they wrote back and said yes she could get a permit to raise coons if two taxpayers would sign her application."

"You see, there's a provision in the law where you can raise wild animals under permit if you agree to turn a certain percentage of the increase loose when they're big enough. So when I told Martha she said, 'You think of everything. I just love you and love you,' and when she looks at you like that and kisses you it does something to you, so now everything's going to be all right."

O'Connor's mouth had dropped open. Now he clamped his teeth on the bit of his pipe and puffed furiously. "Well, why haven't you written a story telling about this permit law, and how the coon came back, and how this girl is going to raise coons under permit," he finally blustered. "You know we have to print all the news."

Jerry shifted awkwardly and hitched up his pants. "I sort of hated to write about myself."

"Well, don't. Write about the girl and the coon."

"That's just it. It's a family affair now."

"What do you mean?" O'Connor yelled. "Has the coon had pups or whatever they have? Why didn't you say so. We'll send a photographer right out."

Jerry blushed. "That isn't what I meant. What I meant was that Martha decided that if she was going to raise coons under permit, she'd have to have help. I don't see how we can do it on my salary, but she's always lived on a close budget in her family and she says we can do it."

"You mean she's going to marry you?" O'Connor groaned.

Jerry gulped and his ears turned red. "She did. This morning."

"Well, it's a story," O'Connor managed. "And if we're going to have to support both of you, you'd better learn to write it. Here, I'll give you the lead." He scribbled across a piece of copy paper and handed it to Jerry.

"Girl keeps coon and catches cub," Jerry read.

The End

Stanley, with youngest son Carl, showing new dress clothes for work—great socks! 1950's

Chapter 6

Picture This: Photography

Stanley Martin in "shooting" mode, late 1950's

In 1906, the year Stanley Martin was born, his father, Frank James Martin opened an office at 681 Wabash Ave. in Terre Haute, Indiana.[21] Inspired by a growing need for blueprint reproduction, Frank Martin began with the oversized copier for blueprint services, and then went on to add commercial photography and portraiture to his venture. Spanning the better part of the twentieth century, the Martin name in Terre Haute became synonymous with photography. All of Frank Martin's children—Willard, Ray, Lawrence, Stanley, Esther, Kenneth and Stewart—were educated and trained in a variety of studio-related skills ranging from basic photography and processing techniques to customer service and administrative details

Martin Family Photo, all the siblings in order, in 1964 Terre Haute. Left to right they are Willard, Ray, Lawrence, Stanley, Kenneth, Esther, and Stewart

Even the grandchildren got in on the action at the Martin Photo Shop. My mother in particular, Nancy Gene Martin Harper, spent the better part of her 14th summer upstairs in the studio on Wabash Avenue, sorting, categorizing and labeling the proofs and negatives amassed in their first forty years or so of business. It is said that this attention to organization and preservation is the key to the archival value of the Martin Photo Collection[22] as a whole, excellent talent and technique notwithstanding.

Stanley Martin, like his siblings, put in plenty of time at his father's studio, reaping the reward of training and experience which he put to use as a photography instructor in the Ft. Monmouth NJ Signal Corps School[23] in 1926-27, U. S. Army.

Willard and Stanley Martin with cameras at the Harper home in Pleasant Hill, CA, early 1960's

Particularly through his younger years, including the Depression era and times of financial challenges, Stanley was able to rely on his skills as a photographer, whether for private side jobs or to acquire full time employment with an agency. His enjoyment of the trade and his days as an itinerant photographer are reflected in Chapter 6's *Night Flash* and *Box Supper*.

An excerpt from my grandmother's memoirs (Stanley's wife Mabel Louella Thomson Martin) reflect the somewhat humorous view of the Frank J. Martin family legacy. Gram was about to have her first child . . . . my mother, Nancy Gene Martin, now Harper. You can bet that in 1934, a full professional photography setup right in the delivery room was definitely NOT the norm!

I told Stanley (it was time) and he called Dr. Duenweg, who said for us to get to the hospital as soon as possible. Stanley locked up shop and we got there in a hurry. The nurses hurried me into the labor room, got me ready to deliver, then to the delivery room with Stanley all draped and with a mask on, standing by my side, holding my hand.

Just as things were getting interesting they gave me enough chloroform to put me out and Nancy was born, rushed to the nursery, washed up and a shirt and diaper put on her and rushed back to the delivery room. There Stanley had his photo equipment set up, Dr. Duenweg stopped what he was doing with me, stood up by the window and Stanley shot a picture of Dr. Duenweg holding Nancy at 10 minutes old and another at 12 minutes old. Then, since I was still out, Stanley gathered up the equipment and headed for the studio to develop the film.

He came back about 6 a.m. and showed me the pictures and then took them down to show Mother and Dad who were just eating breakfast on March 29, 1934, Nancy Gene Martin's birthday. The verse on the announcement:

The Doctor's Doctor Duenweg,
The gal is Nancy Gene.
Her Mom and Pop are Martins,
So Daddy shot this scene.

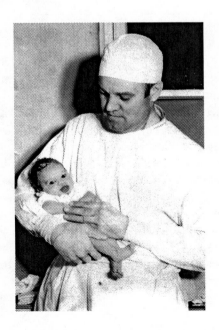

Nancy Gene Martin with Doctor Duenweg, Terre Haute, IN, 1934, Photo by E. Stanley Martin

E.S. Martin
1708 N. 8th Street
Terre Haute, Ind.
Lesson #2, Assignment #1
August 7, 1941

NIGHT FLASH

By E.S. Martin

SUMMARY

High school senior gets jealous when he hears the professor will date his girl for faculty dinner that night. Pouting, takes off on bike with camera to make night-life pictures in woods he had expected the girl to help with. On way home sees prof's car pulling down lovers' lane, and sees chance for revenge in photographing car. In doing so he does the girl and prof a service, catches a thief, and finds he was all wrong.

Stuart Tynan
Madeira, Ohio
August 28, 1941

Dear Mr. Martin;

Instead of ending your short-short story titled NIGHT FLASH with Betsy kissing both Jack and Professor Wood, have her just kiss Jack, because he is really the hero in your story. Don't have Betsy and the professor undressed when Jack rescues them, for this incident is not necessary to the plot. Your opening paragraph is good—it arouses the readers' interest so that he wants to read on to see just what is going to happen. I want you to make the rest of your story like this. Add a couple more of dramatic incidents between Betsy and Jack that will make your script exciting. Describe Betsy some more so that the reader will become more intimate with her, and by becoming more intimate, more interested.

Sincerely,
S. Tynan

E.S. Martin
1708 N. 8th Street
Terre Haute, Ind.
First Revision, Assignment #2
Sept. 18, 1941

NIGHT FLASH

By
E.S. Martin

As soon as the final bell announced the end of the last class for the day Jack Wilson hot-footed it up the stairs from the manual training room to the home ec room to meet Betsy Browning. If the weather held this would be a fine night to try for some more of their "Life in the Woods" series of photographs. Maybe they would be lucky enough to finish the tree toad set.

As he topped the stairs into the crowded main corridor Jack was just in time to see the handsome young science teacher, Mr. Woodford, beckon Betsy into his classroom. Betsy caught sight of Jack through the laughing home-going mob and waved at him. "Wait for me," she called. "I'll only be a minute".

Jack didn't intend to eavesdrop, but standing outside Mr. Woodford's door he heard the teacher saying, "Then you will come with me to the faculty dinner this evening? I can pick you up about six-thirty?" Then he heard Betsy's eager voice. "Of course. I'll be glad to come."

Jack bolted down the hall and ducked out the side door. His ears burned and he was suddenly filled with a terrible aching void. Betsy was going to have a date with Mr. Woodford, and she wouldn't be going to the woods with him this evening.

Jack and Betsy had grown up in the same block. Since they were kids they had played together, fought, made up, and fought again. In high school they had taken the same classes. When they had gone on their first little science field trip to the nearby park four years ago they had both taken their cameras. That's when their "Life in the Woods" series had started. Before the year was out they were spending all of their spare time together with their bikes and cameras combing the fields and woods for subjects. Through the intervening three years they had kept it up and now at the end of their senior year they had an enviable collection of pictures, many of which had appeared in the Sunday supplements and in the magazines.

On his way home Jack took to the alleys and side streets to avoid the inevitable, "Where's Betsy? Have a falling out?" At thought of that question which all of his classmates asked him whenever they met him alone on the street he suddenly realized that in all of the years of their acquaintance he and Betsy had never had a date. Now Betsy was going to have her first date with Mr. Woodford, who wasn't so terribly much older than they were, and she had been shameless enough to make the date where she must have known that Jack could overhear her. Let her walk home by herself this evening and every other evening. He could make his tree-toad pictures without her and she could have as many dates with Mr. Woodford as she wanted to.

Jack's stomach was filled with lead and his chest felt as if someone was squeezing it. He was filled with a sudden need to get into the country and away from any possible nearness to the fickle Betsy. At home he got out his bike, slung his camera and flash equipment over his shoulder, left a note for his mother who was up town shopping, and headed for the woods.

The shadows were lengthening fast when Jack turned off the pavement and negotiated the narrow gravel road to where lover's lane wound up the hill through the underbrush. Here he hid his bike in its accustomed place, followed the lane up to where lover's oak stood majestically alone in its little clearing, and plunged down the hill into the denser woods beyond. It was dusk here, for he had been here many times before. Now, however, the loneliness overwhelmed him, for always before there had been the two of them.

Every foot of these woods was filled with Betsy. Here by this sycamore they had found the wonderful cluster of morel mushrooms. In that grove of Beech she had found the showy Orchids they had sought so long in vain. There lay the treacherous limb that had broken under their combined weight when they were climbing to photograph the oriole's nest. Betsy had landed in a crumpled heap with a broken wrist. He had taken her back to town on the crossbar of his bike, tears running down her cheeks and a jest for his concern on her lips.

He sat down on an old stump. Night settled around him and the stars crept across the sky but he made no move to seek the tree toads that had been the object of his trip. Finally by the light of his pocket torch he looked at his wrist watch, saw that it was nine o'clock, and reluctantly started home.

Getting his bike out of the weeds he heard a car leave the highway and turn down the gravel road. Then before he pushed his bike into the lane the car turned off the gravel and wound up the lane towards lover's oak. And in the moment of its passing he saw that it was Mr. Woodford's car.

All in that instant Jack was fighting mad. So the faculty dinner had been only a come-on for a petting party. Mr. Woodford was a seducer of women. He should be run out of town. Then the camera bumping at Jack's side gave him an idea. A night flash of Mr. Woodford's car parked with the unmistakable and easily recognizable lover's oak in the background would do it. Passed around in the right places, such a picture would force the man to resign.

In a few minutes Jack had wormed his way through the underbrush until the darker bulk of the parked car was in line with where he knew the trunk of the oak stood. He would only show the back end and the license plate of the car. He didn't want by any chance to involve Betsy in this, for he held her blameless.

He heard a mumble of low voices in the direction of the car. Quickly he adjusted his camera and fitted a flash bulb, a job that he had done in complete darkness many times before. Then with a, "That for you, Mr. Woodford," he pressed the synchronous release and started to duck back through the brush.

Almost instantly a shot shattered the night silence, and Jack heard the angry hornet sound of a bullet close to him. He promptly swapped directions and broke back towards the car, for in that instant of brilliant light when the flash had etched the scene before him indelibly on his brain, he had seen something far different from anything he had expected.

He heard Betsy say, "Thank goodness you got him, Mr. Woodford." Then almost in the same breath she was calling, "Jack! Oh, Jack! Are you hurt? Where are you?"

"Here, Betsy," he answered, and thumbed on his pocket torch to see Mr. Woodford sitting astride a disreputable looking hoodlum on the ground who was obviously out. Jack picked up the fellow's fallen automatic and handed it to Mr. Woodford. Then Betsy had her arms around him.

"Jack, I'm so glad to see you," she cooed. "Where have you been? The faculty was awarding us scholarships because of our pictures and Mr. Woodford was to bring us, but we couldn't find you. Why didn't you wait for me after school?" Jack dug his toe in the dirt and said nothing. "You get the scholarship anyhow." Her arms squeezed tighter around him. "And when Mr. Woodford was driving me home we had to stop at the light, and this man got in and made us drive out here. I was so scared. He was just making us get out so he could steal the car when you made that flash and he turned to shoot at you. Mr. Woodford hit him and knocked him cold. Then you came and I was never so glad to see anyone in my life." She kissed him soundly.

Jack gave himself over entirely to this pleasant turn of events. Then he noticed the prostrate gunman beginning to move so he gently disengaged Betsy and slipped the carrying strap from his camera and helped Mr. Woodford tie up his prisoner. "A nice job, Jack," Mr. Woodford was saying; "I appreciate it," when Betsy spoke again, very softly.

"Jack, what were you doing out here?"

"Oh, I was just trying for some night flashes," he said airily. "And, boy, the one I got is a honey."

THE END

Sept 30, 1941

Dear Mr. Martin;

Your assignment script, Lesson #2, has been placed on the complete rounds of the markets. Keep your fingers crossed, and here's hoping.

Sincerely,
Stuart Tynan

(Original in your office file)

Dear Mr. Martin;

Your story which I accepted for marketing on the first revision of Lesson #2 has been placed on several markets and only this week has been returned home.

The failure of this script to "click" in one of the editor's hands was due to that recurring fault in your writing, which has shown up clearly in this story now, of the loose relationship you have between the climax-situation and the opening and build-up problem. I am going to smash this weakness if it necessitates a full hundred letters dictated on the point about your future writing. Watch it constantly. It is consistently your error in plotting. I am going to jump on it equally hard to make you see the importance of this twin-like unity between the opening and climax. The failure of this story to sell SHOULD NOT WEAKEN YOUR ENTHUSIASM. It should be counted as one-lesson-learned-in-writing and applied to YOUR FUTURE WRITING. I want you to get right on this new work you are to turn out—and keep turning it out! I shall call for a new application of this script's idea later.

Sincerely Yours,
Stuart Tynan

Box Supper

Stuart Tynan
(Manhattan Studios)
2010 Raymond Commerce Building
Newark, N.J.

Dear Mr. Martin;

It has been in my mind for sometime that there is one unrelenting obstinacy in your fiction technique which stands hidden under your willingness to shape your productions accurately, yet is like a thorn sticking through every script.

I want you to take one week upon receipt of this letter, six or seven short-short stories published in the very best publications which use them, and RECOPY NO LESS THAN A HALF A DOZEN WORD FOR WORD on your typewriter. Do one a night if you possibly have the time. Forget all about your own scripts. After you have them copied word for word, underline the LINES WHICH SEEM TO YOU TO BE THE CLIMAX IN EACH SCRIPT. I don't want you to just underline the lines in the published stories, but RECOPY EACH and underline the typewritten pages.

Send two of those stories to me with fifty words or so telling me why your underlined sections seem to you to be the climax. Along with those published story scripts, send me this one back, also changed.

In your short-short story titled BOX SUPPER I think that you could greatly improve your opening paragraph if you would start it out with Rod asking Mary if the teacher is in. Then you could tell the reader about the two of them—describe Mary like you did on the first page. I want you to add another incident between the two of them, and make your story funnier than you have it at present. Give it a humorous touch.

Sincerely,
Stuart Tynan

E.S. Martin
1708 No. 8th St.
Terre Haute, Indiana
November 21, 1941

Mr. Stuart Tynan
Madeira, Ohio

Dear Mr. Tynan;

I have your undated letter of late October concerning my script, BOX SUPPER, before me. I am sorry that I have not been able to respond to your suggestions and revise my script sooner, but my work has been interrupted by a business trip to Washington. I am now back at my desk, however, (from 4 A.M. to 6:30A.M., those being the only hours I have available for writing) and hope to get caught up on my writing again soon.

As I told you in my first letter, I favor the Collier's story. The short shorts that I have copied according to your instructions therefore came from my stack of fifty or sixty tear-sheets from their book. I don't need fifty words to tell you why I underlined the sections I did for the climax in each case. These are very obviously the culmination or acme of the story.

Perhaps I have been going astray in reading too darned many syndicate shorts in the papers I have available here, particularly the Chicago Daily News. Many of them seem to violate more rules than I do. It is natural for me to feel that way I suppose.

BOX SUPPER has been muchly revised and polished since I copied these stories. It probably still stinks, but I have a certain feeling of satisfaction towards it now that I haven't had towards my other stories. You and the market may not like it, but I sort of do.

Incidentally, how do we stand financially? My record is incomplete on my payments, but I know I've gotten more than I've paid for so far. Why don't you send me a statement and see if I won't send you some more money? Of course, if you're not worrying about it, I won't either.

Will revise the other two scripts as soon as possible.

Sincerely,
E.S. Martin

E.S. Martin
1708 N. 8th St.
Terre Haute, Ind.
Second revision, Lesson #5
December 16, 1941

BOX SUPPER

By E.S. Martin

Rod Gale parked his car among the other cars and walked across the moonlit yard towards the brightly lighted schoolhouse. He wondered if he was letting himself in for a bum evening. After all there would be no person here he had met before excepting the pretty little school teacher, Mary Monroe.

She greeted him just inside the door of the crowded schoolroom. "Mr. Gale! I'm so glad you came!" Lights danced in her brown eyes, and the beautiful oval of her face framed with auburn hair glowed with excitement. She was even more attractive than he remembered and he was glad he was there.

Then, almost in the same breath, she plucked a girl from the crowd. "Ann, I'm going to be busy for a while. Will you take charge of Mr. Gale, and introduce him to the others? Miss Monroe, Mister Gale." She included them both in an intimate, warm, smile.

"If there are any more as nice as you two, I don't think I'll be able to stand it", he acknowledged the introduction.

Mary gave Ann a bright, knowing look. "Didn't I tell you?"

"You work fast, don't you Mr. Gale?" Ann had a nice smile, and she'd been around some. State University maybe, he thought.

"I have to. Some of these men have known you for years, and I have but one evening to overcome the handicap."

Mary interrupted. "You two will do. You must excuse me now. The auction is about to start." She started working her way through the crowd towards the front of the room.

"How will I know your lunch when it is offered?" Rod called after her.

"You must take your chance with the rest," she retorted with a quick smile over her shoulder.

He turned back to Ann. The name is Roderick, but you may call me Rod."

"Thank you . . . . Rod." She curtsied prettily.

She was slender and blonde, a little taller than Mary, and her eyes were a serene sort of deep blue. Her emerald green dress was wisely chosen, and it hadn't come from a mail order catalog. Except for the differences in coloring her face and Mary's face were remarkably similar. A very pretty pair of sisters, Rod thought.

"You Monroes are attractive people." He said.

"Flatterer!" She took his proffered arm and turned him towards the noisy group clustered around the cloak hall door. "Like to meet the gang?"

But the sound of rapping silenced the assemblage, and they turned with the others to face the front of the room where a tall, jolly, middle-aged man stood by the teacher's desk heaped high with attractively wrapped boxes.

"Folks, we're ready for the auction!" he was saying. "Remember the rule! Even if you guessed wrong, the successful bidder must eat with the fair lady who prepared the box you buy! Now, the first offering! A right handsome box! What am I bid?"

A stocky middle-aged farmer bid fifty cents. A blushing carrot-topped lad of about sixteen squeezed in beside Rod and bid seventy-five. The man bid a dollar, and Rod could feel the boy tense as he bid a dollar ten. All he's got, Rod thought. The man bid one twenty-five.

"That man doesn't want that box especially," Ann whispered. "He's just hungry. He should eat with some of our old maids. They fix fancy boxes. He's going to break up Red Tompkin's romance if he isn't careful."

The auctioneer turned back to the carrot-top, but the boy shook his head sadly. His opponent saw, and stood up suddenly. "May I withdraw my last bid?" The auctioneer shook his head. "Against the rules."

Rod pressed a quarter in the clenched hand of the boy. The carrot-top stared at it unbelievingly for an instant, muttered "thanks" and bid one thirty-five. The crowd clapped happy approval as he won the bid and was joined by a blushing fifteen year old girl. Ann gently squeezed Rod's arm.

Rod felt strangely at home here. He was a city boy, a photographer, photographing country schools for a living. When he had called at the schoolhouse this afternoon and found Mary Monroe and her pupils decorating for this box supper, he had been reluctant at first to accept her invitation to attend. But one look had told him that Mary Monroe was his kind of girl . . . the kind of a girl he wanted to marry when he settled down . . . and he was ready to settle down . . . so here he was. He watched Mary, gaily smiling, eagerly alive, as she helped the auctioneer. The kind of a woman who never grows old . . . his kind of girl. He turned to Ann.

"How will I know Mary's box when it is offered?"

Ann wrinkled her nose at him. "So you don't want to eat with me?" He patted her hand on his arm and smiled. "Of course I do! I'd love to! But I came here this evening especially to eat with Mary!" Ann turned suddenly to look at the young folks in the corner who were noisily cheering a successful bidder.

Rod watched Mary collecting for the boxes as they were sold. He caught her eye and she smiled and nodded gaily. He liked this community . . . these friendly people. He could set up his darkroom here . . . . He might even learn to do a little farming . . . . With a girl like Mary . . . He turned back to Ann.

"Any place around here where a man could settle down?"

"There's a nice little place just below home. Doesn't look like much, but it could be fixed up. I always thought I'd like to live there."

"Swell!" Rod said. "Maybe I'll take it." Ann's a nice kid, he thought. "You'd make a swell sister-in-law," he told her.

"I hope you don't get hurt," she whispered, but Rod was watching the bidding, waiting for Mary's box to be offered.

Finally but two boxes remained to be sold. One was wrapped in plain white paper. That one's Ann's, Rod thought. The other was wrapped in pink, and tied with blue ribbons. The auctioneer held it up. That's the one! That's Mary's! "Five dollars," he bid.

That was higher than most of the bids had gone. A surprised murmur ran through the room which wasn't so crowded now, since many of the youngsters had gone outside with their boxes to eat in the moonlight. At Rod's bid, one young fellow shrugged and went out. Another, a nice looking young fellow, well dressed, personable, bid six. Rod liked the fellow's looks, but he wanted to eat with Mary . . . .

"Seven!" "Eight!" "Nine!"

Rod's opponent called across the room to him with a grin. "The rest of the folks want to eat. How high will you go?"

Ann's fingers were digging into Rod's arm. He grinned back. "Top any bid!"

"Good enough. That's all I wanted to know." The young fellow waved his hand, indicating he was through.

Ann's fingers dropped from his arm and he moved up to the desk. He pulled a ten from his billfold and handed it to Mary with a broad smile. "Shall we find a place to eat now, or will you want to wait until the other box is sold?"

Silence . . . . sudden, tense, silence . . . . Fell over the room. Mary stared at him, her eyes suddenly wide, her face blank.

"What's the matter?" Rod asked.

The auctioneer caught the situation first. He smiled, and Rod heard a sigh of relief run through the room. "The rule requires you to eat with my daughter standing behind you," the auctioneer said. "I will eat with my wife myself." He indicated Mary.

Rod turned. Ann stood just behind him.

He turned back to stare at Mary Monroe. The kind of a woman who never grows old . . . .

He took the pink and blue box from the auctioneer and offered Ann his arm. "Tell me some more about that nice little place you'd like to live in."

THE END

Stanley and brother Ray with cameras in Santa Rosa, California, late 1950's.

Chapter 7

Death and Taxes

Come on, you'll miss some fun if you skip this chapter—Gramps had a healthy, if dry, sense of humor.

In a letter to Jean-Baptiste LeRoy, in 1789, Benjamin Franklin made a sort of "state-of-the-union" comment that has become a household saying in America: *"Our new Constitution is now established, and has an appearance that promises permanency; but **in this world nothing can be said to be certain, except death and taxes.** "*[24] Stanley Martin had reason to grapple with both issues in his lifetime, as much or more than most. As an agent of the Internal Revenue Service, Department of Alcohol Tax, his career centered on the second of these certainties, and he often made quips or even humorous poetry on this theme. He was forced to deal with the accidental and relatively untimely death of his beloved father, Frank, when Stanley was still a young adult and recent father himself. The passing of his mother, Ella, in 1956, was an event that precipitated the release of his story-writing ambitions, in order to put all his focus of energy into building a comprehensive genealogy of the extended Martin family history. Both were life-changing events for Stanley.

The strong work ethic and entrepreneurial spirit that Frank Martin instilled in his offspring helped each one of them to make ends meet and further succeed as they followed their hearts in their life work. That isn't to say that there were not slim times for all the Martins, both in their childhood and as they grew to adulthood during the Great Depression. Gramps moved often, relocating for work and then traveling away from wherever home was at the time, a rather nomadic existence which inevitably impacted and challenged his wife and children. He surely knew the value of a dollar saved[25].

Frank James Martin. A Photo by Martin, Stanley's daughter Nancy says that "Uncle Willard captioned this photo Keeper of the Shop, a sobriquet fondly given to him by the family"

The story *Handout* is a character study about Stanley's adventures freight-hopping from Chicago to Seattle in the early 1920's, and shows just how valuable some pocket change could be to three hungry young men hitching across the country. More money issues in *The Treasure Chest* also involve brother and father relationships which reflect some of Stanley's own family values and early experiences.

The Policy is a tale that focuses on the practical money issue of life insurance, and of course its inevitable partner, death. This tale, like many of Gramps' stories, shows a slice of Midwestern family life of the times, but with a surprising twist. In his other tale of the hereafter, *R.I.P.*, he has imagined a truly science fictional setup of radio communication with the dearly departed. Why does that make me curious about the experiments and discoveries in the darkrooms of the studio on Wabash Avenue? All it takes is some mixture of imagination, talent, and hard work—you never know what one of those Martin boys might come up with . . . .

Handout!

By
E. Stanley Martin

Image of an early freight train

It was the wee small hours of a late August morning in 1926. By the sound of the switch frogs we had been bumping across, and the glimpses of signal lights, we knew that the train was pulling into a division point yard. Sticking our heads out the partly open car door we could see the round house and the smoky glare from the shops ahead.

"You boys ready to jump?" I asked. "We're about in."

"Just a minute," the Polack said, as he finished rolling his tarp and pulled the sling rope tight.

Marvin tucked his shirt-tail in and hitched up his belt. "I'm ready," he said. "Let's go."

The engine was puffing laboriously now and the freight had slowed to about ten miles an hour. We'd be in the middle of the yards in another minute if we didn't get off now, and I wasn't in the mood to argue with any railroad dicks this morning, I jumped down to the cinders and ducked in between two box cars. I heard the other two boys hit the cinders, and soon they joined me.

"I think the town's over this way," I said. "I need some chow. Let's see if we can find a restaurant."

"Maybe we can wash dishes for some grub," the Polack said. "A good go at pearl diving is just what I need to get some of this grime off me."

I nudged Marvin. "You got any money left?" I whispered, so the Polack wouldn't overhear me. "I'm broke."

"I got a buck I been saving," Marvin told me, and pretty soon he slipped a folded piece of paper into my hand.

We crawled through a string of empty coal cars and found ourselves on a street at the edge of the yards. Marvin and I waited for the Polack to catch up. There weren't any street lights, and the stars weren't very bright so we could only guess at the town. A couple of blocks away we saw a light shining from a store window onto a weather-beaten sign.

"That looks like a restaurant," Marvin said.

We struck out in the direction of the light. We didn't go very fast because we were cold and stiff from trying to sleep on the jolting box-car floor. Even the Polack's tarp hadn't helped too much.

Marvin and I were four nights out of Chicago, headed for Seattle. We were just out of high school and had been working in Chicago when we had decided we wanted to see the west coast. We had no money saved, so we each put on an extra shirt, poked some socks and a razor inside our waistbands, grabbed a handful of freight train, and here we were. The Polack we had picked up in the Milwaukee yards in Aberdeen. He had told us that he had been gassed in the war, and so had only one lung, and was just wandering around the country looking for a good place to die. He looked the part.

"Miles City Restaurant. Open all night!" the sign said.

"Miles City. That's in Montana, isn't it?" I asked.

"Yep," the Polack said. "We been in Montana since a little after dark."

We pushed open the door and were greeted with the mouth-watering aroma of frying ham and bacon and coffee. We could hear something sizzling in a skillet in the kitchen. A blonde waitress was setting heaping plates in front of two railroaders, their lanterns sitting at their feet. Three men who looked like cowboys were sitting at the far counter sipping coffee and jibing with each other.

"Where's the wash room?" the Polack asked the blonde.

She pointed to a door in the far corner. We pushed in and soaped some of the grime from our faces and hands. We couldn't tell just how clean we were by looking at the roller towel when we dried, but at least we felt better.

"We going to hit 'em up for dishwashing before we eat?" the Polack asked me.

"Naw. Let's eat first. I'm starved," I said.

"Okay," he shrugged. "Maybe they feed good in their jail here."

We climbed up on the counter stools and I picked up the fly-specked menu. I looked over the breakfast specials and felt of the crumpled piece of paper Marvin had handed me in my pocket.

"Hot cakes, bacon and coffee—25 cents," the menu said. With three of us eating that would come to 75 cents. That would leave us two bits to get the last thousand or so miles of our trip to the coast. Oh well, I'd been broke and hungry before.

"How about some hot cakes, bacon and coffee?" I asked.

"Sounds good to me," Marvin said.

"Suits me fine," the Polack chimed in.

"Let's have three stacks with bacon and coffee," I told the blonde. She set the coffee on the counter and then went back to the kitchen door to call in our orders.

The Polack pulled out a bedraggled sack of bull and we each rolled a smoke.

When the hot cakes came we slopped plenty of syrup on them and took our time enjoying them. Marvin and I talked of some choice meals we had had in high school. The Polack relapsed into silence. After our second cup of coffee, which was well doctored with cream and sugar, he nudged me.

"Don't you think we better get it over with?" he whispered.

"Relax," I told him. "I think I can talk our way out. You and Marvin head for the door while I talk to the blonde."

I walked over to the cash register while Marvin and the Polack headed for the door. I unfolded the wrinkled buck and handed it to the girl.

She didn't even look at my dollar. Maybe she was tired after a long night. She just poked it in the till, clinked around among the silver, and then handed me a two bit piece and four big shiny cartwheels.

I reckon my jaw fell open and I must have been staring at that hand full of sudden wealth. I had been brought up to be honest and an inner compulsion urged me to tell the girl she had made a mistake, but I was too stunned to speak.

Just then Marvin nudged me and said "Come on."

Suddenly I realized our position. A thousand miles or more from our destination with only a lousy two bits if I gave back the four bucks. I shoved my hand in my pocket and we headed out the door.

As soon as we were outside we made it a point to disappear into the darkness of the yards as fast as possible, and we stayed out of sight until a freight pulled out headed for the west, and we caught it at the last possible minute. Just in case the dicks were looking for us.

We had to tell the Polack what had happened and he got a big bang out of it. He'd been in this part of the country before.

"You see," he said, "This is silver country out here. Everybody uses cartwheels. There isn't any paper money here smaller than a five dollar bill. That girl didn't even look at the bill you gave her. She knew it had to be at least a five, and she could tell by looking at you that it wouldn't be more than that. I hope the boss doesn't take it out of her pay."

I hoped so, too, and I've always thought that I'd like to go back to Miles City sometime and pay back that four bucks. Maybe I will yet.

The End

The Treasure Chest

By E. Stanley Martin

"Do you think Dad's got that much money?" Although it wasn't particularly warm, Mark wiped first his forehead and then his palms with his handkerchief.

I knew in my heart that it was a forlorn hope asking Dad for the money. I knew from his letters that he wasn't well, and that the chickens weren't laying like they should. "I don't know. That's a lot of money."

From the way Mark was fidgeting and tossing half-smoked cigarettes out of the window of my ancient coupe, I knew he wasn't optimistic, either. Of course he was under a strain. It was he who needed the thousand dollars.

We weren't talking much on the drive up from the city. There wasn't much left to say. Mark had come over to my room last night and told me the whole sordid story.

"That Dorrie was a cute chick," he had told me. "But she was expensive. The first time she wanted to take in the International Settlement, I didn't have enough dough so I borrowed fifty from the safe. I was going to pay it back. Then she had to do the Top of the Mark, and that took another hundred. And there were other times. This morning I overheard the boss call the accountants on the phone and they're coming over Thursday for an audit, and my books are short by a thousand dollars. If I don't get that dough back by Thursday, it's San Quentin for me."

I had wanted to blow my top, but habit was too strong. After all, this was my little brother, Mark, and my job was to look after him. Ever since he was three I had been looking after him. I was six at the time. We were in the barn and he had pulled the old cow's tail and she had kicked him and broken his leg. After we got back from the doctor with the leg in a cast, Dad had said in that quiet way of his, "You should look after Mark, son. He is younger than you. Don't let him get hurt like this again."

So I had been looking after him for more than twenty years, and now he had come to this. He had had girl trouble all his life, but so far as I knew, this was the first time he had stolen anything. I had fought more than one boy who wanted to black his eye for messing around with his girlfriend, and in high school once it had looked like a shotgun wedding for Mark with a pretty little redhead. I never had heard how he got out of that one. And since we got jobs in the city Mark had kept me broke hitting me up for a ten or a fifty to tide him over until he could find another job or to pay off some dame.

It must have been this same Dorrie that Mark had been making a pass at when his car had gone out of control coming down Post Lane last month and wound up in the show window. He never had believed in insurance, so it cost me better than twelve hundred dollars to pay him out of that one—the money I'd been saving to buy ME another car. That's how it happened that I didn't have the money to keep Mark out of jail, and why he was riding with me in this beat-up crate of mine.

"What about Dorrie?" I asked. "Have you told her?"

"No," Mark said, and slammed another cigarette out the window. "She went east with a sailor last week."

As I held out my hand and made the turn up the hill towards Dad's little white house, Mark turned towards me.

"You'll do the talking, won't you?" he asked.

"I'll do the talking," I said.

"And you won't tell Dad about this mess I'm in?"

He wanted to keep on being Dad's fair-haired boy. "I won't tell him," I said. I didn't add "But this will be the last time," as I wanted to.

"Don't chide him, son," Dad had told me once, when he had caught me giving Mark what-for over one of his smart tricks. "Some day he will come face to face with reality, and then he'll grow up." But it looked like Dad had been wrong. And when it came to plain stealing, that finished him in my book.

Dad was just sitting down to dinner when we arrived. He insisted on hobbling around and brewing a pot of coffee and opening up some jars and moving it all into the dining room from the kitchen table so we could join him in style. After we had finished eating and he had poured the coffee he lifted one shaky leg and crossed it over the other, leaned back in his chair and got a little of the old sparkle in his rheumy eyes. He peered first at Mark and then at me.

"Well, boys," he said. "It's been quite a spell since you were both up to see me at once, on such a pretty Sunday, too. Something on your mind?"

Dad had always been pretty observant, except where Mark was concerned. I always got up to see him at least once a month, but Mark only made it occasionally on rainy days in the winter.

"Well, yes Dad, there is." I didn't quite know how to tell him. Mark scooted back his chair and tried to light a cigarette and burned his finger on the match.

"As a matter of fact, Mark has a chance to make a little investment in his company and he needs a thousand dollars to do it."

I hated to lie to him, and I never had except when Mark was in trouble.

The sparkle went out of Dad's eyes. "You couldn't have come at a worse time. You know I can't take care of as many chickens as I used to, and the ones I have are molting and not laying good. Yesterday I had to have the feed bins filled and I'm strapped."

Mark stalked over to the window and stood with his back to us, his shoulders sagging.

"Does this chance mean a lot to Mark, son?" Dad spoke in a low voice to me, but I noticed Mark cock his head a little.

"It really does," I said. "It probably means his job."

Dad's eyes had a sort of glint to them and he was staring across the room. I turned to see what he was looking at. He was eyeing the "treasure chest" on top of the buffet.

I hadn't really thought of the treasure chest for years. For as long as I could remember it had sat there on top of the buffet, right where it was now. Dad had always told us it contained the family fortune. When Mark and I were kids and times were hard, I remember more than once hearing Mama and Dad trying to decide if that was the time to dip into the chest. But they had always held out and found some other way to get over the rough spot.

The treasure chest wasn't much to look at. Just a plain black wooden box maybe sixteen inches long, half as wide, and about six or eight inches high.—and it was as heavy as lead. I knew. I had tried to dust under it once when I was a kid. Dad had told us that it had been passed down to the eldest son of each generation from his great-great grandfather who had been a forty-niner, with the admonishment that it be resorted to only in the direst necessity. The box was locked with a little cabinet lock and Dad carried the key in his purse.

As a boy I had dreamed of the chest being filled with gold coins and stacks of paper money—maybe a million dollars. That is, I had until one day when Mama and Dad had gone to town shopping and I came in the house and found Mark up on a chair at the buffet with a hairpin in his hand and the box open.

"So this is the family fortune, huh?" he had snorted. "Nothing in here but a rusty old gun and a book. See for yourself."

I hadn't wanted to look but I did take one little peek before I closed the lid and made Mark lock it again with the hairpin, and he was right—nothing but a pistol and an old book. I really gave mark what-for that day. Only time I ever really laid hands on him.

Dad woke me from my reverie. "Bring me the treasure chest, son," he said.

Mark whirled around at the window and watched with a funny look on his face as I got the chest and brought it over to the table. It *was* heavy—too heavy for what I knew was in it.

"You know, son, this chest would pass on down to you one of these days soon in case you didn't have to bury me out of it. Do you think Mark needs it badly enough to justify opening it now?"

I had a funny feeling in the pit of my stomach. I looked at Dad out of the corner of my eye but he was fumbling in his purse for the key. Did he really think there was something of value in the chest, or was he going off his rocker from living alone these past five years since Mama died and Mark and I moved to the city? I hoped the shock wouldn't kill him when he opened it. Maybe now would be a good time to do it, when Mark and I were both there. I noticed mark coming back to the table a step at a time, as if drawn by a magnet.

"I think now would be the time to open it," I told him.

Dad fumbled the key into the lock, turned it, and laid back the lid. He reached in and took out an old cap and ball revolver and a tattered leather bound Bible and laid them on the table. "These things came west with my great-great Grandpa," he said.

Then he lifted out the felt pad on the bottom of the chest, turned the box over, and there in his shaking hands was a flat plate of dull gold just the size of the box bottom. He set the chest aside and put the gold on the table in front of him. It must have weighed eight or nine pounds. His shaky finger pointed to crude lettering on the plate. "Thos. Jones—Hangtree—1853—10 lb Troy," it read.

"Well there's the family fortune, boys," Dad said, and he peered up at Mark. "Ten pounds of California gold. You'll have to take it to the mint to cash it in. It should be worth better than three thousand dollars with gold at thirty-five dollars an ounce."

I felt silly. The gold had been in the chest all the time. Then I looked at Mark. He ought to be relieved.

Mark was staring at the gold as if it fascinated him. His face was pale and the muscles in his cheeks were twitching. He pulled out a cigarette and lit it, and his hands were shaking.

"Will that do what you want, Mark?" Dad asked him, and his voice sounded almost harsh. I glanced back at him and he was peering at Mark with that glint in his eyes and the lines of his face were set.

Mark was looking at Dad, too. His eyes took in the set look of Dad's face and stared into his eyes, as if it was the first time he ever had really looked at Dad. Then his face stopped twitching, his shoulders came up, and he reached over and quietly stomped out his cigarette in a saucer.

"Thanks, Dad," he said quietly. "You've been very generous. I'll figure my way out of this one by myself."

Then he looked at me. "Shall we go?" he said, and started for the door. But he left the gold there on the table.

Dad had sort of wilted down in his chair. I started to call to Mark and ask him about the gold, but he was already out the door. I started for the door, but Dad clutched at my arm.

"It's been a long time," Dad said, "but I think you've made it, son. You boys come back and see me again sometime."

In the car Mark looked like he didn't want to talk, so we were halfway back to the city before I asked him "Did you think of someplace else to get the money?"

"No, and I'm not going to try," he said quietly. "In the morning I'm going to the boss and tell him the story and ask if I can work off what I owe him a part at a time. If he won't go for that then I'll go to jail."

I couldn't think of anything to say. After a while he put his hand over my knee and squeezed a little.

"You and Dad have been too good to me," he said. "You should have beat some sense into my head years ago." He lit a cigarette and inhaled deeply. "You know that hunk of gold out of the chest that Dad showed you? It's lead, and I think he knows it."

"Remember that red-headed girl I got mixed up with in high school? The doctor wanted real money to take care of her. I didn't know where to get it so I took the gold out of the chest, made a plaster cast of it, and filled it with lead. Then I gilded the lead and put it back in the box." He puffed a couple more times and let the smoke drift out the window. Then he went on in a friendly conversational tone he'd never used with me before.

"You know that old guy at the pool hall? The one that used to buy false teeth and old watches? He was the only one I dared go to with the gold. Know what he gave me for it? Two hundred lousy bucks."

THE END

The Policy

By E. S. Martin

He had to get out of there. Tears and sadness were too much for him. He sidled to the half open door, watching with absent-minded fascination as Doctor Gregg pulled the sheet up and over the head of the still form on the bed.

"It must have been quite sudden and painless," the doctor was saying to Margaret, who stood near the foot of the bed, tears silently slipping down her cheeks, her hands twisting and un-twisting a handkerchief. "Apparently the heart just stopped and that was it."

Margaret's shoulders started convulsing as great sobs shook her slender figure. He should go over and take her in his arms, and kiss her graying hair, and comfort her with tender words. But he couldn't now. He had to get out and get a breath of fresh air.

He slipped silently out the door, along the hall, and down the stairs. The morning sun was streaming in the east windows. Margaret hadn't closed the drapes as she usually did as soon as she arose. The sunshine looked warm and comforting, and full of life and promise.

The morning paper lay on the end table, unopened. He thought of easing into the big rocker and reading it, but let the idea pass. Printed news held little appeal for him at the moment.

Through the front window he saw a car slide to a halt. His daughter Peggy, her husband, Joe, and their four year old daughter Jenny emerged and came hurrying up the walk. Much as he loved them, he didn't want to see them just now. He moved quickly across the room and out the side door into the garden.

The late spring sunshine was bright and warm. The perfume of the roses was on the air, and a robin sang in the maple tree. The lawn was a velvet carpet of green and still had little jewels of dew flashing here and there. He was glad he had mowed it yesterday. That would be one less thing for Margaret to worry about.

Mabel and Stanley Martin with their grandson Robbie (Nancy's eldest) in the garden, early 1950's California

He walked towards the rhododendron and met his father coming around the corner. News travels fast, he thought.

"Good morning, Dad," he said. "You're looking well." As a matter of fact he was looking better than the last time he had seen him. How long ago was that—?

"Thank you, son. You're looking very fit yourself. How is Margaret?"

"She's taking it pretty hard, just now. You know how it is. People are never ready for these things."

"And Peggy?"

"She and Joe and Jenny are upstairs now. We didn't see them over the weekend, but I'm sure they're all well."

"That's fine. Well, son, I know you're wondering why I'm here. I hurried over as soon as I heard the news. I wanted to see you before you made any plans. It occurred to me that this might be a good time to take that trip we have talked about for so long. You know, Hawaii, the South Sea Islands, the Orient."

Dad's hands moving in the shape of a voluptuous female, his hips moving in a rheumatic Hula, brought a smile.

"Well, you may be right." Things *would* be different now. "As a matter of fact, I think I might enjoy it, but I'll need a few days to see that Margaret gets straightened around. Say a week. Suppose we get together in about a week and then we can really put our minds to that trip of yours."

"Okay, son. In a week, then." Dad waved his hand and disappeared around the corner of the house.

Dad and his trip. He had been talking of it for years. Just the two of them. The South Seas! Romance! Adventure! But there had always been something to keep them from going. Time—money—Dad's Rheumatism—He was certainly looking chipper this morning.

His glance dropped to the mulch at the foot of the Rhododendron. The ground was being slowly pushed up in a moving ridge. That would be the mole that had been giving him trouble. He saw Spot, the terrier coming up the lawn towards him. Spot would make short work of that mole.

"Here, Spot. Mole!" he called.

Spot stopped in his tracks, looked at him a minute, growled deep in his throat, tucked his tail between his legs, turned and slunk away. What had gotten into him all of a sudden, that he was afraid of moles?

The casket was in the hearse. The pall-bearers were climbing into their car. Margaret and Peggy and Joe were already in the car allotted to them. Jenny had not come to the funeral. She had been left with the neighbors. He was glad of that. So much sadness and tears for one so young. The other mourners were moving to the long line of flagged cars at the curb. For Margaret's sake he was glad that there had been so many friends who remembered and took the time. He glanced along the line of cars for one that might have room for him. Doctor and Mrs. Gregg appeared to be alone. He slipped into the back seat of their sedan.

Driving towards the cemetery in the long parade of cars in the noon sunshine was relaxing. He watched the flower decked lawns gliding by and paid no attention to what the Doctor and his wife were saying until he heard Mrs. Gregg mention Margaret.

"—So hard on Margaret," she was saying.

"But if you have to go, that is the easiest way I know," the Doctor was saying. "Go to bed alive and healthy, and wake up dead. If I had my choice, that's the way I'd choose."

He nodded to himself. His feelings exactly.

"Hope he left enough money to pay my bill," the Doctor said.

"Why, you charlatan," he thought to himself, but said nothing. They were pulling up in the cemetery drive. But Doc Gregg had never been one to hound you on his bills. He slipped out of the car and moved along the fringe of the crowd.

This hillside plot was the most beautiful spot in the cemetery, he thought. Always had thought so. And it was never more beautiful than now, covered as it was with summer flowers in their first bloom.

The minister spoke quietly in his most comforting tone. Reverend Hill was a fine man at funerals. He made you feel that your loved ones were not far away. Margaret stood quietly through the eulogy, dry-eyed and reconciled. Peggy was weeping. Joe had a firm hand on each of their arms, his face immobile.

The service was over. The casket was lowered slowly, part of the way into the grave. The people turned back to their cars. He was glad Jenny had not been here to see her grandfather lowered into the ground. He turned and strolled leisurely across the cemetery towards the entrance.

Margaret, Peggy and Joe were in the living room. George Black, the family lawyer, was in there talking to them. Out on the lawn, Jenny was playing with Spot, tossing a ball for him to retrieve, from the sounds they were making. From his easy chair in the den, he listened to the lawyer.

"We cleaned out the safe deposit box. We found insurance on the house, on the car, a policy on you and one on Peggy, and a few government bonds totaling fifteen hundred dollars. The bank tells us there is about six hundred in the checking account and eleven hundred in savings. Then of course there's another six hundred yet to come from the firm. And that looks like the whole picture, unless you have some other ideas. Of course the house is paid for, and there's the car, too, but $3800 isn't going far these days."

He heard Margaret catch her breath. "But I'm sure there was a ten thousand dollar insurance policy with Gibraltar. He carried it for years. And there should have been more bonds than that. I know there were several thousand dollars worth."

"There was a ten thousand dollar policy," Black said. "We checked with Gibraltar because we found checks for the premiums among the old statements. The policy was cancelled on payment of its cash surrender value two months ago.

And we can find no trace of another policy through any of the local agencies. As for the bonds, Joe was with me when we opened the box, and there were only fifteen hundred dollars worth. Unless you know of something, it looks like there won't be much left after the funeral is paid for."

"There must be some mistake," Margaret was saying.

"We'll see that you're taken care of, Mother," Peggy was saying.

Why hadn't they found the insurance policy, he wondered? Then it struck him. Why, Indeed? Because he had forgotten to put it in the box. And why hadn't they found trace of it? Because he had paid cash for it instead of banking the money and writing a check as he should have, and because he had gone to the city to make the deal because the company there offered a unique policy that he wanted. That's why he had cashed in the old policy and the bonds. And where was the policy now? Oh yes, it was in the legal advisor book where he had been checking it and left it when he was interrupted. He rose from his chair and moved over to the bookshelf. There, he could just see the policy jacket protruding above the top of the pages.

He reached for the book to take it from the shelf, but the book remained in its place. He took both his hands and tugged, but he was powerless to move the little volume. But he had to tell Margaret about this policy. He spied the desk. He went to it and started to pick up a pencil to write on the sheet of notepaper lying on the blotter, but the pencil wouldn't move, either. He gave it up, and strode into the living room.

"I don't know what I will do," Margaret was saying.

"I'll tell you what you will do," he said firmly, but she kept on talking.

"I suppose the smart thing to do would be to sell the house," Margaret was saying.

"You won't have to sell the house," he said, but she kept on talking. He moved directly in front of her, between her and Black, and laid both his hands on her shoulders.

"Margaret," he said. "You don't have to sell the house. There is an insurance policy, and a darned good one," but she kept right on talking to George Black just like she couldn't see him or hear him.

Exasperated, he yelled, "Will you listen, everybody. There is an insurance policy!" But they kept right on talking, and paid him no attention. Only Spot, out in the yard, quit barking suddenly, and he could hear Jenny calling "Here, Spot!" He gave up and stalked back into the den.

In a few minutes Jenny sidled through the door of the den and plopped herself down on the chair at the writing desk.

"Hi, Grandpa," she said. "Mommy and Daddy said you were gone, but you aren't at all, are you?"

"I'm not sure," he said. "Have you and Spot been having fun?"

"We were playing ball, but all of a sudden he quit and sneaked away."

"Who are you talking to, dear?" Peggy called from the living room.

"To Grandpa," Jenny replied.

He heard Margaret's sudden burst of tears in the silence. Suddenly he had an inspiration.

"Jenny, doll. Would you do something for Grandpa?" he whispered.

"Sure, Grandpa. What?"

He pointed to the Legal Advisor. "Take this book in to Grandma and show her what's in it."

"Will you hand it to me? I can't reach it."

"Pull the chair up and stand on that," he said.

"Mommy doesn't let me stand on chairs," she reminded him.

"That's all right, honey. You tell her I said you could this once."

Obediently, Jenny pulled the chair up to the bookcase, lifted down the book, and took it proudly into the living room. He followed her out the door of the den, moved behind her across the living room, and gained the side door to the garden, as Jenny handed the book to Margaret.

He smiled to himself at the strange look on Margaret's face as Jenny said, "Grandma, Grandpa said show you what's in this. Are there pictures, Grandma?"

And he felt an inner satisfaction as he saw Margaret, unbelieving, take out the policy and open it. That fifty grand should be a comfort to her.

He passed through the door and hurried to meet his father, coming across the lawn.

"Things are all set here now, Dad. Shall we take that trip we've been dreaming about?" he said.

The End

R. I. P.

Collier's
640 Fifth Avenue
New York 19, New York
Plaza 9-1000

Thanks very much for showing us this story. We're sorry to have to report that it isn't one we can use.

Please keep us in mind for the future. We're always looking for stories, and we're glad to read them; and we're particularly pleased when we can publish the work of a new writer.

We'd like to comment individually on the manuscripts we receive, but we receive so many that such comment isn't possible.
We appreciate your thinking of us; we hope you will again.

Sincerely,

The Editors

Earl S. Martin
10945 Graton Rd
Sebastopol, California

R. I. P.

By
E. Stanley Martin

As a creature of habit, I dined in the cafeteria and then strolled leisurely across the campus through the golden September twilight to my bachelor quarters. From the mahogany stand just inside the ornate Victorian door of my rooming house I picked up the French journal and an advertisement from a book house that constituted my share of the day's mail, and climbed the stairs with their worn carpet to my room.

Greg and Jen had often fussed at me for living in such shabby quarters, but I found it comfortable. It was quiet and respectable, and the landlady deferred to my idiosyncrasies.

As I placed my hat on the shelf and slipped my coat onto a hanger, I thought I would indulge myself for a half an hour with the crossword puzzle in the new French journal, before continuing my early Italian translations. As an associate professor of romance languages I find such little indulgences both pleasant and profitable.

I was just settling myself in the old leather chair with the magazine and a pencil when something prodded my inner consciousness. "It is Tuesday evening!" I remembered. "I promised Greg that I would warm up his set and try to tune him in on Tuesday evenings!"

As I put my hat and coat on again and started down the stairs, I wondered how I could have forgotten, with Greg not yet two weeks dead! One did not lightly ignore Greg's wishes, be he alive or dead! Could it have been that odd mechanism of the mind that pushes into forgetfulness those things we resent or in which we have little faith?

Two blocks down the street and around the corner I turned in at the flat-roofed modern cottage with the short wave antenna atop a steel mast behind it. Genevieve Johnson opened the door in response to my knock. After twelve years of childless marriage to Greg she looked no older than she had that first night I met her at the USO in Washington, I thought. The soft light behind her made a halo of the honey-colored hair around the oval of her face.

"Good evening, Jen," I said. "You're looking lovely tonight."

She managed a little smile. "Thank you, Ab. Won't you come in?"

"I don't see much of you on the campus," I said, as I placed my hat on the table and eased myself carefully into a campaign chair. "How are the art classes this semester?"

"Abstract is loaded, and the figure class has a good enrollment—mostly men, as usual. How are the romance languages?"

"I offer no cinch courses, so my enrollments are moderate; I like it that way. Are you getting adjusted to your new life?"

"Oh, I do alright on school days with my classes and all the campus activity. I don't think I'll ever get used to the nights and weekends, though. Not that we ever did anything, Greg and I. He was forever tinkering with his radio, and I'd sit and read, or paint and putter around. But I was used to it. Will you be over Saturday evening as usual?"

For the past ten years I had customarily dined with Jen and Greg on Saturday evenings. Greg's death put a new aspect on these pleasant evenings, however. "Perhaps it would be better," I said, "if we dined out this week at some quiet little spot."

"I'd like that, Ab!" she said, and her brown eyes were bright. "It's been a long time!"

"The reason I came over this evening," I said, by way of changing the subject, "Is that Greg exacted a promise of me some weeks before his death. He may not have told you about it since he refused to tell you about his heart condition, even after the doctor warned him that it might prove fatal. He was working on a complex theory of radio communication with the other world, which I don't pretend to understand. He insisted that, in the event of his death, I agree to come over here on Tuesday evenings and tune in his set against the possibility that he would contrive some way of establishing communication with us. I couldn't refuse, of course. I was never able to deny Greg anything he insisted on." *Even you*, I thought to myself.

"No, he didn't tell me," she said. "But that sounds very like him. I knew that he was toying with the idea of communication with the other world, but I just supposed it was a pipe dream. Do you think he can really get in touch with us?" I noticed that she frowned a little and that there was an odd inflection to her voice.

"I wouldn't build up any hopes on it. Radio held very few secrets from him. But when I flew to Rome at the end of summer session he had not yet worked it out, and that was just three weeks before he died. I didn't come over last Tuesday because of the opening of the semester and because I knew you were too broken up over his passing."

"I hope he told you how to operate the set. He was never able to teach me the first thing about it. Would you like to go in there now?"

"Please." Might as well get it over with.

I followed her willowy, nicely rounded figure to the den, which Greg had converted to a short wave station and radio workshop.

"I haven't been in here since Greg passed away," she said as she opened the door and flipped the switch. "For heaven's sake! Who could have left that turned on?" she exclaimed.

I looked at the workbench and saw two spools of recording tape turning and feeding the tape through a recording head. They were not on a standard machine. They were on some weird device that Greg had concocted, apparently. The whole top of the bench was covered with coils and condensers and resistors, with one out-sized tube glowing in the midst of them.

"I don't see any switch for it," Jen said. "I'll just pull the plug."

There was a microphone on a short stand by the recorder, and as Jen reached to pull the plug from the wall socket over the bench, the mike seemed to fall over into the mess of equipment. There was the crash of broken glass and a flash of sparks as she pulled the plug.

"Oh, dear!" Jen said. "What have I broken now?"

I set the microphone up again and looked over the equipment. "I don't see any damage but a broken tube", I assured her. "I'll replace it. Greg always had a spare for anything that could burn out."

I opened the parts cabinet. There was a shelf of tubes all in the original cartons with identifying numbers on the end, some of which I recalled from the days when Greg and I were in Signal Corps OCS together. It didn't take much looking to tell me that there were no cartons in the cabinet large enough to hold a tube the size I was looking for. I poked among the broken glass on top of the bench to find the part with the symbols etched in the glass, but I could find no symbols.

"I'll have to get help from an expert, I guess," I told Jen. "I don't see another tube like that one in here. It probably is of no consequence anyway. Why don't I tune in the set now?"

"You do that!" Jen said. "I'll run out to the kitchen and put on a pot of coffee."

I turned on Greg's receiver and gave it a chance to warm up. Then I plugged in the headphones and settled them over my ears. The frying noise was abominable, so I turned down the volume and adjusted the tuning dial. I picked up my ears at an Italian voice, clear and crisp, but after a few words I realized that it was a newscast carrying the same world news that I had read in the evening paper over dinner. I turned the dial again. Conscientiously I tried to tune in a station at each change in the hum and crackle on the phones.

This is just like Greg, I thought. Imposing on my leisure time in pursuit of the impossible, even in death.

I had first met Gregory Johnson on our first day of basic training at the old New Jersey National Guard Camp near Fort Monmouth. As the tallest man in the platoon he was shuffled to right guide and I wound up at the other end of the line. But as college professors we had something in common and bunked in the same tent. I cleaned his rifle after the supply sergeant refused to accept it because it was still dirty. We went on into OCS on the same orders, and bunked side by side again. Greg wound up as battalion commander and I stayed in the rear rank. When we had a few minutes to spare, Greg decided what we'd do and I did it.

The dial turned past a quick oriental voice and I tuned back carefully. I was disappointed to find that it was not one of the two Chinese dialects that I understand, and I tuned it out reluctantly.

From OCS I had been assigned directly to Washington as a cryptographic officer because of my language familiarities. That's where I had met Jen. After decoding and translating Italian all day I was pretty well done in by evening. For a change, I dropped in at the USO one evening, and there was Jen! She was in Washington sacrificing her career to do drafting of some sort for the Navy. She was also taking classes in painting two nights a week, but she still managed one night a week as hostess at the USO, and I had picked the night.

I finished the band I was working, switched coils, and started working another wavelength. After all, I had promised Greg I would do this.

Jen and I had gotten along very nicely. We had reached the point where we were having dinner together each evening, and on her free nights would stroll around the town, window-shopping or just talking. Then Greg called me one day to say that he had been assigned to duty in Washington, and of course he had to meet Jen. He hadn't known her three weeks until they were married. That was Greg for you, he always knew what he wanted, and usually got it.

I was startled to hear a voice very like Greg's. I turned square on, but it turned out to be a Fresno operator answering a CQ. I continued turning the dial.

When the war was over, Greg was wearing a Major's gold leaves, but I felt myself lucky to be a first lieutenant. Greg thought I should come out here where he had been teaching physics before the war and join the faculty. I liked the little college where I had been teaching, but in the end I did as Greg had suggested. These past ten years had been rather pleasant, too, for an old bachelor, set in his ways. There had been dinner on Saturday nights with Jen and Greg—an occasional quick trip to Rome for research on the book of translations from the early Italian that I was working on.

As I reached the end of the band I was working and started to change over to another, my glance wandered over to the workbench and stopped at the rolls of recording tape. I eyed them speculatively. Which way had those tapes been turning?

Jen came in carrying a tray loaded down with coffee pot, cups and saucers, and little cakes. I took off the phones and turned off the set.

"Any luck?" she asked.

"I didn't contact Greg," I said, and accepted a cup of coffee. I thought she looked somehow relieved. "You told me you hadn't been in here since Greg passed away. Was anyone else in here this evening?"

"No! Why do you ask?"

"I'm thinking about that tape recording device. It wasn't here when I was in here just before leaving for Rome. It seems to me that there isn't more than ten or fifteen minutes of tape on the pickup spool. If that is true, it hadn't been running long when we came in here a while ago."

"That's right! If Greg had left it on it would have run through days ago! But I'm sure there hasn't been anyone in here, Ab. My last class was over at four and I came straight home. There has been no one here this evening except you. Do you suppose—?" Her eyes were wide and questioning.

"I intend to find out. Do you have another tape recorder here?"

"Not that I know of."

"I'll run over and get mine. I want to see what's on that tape."

I have a recorder that I use for dictation on my trips to Italy. I find it so much faster and more satisfactory than writing. I was back with it in five minutes. Jen had set up a card table for me. I took the spools from the workbench, rewound the tape, and threaded it up to play. I turned the recorder on to warm up, took a sip of tepid coffee, glanced at Jen, staring with a sort of morbid fascination at the tape I thought, and started the tape.

"Hi, Doc!" the recorder said, and it was Greg's voice, alive and vibrant with energy. He had always called me Doc, with reference to my degree, in preference to Abernathy, or the more familiar "Ab" that Jen used and that I preferred.

"As you can see," the machine continued, "I finally figured it out. I am talking to you from what we have always heard referred to as the "great beyond", only it isn't so far away, really. Here I am, right in my own radio room. It's Tuesday evening and you will be here any minute now. I just saw to that! To think that I had to poke you in the conscience to keep you from settling down with that silly French crossword puzzle instead of coming over here as you promised.

I moved in my chair. It didn't feel comfortable. Looking up I noticed that Jen was trying to get her cup back onto the saucer and the whole thing set down without spilling. Her face was white, and her eyes, watching the tape, were bigger and darker than usual.

"I don't have much tape for this first séance," the recorder continued, "so I'll talk right along. Later you can put longer tapes on and I can really give you something to write a book about. Should be a best seller. I think you'd better marry Genevieve, Doc, so you can move in over here and keep putting tapes on this device."

I looked up to find Jen looking at me. There was some color in her face and a new warmth in her eyes that was disturbing to me. "The conceited ghost!", I thought. "Why doesn't he mind his own business? But he has a point there, marrying Jen, I mean."

"You know, Doc, I was trying to work out a system of contact by radio, but it wouldn't work for reasons that I'll explain later. I was working from one of Einstein's formulas and the only way I could figure out that it would work was on a tape recorder hookup. I ran into Doc Einstein the other day and he told me that I was the first one that had figured out any practical use for the formula. He told me that when we get this system working he will record a new formula that he's been working on—one that could bring total peace to the world just as his earlier ones paved the way for the atom bomb."

"You and Jen are probably wondering what it's like over here. I know I used to. Of course I haven't been here very long and I don't know my way around too well as yet, but it isn't a great deal different from what I'm used to. We look the same here as we did on your side in the prime of life. There is no element of time here, so no one is old. The nearest I can explain our state of being to you is that we are energy in vibration much like light waves or heat waves. That's why you can't see us even when we are in the same room with you."

"What do we do over here? Whatever we want! Many of us that are still here on earth are doing what we did before—studying—experimenting. Of course most people when they come over are tired of working and glad to be through with it. They just take off out through the galaxy to look around. Natural born tourists, most of them. The traveling is easy, you know. Since we are in a state of vibration we can travel through space at the speed of light and with no more trouble. We just decide where we want to go next, head in that direction, and there we are. I have talked to Marco Polo and Columbus and some of the other old timers that have made the tour, and they tell me that some of the more remote worlds are quite unique and interesting."

"That's enough about this side for now. Later I can give you a complete rundown on things over here, and I know that there will be hundreds of ideas that various of us will want to record for the information of you people when we get into production on this device. Right now I want to tell you about this machine I rigged up so that you can duplicate it in case something should go wrong with this one."

"You'll want to know something of the theory of it. This machine is designed to operate on a frequency resonant to the frequency at which we on this side vibrate. Resonant to the frequency of light, in other words. You remember about resonant frequencies, of course. That's the deal I spent so much time explaining to you in the radio class when we were in OCS, that allows waves of one frequency to come in at any resonant multiple of that frequency."

"I set up this machine just before I died. It had to be connected to a power source for operation so I had to fix it to be turned on by voice control. At the word 'Start!' the microphone generates enough micro-amps to operate a relay that turns on the power. At the command 'Stop!' the machine turns off. You can try it yourself."

"I won't bother to explain the hookup to you. It is obvious. Just trace it and draw a diagram. All of the parts are standard except the tube. It's the tube that I want to tell you about, and for heaven's sake don't let anything happen to it until you get duplicates built! I had quite a time designing it and building it, and there isn't another one like it on earth. First of all, the filaments are—"

"—been in here since Greg passed away." That was unmistakably Jen's voice.

"Oh, there you are!" That was Greg's voice again. "You're looking well, Doc, and you were never prettier, Jen."

"For heaven's sake! Who could have left that turned on?" It was Jen's voice again. "I don't see any switch for it. I'll just pull the plug."

"Wait just a minute, Jen!" Greg's voice was urgent. "I have to tell Doc—skreek!"

That was all. There was just the hum of the motor and the whisper of the tape feeding through the recorder head. It ran for a minute before I could raise my hand to turn it off.

When I looked at Jen she was trembling, staring at the microphone and shattered tube on the bench. She needed something to do with her hands, I decided. I gathered up the cups and saucers, put them on the tray with the pot and handed the tray to Jen.

"I didn't do it on purpose, Ab. I didn't know—"

"Of course not!" I assured her. I managed to sound more matter-of-fact than I felt. "I think we need another cup of coffee. Would you mind brewing another pot?"

"That would be nice." She took the tray and walked out of the room, moving as if in a trance.

After she was gone, I slumped down in the chair again and stared at the tape on the recorder. Was the man going to run my life forever? Couldn't he stay respectably dead like other people?

I got up and looked at the recording hookup on the workbench. It wasn't too complicated. Even I could diagram it. Except for the shattered glass, even the tube looked duplicable.

"It would be nice to give Einstein's new formula to the world," I thought. "And how about the others?"

Yes, how about the others? How about Genghis Kahn, Napoleon, Joe Stalin? Suppose they had something to say. If they did, Einstein's formula wouldn't be enough.

"The man's mad," I thought. "This device of Greg's is a machine of the Devil. The world must never know about it!"

I turned to the recorder and jerked the tape from the reel. I dumped the mess into the metal wastebasket and struck a match to it. It didn't burn fast enough, so I tore pages from Greg's radio log, crumpled them and put them under the tape and lit them. The tape disappeared in the smoke.

At the workbench I started tearing the components out of Greg's hookup. As I jerked each piece away, I laid it over the vise and hit it with a hammer until it was unrecognizable. When I got to the tube I went at it with pliers and wire cutters. I bent each part out of shape, and then beat the whole thing into a shapeless mess. I dumped the whole pile into the wastebasket on top of the ashes.

Carefully I closed up my tape recorder and took it out and placed it on the table beside my hat. Then I folded the card table and set it outside the door. Finally, I picked up the wastebasket, walked to the door, and turned for a last look before closing the door on the room.

"*Requiescat in pace*, Greg!" I whispered, flipped the switch, and closed the door firmly.

Jen said nothing as I walked through the kitchen and carried the wastebasket out to empty it in the garbage can. When I came back she poured two cups of coffee and set them on the table. She was completely composed, and there was a gentle smile around her mouth.

"Thanks, Ab," she said. "I know that was hard for you. He was almost as irresistible dead as he was alive, wasn't he?"

"I hated to do it," I told her quietly, "But it was too dangerous. The world isn't ready."

I sipped my coffee and looked into the now serene depths of her brown eyes.

"I meant to ask you years ago in Washington," I said. "Before you met Greg. When will you marry me, Jen?"

"Whenever you think it's decent. As soon as you wish. Tomorrow if you like."

I smiled and slipped my hand over hers, the most intimate gesture I had ever made towards her.

"After waiting this long we can wait a few more months to observe the niceties of convention," I told her. "But remember! We have a dinner date for Saturday night. I'll pick you up at six."

"I'll remember," she said.

The End

Chapter 8

The Love Angle

In July of 1932 my grandmother Mabel Louella Thomson was active in the choir, Sunday School and youth group of the Breden Memorial United Brethren Church in Terre Haute, Indiana, where she was befriended by Stanley's sister, Esther Martin. My Aunt Esther brought her brother Stanley along to several of the youth dances and gatherings, where he soon had a romantic eye on Mabel, which evolved into a courtship. By early fall he knew she was the one for him, and Gram writes in her memoirs:

> *He was very romantic when he proposed to me while we were sitting on the banks of the Wabash River in what is now known as Fairbanks Park. I shyly dropped my eyes and said I'd have to think about it. This—he knew and I knew—was for effect only. I didn't want him to think I was too anxious. Anyway he didn't take me very seriously but went ahead making his plans to marry me. He even went out and got a job.*

Gramps was doing freelance photography at that time with a friend, traveling around Indiana, Kentucky and Ohio making photographs of anyone interested, and then checking into a cheap motel to develop the photos and deliver them the next day. The income was barely enough to keep the two of them working, but certainly not enough to support a wife and family. Still, when Stanley came home over Labor Day weekend, he and Mabel decided to go ahead and get married, quietly. It was important to keep their marriage a secret, as Gram was a teacher at that time, which carried a prerequisite of being single. They were married in Marshall, Illinois, on September 3rd, 1932.

After Labor Day the newlyweds had to part, with Stanley heading back out on the road, and Mabel settling in to a rented room near her new teaching job in Greencastle. Unfortunately, the news of their marriage somehow became known to the school principal by mid-October, and Gram was forced to leave her teaching position, which in any case coincided with a severe cystic infection of her leg which kept her from working until after Christmas. And of course these events made a public wedding announcement necessary; thus began the married life of Stanley and Mabel Martin.

The wedding photo of Stanley and Mabel Martin, taken in 1932,
Photo by Martin Studios

Gram talks about Gramps in her memoirs, saying: *As for the man I married, Earl Stanley Martin, and who became the father of my children, I can only say, "He's tops." I can truthfully say we never had a serious disagreement. We had differences of opinions, but each of us exercised psychology on the other and usually worked things out to my way of thinking! We had our ups and downs financially, but I believe our reverses helped to draw us closer together. Even with all of our reverses, Stanley, like my father, always provided an adequate living and we never went hungry or without proper clothing and shelter. Stanley was always generous and thoughtful with me and his children. Whenever he got out of line I reminded him of what an elderly cousin of my mother's used to say to me before I was married. He would say "Mabel, when you get ready to get married—pick out a man who has a face like a horse and who is good to his mother and he will be good to you." Well anyway, Stanley was good to his mother . . .*

Gramps had a good deal of romance in him, and his stories in Chapter eight reflect a variety of themes such as first love; the old "which sister" question; infidelity; and what we might refer to today as "Mars-Venus" issues. But my favorite stories in this section are the short slice-of-life vignettes of John and Edith Osburn, which have such mundane yet humorous elements of real life, underlaid with the kind of committed and lasting love I believe he shared with my grandmother for thirty-seven years[26].

E. Stanley Martin
Oct. 9, 1956

Little Sister

(story starter)

"Hi-ya, Pest. Is Gloria home?"

"Hi, Plumber. Come in. Of course she's home. You have a date with her tonight, don't you?"

I sure do, babe. We're going to Fisherman's Wharf for dinner, and then to the Paramount."

"That's a long drive for a sardine sandwich and a movie. Better sit down and rest while Gloria finishes putting on a new face. The one she wore this afternoon with Gerald got a little smudgy."

"Was she out with that square again?"

"Mister Square to you, Plumber. Remember that he designs the houses and you just install the plumbing where the plans say. He took Gloria up to see his latest dream home up in Mayacamas Highlands. Must have been windy. Her hair was a mess when she got in."

"That guy has been dogging me ever since he and Gloria and I were in Freshman English together. If he doesn't lay off Gloria I'm going to punch his nose so hard it'll drip down the back of his neck."

"Such uncouth language for a U.C. Grad. Can I hold your coat while you punch him?"

"Rosemary O'Brien, your Irish blood is showing. You must have inherited it all. Gloria doesn't have any. Yes, you may hold my coat while I punch him. And after I do Gloria will marry him out of sympathy, and your dad will fire me, and I'll have to figure out some other way to get enough money to set up my contracting business."

"Oh, is that what you're after? A contracting business of your own? I thought you were planning on marrying one."

"Look, Brat. You've been needling me ever since the first time I carried Gloria's books home from high school. You must have been in the fifth grade then. You have seen enough of me by now to know that I'm not about to marry a contracting business. When I marry Gloria I'll have my own business. And it shouldn't be too long now."

"Sixth grade, and I've grown some since. You mean those three houses you're building in your spare time?"

"I do. I didn't know you knew about them. In another three months they'll be ready to sell and the bank has already told me they'll back me on another twenty if those clear FHA."

"Oh, Ralph! I'm glad! I thought you were going to marry Gloria for her money. I think I hear her coming. Here! Let me see if you got the grime out from under your fingernails!"

"Well, if I'm interrupting something, forgive me. I didn't know you two cared enough for each other to hold hands. Shall we go, Ralph? Or do you want to stay and play pat-a-cake with Rosemary?

Today is the Day

By E.Stanley Martin

"Today is the day!"

The words were singing inside David Bromley as he popped his eyes open to the bright June sunshine in his room. He flung back the blanket and whirled his feet to the floor in a single motion.

He tossed his pajamas on top of the cap and neatly folded gown on his dresser, reminder of his graduation last night, and hopped into the shower. As he soaped and rinsed, he caught himself humming the class song and stopped abruptly. That was from last night. His graduation had been important but it was over, and today was *the* day.

"Susan comes back today," he thought. "I'll climb the pinnacle for her, and I'll collect my kiss."

He started to sing a chorus from the top tune of the Hit Parade, but it dwindled away until there was only the sound of the water splashing on the shower curtain.

He *would* get his kiss, wouldn't he?

This was the day Susan Wentworth and her family should return to their summer home adjoining the Bromley ranch. He could climb the pinnacle for her as he had told her three years ago that he would, and Bernard wasn't home from U.C. yet to louse up the deal. At least he hadn't heard Bernie drive in during the night.

David toweled briskly, slipped into a bright sports shirt, slacks and crepe soles, and ran a comb through his dripping black curls. Then he started down the stairs, holding the banister and favoring his left foot as much as possible. After three years and five operations it still wasn't as good as it should be, and never would be, he guessed.

"Good morning, David. Will you have orange juice or tomato?" his mother greeted him as he strode into the kitchen with almost no limp.

"Orange juice, please. Did Bernie get in?"

"Not yet. He probably won't leave Berkeley until mid-morning."

Her back was to David as she squeezed the orange juice, but from long observation he noted the softer tone in her voice as she spoke of Bernard, two years older than David and just finishing his sophomore year at U.C.

"She probably doesn't even suspect that she favors Bernie, much less suspect that it shows," he thought, but he had known it almost since babyhood.

"Thank you Mother," he said as she set the juice in front of him and dropped bread into the toaster.

"What are your plans for the day?" she asked.

"Thought I'd just goof off this morning and get the feel."

"Your father left early for a sale up at Willits. He suggested that you check on your lambs before you go anywhere. He didn't have time. He thought your valedictorian address last night was fine."

"I'll look at the lambs," he told her. She hadn't said how she liked the speech.

David gulped his breakfast hurriedly and headed for the pasture where his lambs were grazing. A quick look assured him that the lambs were in good shape, so he walked on through the pasture, taking the path around the hill towards the Wentworth place.

It would have been closer to go over the hill, but because of his foot David preferred the longer path. It was early enough that David should be able to reach the pinnacle before Susan came cantering over on her roan mare to begin another lively summer.

Susan Wentworth was David's own age. Last summer she had been gangly with brown hair and brown eyes in a deep-tanned face. For ten years that he could remember, she and her family had spent the summer at their home adjoining the Bromley ranch. Susan had spent her time for the most part, as he recalled only too well, romping, riding and swimming with the two Bromley boys.

David knew that Susan was filled with an eagerness for living and a zest for action. Susan's mind seemed to be filled with ideas, sometimes daring, sometimes whimsical, so that there was never a dull moment when she was around.

As David's left foot slipped on a rock in the path and the pain shot up his leg, he was reminded that it was one of Susan's whimsical moments of three years ago that had been responsible for the injury to his foot.

He and Susan and Bernie had been stalking each other through the brush in the valley along the edge of the Bromley property toward the Wentworth's. Susan had just flushed the two boys from cover when she had spied one of the Bromley rams on top of a high rock projecting from the base of the hill.

"Look at that old ram standing on the pinnacle," Susan had said. "He's looking at the scenery. I'll bet there's a pretty view from up there."

"Want me to go see?" Bernie had asked.

"I'll go if you want me to," David had offered.

"You couldn't get up there if you tried a week," Bernie had scoffed.

"I could so," David had retorted. "I have a big kiss for the one that gets there first," Susan had said.

Bernie took off for the far side of the big rock. David had headed for what appeared to be a pathway of some sort running up the face of the rock.

How it happened that they had not climbed that rock before, David could not recall. Perhaps it had not occurred to them or had not seemed worth the effort.

The rock on which the ram was standing was a rough pillar of basalt with almost vertical sides projecting twelve or fifteen feet above the clustered boulders at its base. It appeared to have a flat top possible three feet in diameter. On the side David approached, erosion had taken its toll, for there appeared to be a trough or chute of crumbled rock leading to the summit, steep but not too steep for the old ram to climb.

David had clambered over the lower boulders and reached the floor of the slide. Here he had to go on all fours because the path was steep and slippery. He had glanced up once to see the ram pawing the ground, almost dancing in his excitement. "Hope he doesn't jump off and kill himself," David had thought. "Dad would be mad."

Halfway up the slide, inching along with his fingernails digging into the rock, David had heard a sudden clatter on the rock above him and raised his head just in time to see the ram hurtling at him.

The next thing David remembered was waking up in the hospital with his mother and Susan sitting by his bedside. His mother had been wringing her hands. Susan had been sitting quietly with her hands in her lap, still dressed in her sweater and riding jeans.

When his mother had noticed that his eyes were open she had said, "Thank goodness you're awake at last! I'll have to go and call your father."

When his mother had gone Susan had scooted her chair over and held his hand. "How are you feeling, David?"

"I hurt all over," he had said.

"I know," Susan had told him. "Bernie scared the ram and he knocked you into all those rocks. One of the rocks rolled on your foot and crushed it. And do you know," she had added indignantly, "That stinker Bernie wouldn't even help me try to get that rock off of you. He was so scared he ran all the way home to get help."

"Did he get his kiss?" David had felt the words dragged from him.

"He did not, and if he asks me for it he'll get his face slapped. You get the kiss," and she had bent over to give it to him.

"I didn't earn it," he had protested and turned his face away. "When I get out of here I'll climb that rock for you and I'll earn my kiss."

Why he had been so perverse he couldn't imagine, unless it had been his chagrin that Bernie had been first again. Bernie was always first. He could do things easier and faster and with less effort than David could, and was the first to point out that fact.

David was just coming around the foot of the hill to a point where he could see the pinnacle when he heard someone whistling. He stepped behind a Manzanita and looking up the hill saw Bernard striding over the crest and down towards the Pinnacle. He was carrying a coil of rope that looked like one of the old lassos out of the barn.

The sight reminded David that on that day three years ago when he had hurt his foot Bernie had been carrying a lasso that he had been using in a game of cowboys and Indians.

David felt a sullen indignation rising in him at Bernie's being here on this day when he wanted to climb the rock for Susan and earn his kiss. But he was also curious as to just what Bernard was up to. He edged around the Manzanita so he could watch.

Bernie was on the side of the pinnacle opposite that where David had made his disastrous effort to climb three years ago, the side where Bernie had made his successful climb. David had never studied the pinnacle on this side particularly, for it did not appear that there was any practicable way to climb the rock on this side. Looking at it intently now he saw that this was true. There *was* no way up the rock on this side.

But Bernie didn't hesitate. He knew that Susan would be coming along this way any minute. He walked to the cluster of rocks, shinnied his way up to the base of the pinnacle, uncoiled his rope and tossed it over a projecting shoulder of rock at the crest of the pinnacle. Up the rope he went, like a monkey on a string. He swung an arm over the top and then swung himself up to sit astride the peak.

"Just like that," David thought. "No effort at all. Leave it to Bernie to find the easy way."

Sitting there David thought of the agonizing weeks that he had spent in bed, the high school classes that he had attended in a wheelchair, the five operations that he had undergone in an effort to salvage the crushed bones of his foot. He thought of the hours he had spent after he was allowed on his feet coming out here to the pinnacle to crawl on his hands and knees, trying to work his way up the slippery chute on the far side, and how proud he had felt when he had finally succeeded in clawing his way to the top.

That was the difference between him and Bernie. Bernie used his noodle. David used his muscle. And there was Bernie sitting on the pinnacle waiting for Susan.

"Well, that ruins my plans for the day," David muttered to himself. "I guess I might as well go home."

"What were your plans?"

It was a soft voice, almost in his ear. He whirled around and there was Susan. Not the Susan he remembered, but a well filled out and finely modeled Susan in a gray tweed jacket and skirt.

"How did you get here?" he demanded.

"A fine greeting." She smiled at him. "I've been here all the time, on the other side of the bush. You were so busy watching Bernie you didn't even notice."

"How did you get here so early? Where's your horse?"

"We drove up last night. It was such a pretty morning that I left the mare in the pasture and walked. And I got here before you country sleepyheads. In fact, I got here in time to see you come trudging around the hill while Bernie came over the top and beat you to the pinnacle. There he is, sitting on top, watching up the valley for me to come riding down so he can claim a kiss. And did you see the slick way he got up there?"

"I saw it," he said, and maybe it was the way she had spoken, but there was no bitterness in his voice. "That's Bernie for you. If there's two ways to do a thing he sees the easy way and all I can see is the hard way."

She smiled at him and there was an odd light in her eyes. "You know, David, I think you're growing up. That's the first time I have ever heard you speak a kind word about Bernie."

"Well, it's the truth," he told her. "For three years all I have been thinking of is climbing that silly rock so I could prove I was as good as Bernie, and so I could earn a kiss. I've practically killed myself trying to climb that rock slide on the other side, and I can do it, too. Only now I don't want to. You'd better go down and give Bernie his kiss. I have to go look after my lambs."

He started to turn back towards the path home, but she took his arm firmly and turned him to face her.

"I'm not about to go down and kiss Bernie. That was a silly kids' deal three years ago because I wanted an excuse to kiss stubborn, persistent little you. You broke your foot, and then you broke my heart when you wouldn't let me kiss you for all the misery I had caused. These past two summers have been plain agony for me, playing checkers with you in a wheelchair and then going swimming and dancing with Bernie. This summer, if I have my way, it will be you and me."

All of a sudden the sun seemed to be shining brighter and the birds were singing more gaily in the trees. Blood seemed to be coursing faster through David's arteries, and his foot didn't hurt. Then he thought about Bernie, sitting on the rock.

"But how about Bernie?" he asked.

"The world is full of clever people like Bernie," she told him. "And they're like cats. If they fall, they always land right side up."

He didn't quite get what she was talking about, but looking in her eyes he decided it didn't matter. For the only message that he could see in her eyes was that this was the moment to collect his kiss.

And he did.

THE END

Modern Course in Syndicate Fiction Writing
2010 Raymond Commerce Building
Newark, New Jersey

October 28, 1941

Dear Mr. Martin;

In your short-short story titled EASY SPARE (later changed to "I Can't Understand Them"), don't have Winnie ask her husband George if it is all right if she goes to the Lyric while he played his game, but make her willing to go with him at first and then have something come up which will make it impossible for her to go with him. Then you can think up a situation in which he can easily win the game after all. Don't end your story quite so abruptly.

Sincerely,
Stuart Tynan

E.S. Martin
1708 N 8th St
Terre Haute, Ind.
First Revision
Lesson #6
November 28, 1941

I Can't Understand Them

By
E.S. Martin

"But honey! You simply *have* to go with me this evening! This is the big night tonight for our team. Can't you send your mother to the hospital, and see her after the game?"

George looked so pathetic, I was almost sorry that we'd told Winnie we'd help her out. And I thought for a minute Winnie was going to weaken and give away the play. But she didn't. She's the prettiest little blonde I've ever seen, and she's got spunk. She got her fur up and came right back at him, and she wasn't just putting it on.

"George Porter, are you asking me to let them cart my poor mother off to a hospital with a broken arm while I go to the bowling alley and watch you play your silly old game?

I've read about sparks shooting out of people's eyes, but I never saw it happen until I watched Winnie right then. But George has a single track mind.

"But honey, you're my talisman! My luck! I can't play unless you're there to watch me!"

She was as cold as a tray of ice cubes. "For our honeymoon you took me to a bowling tournament! For two years I've had to go every Friday night and watch you bowl, whether I wanted to or not. If I knew anything about the game it might be different." Then she opened the draft and sparks started flying again. "Now you get out of here and go to your dumb old bowling alley so I can call a cab and go to Mother's and take care of her."

George didn't even ask me to drop her off at her mother's on our way to the alleys. He just picked up his ball and his shoes and went out the door. As he climbed into my car he slumped down in the seat. Then he shrugged his shoulders and set his ball and shoes on the floor between his feet. "Women!" he sighed. "I can't understand them!"

George and Winnie and I grew up together and went through school together. He was always one of those Honor Roll students that had to work like the devil to stay on top. But he stayed on top, so he didn't have time to learn to play.

When I went with American as an office boy, he went to a commercial school and studied bookkeeping. A year or so later he came to American as a bookkeeper. He worked hard at his job all day, and nights he continued his classes at commercial school. He told me he was going to be a C.P.A.

A couple of years at American and George had a breakdown. Nothing serious, but the Doc told him to quit night school, and to get some outside interests. So we organized an office bowling team and got into the plant industrial league. First thing I knew George was bowling five or six nights a week, trying to get the hang of it.

Then one day he discovered Winnie operating the plant switchboard. I'd known she was there all the time, and had tried to make some progress in her direction myself, to no particular avail. But George went after her like he did everything else, single track, full steam ahead. About the time he began to get the hang of bowling was when he started bringing Winnie to the alleys with him to watch him play. So he got the idea she brought him luck, though how a guy that works as hard as he does can get the idea there's any luck in anything he succeeds in doing, beats me.

They got married just in time for him to take her to the state bowling meet for a honeymoon. Then he remembered his C.P.A. ambitions, and started working on that by correspondence. A fine life for a bride, hubby working all day, studying every evening except Fridays, when he drags her off to the bowling alleys to watch, and be his "luck".

Winnie had had two years of that, and she couldn't convince him that he could bowl just as well without her there. Then when I stopped by to pick them up this evening, just as I got in the door the phone rang. Winnie was standing right by it, putting on her hat, and when she answered it someone said her mother had broken her arm, and would Winnie please come right away . . . And now, headed for the alleys without Winnie . . . because she preferred to go and comfort her mother and her broken arm . . . George couldn't understand women. I kept still.

"I'm whipped before I start," George said, as he got up to roll his first frame. And he looked it. That's how low he was.

The other three boys and I on the office team looked at each other; and the Engineers that we're bowling against grinned among themselves knowingly. We're tied with the Engineers for first place and the season is nearly over. Whichever team takes two out of three games tonight will probably finish the season on top, for a free trip to the state tournament, and it looks like we're sunk, starting out.

George walks up to the foul line, lets go of his ball, and starts back without even watching. When we all cheer, and he looks around and sees the wood cleaned off the alley, he shakes his head like it's a mistake and sits down and pays no attention to our applause. The second frame he does the same thing, but the third frame he stays at the foul line to watch. He hasn't anything on the ball, and the pins fall every direction, half of them staying on the alley. But it's a strike, and I see a strange look in his eye.

"Looks good on paper—only," he admitted, but the team was perking up and began staying right with him. That first game I think George could have shut his eyes, tripped over his own feet on the way to the foul line, and still made strikes. He made six straight, a nine and a spare in the seventh, and struck out for a two-seventy-nine; the highest score he'd ever made. And the team had stayed with him, so we had the Engineers by more than a hundred pins.

"We can do better than that," George says, a grin spreading over his pan, when he looked at the score. "Come on, team! Let's get 'em good!" We were so surprised we forgot to be anxious and tighten up, and the pins really started flying.

We had the Engineers so rattled, they were rolling better than three balls to our two, so we had plenty of time to chatter and exult, waiting for them to finish so we could roll our next frame. And George laughed and shouted and exulted with us, and clapped us on the back when we got up to roll, and said "Get 'em, boy!" He was really being human and enjoying his game for the first time in his life. We took the Engineers by two hundred and twenty-six pins that game.

The third game was a real farce. We just shouted and rolled, and the pins fell down. I'm not sure but what the pins laid down of their own accord when they saw the ball coming, at least part of the time. When George leaned over, his face serious, and said "Al, I wonder how Winnie's mother is?" I was afraid it was all over. I said real quick, "Don't worry about her, George. She's all right." "Okay," he says, and starts shouting again. He just side-tracked her in his mind and went mowing the pins down, and I knew he was a changed man.

We had a real gallery behind us that game. I think every spectator in the place was back there sheering us on. The Engineers wound up with an even seven hundred pins, and we had one thousand and three. As we worked our way through the crowd towards the locker room, George with his arm around me, I was afraid my shoulder would never get well from the beating it was getting, and I knew I'd never be able to hear again. And then, right on the back edge of the crowd, there was Winnie.

"Oh George, you were swell!" she said. Her face was beaming with pride, and she really had her heart in her eyes.

George stood and studied her with a sudden frown, like he would an audit that didn't balance. "How about your mother?" he asked.

Everything was funny to us then, and the whole team just roared. George's ears got red, and Winnie looked a little scared.

"You mean it was a set-up?" he said, and he could see by looking at us that it was. We began to be a little worried too.

"So you think that much of me, do you?" they heard him mutter to himself, and I saw two little bitty tears in his eyes. But his face lit up like the sun coming up in the morning, and he squeezed my shoulder. He included all of us in his grin.

"Well, it worked," he said. Then he looked at Winnie. "I'm going to see that you get some fun out of life from now on. We're going places . . . and you won't have to watch me bowl any more."

Winnie had some tears in her eyes too. "Oh yes I will! I thought I hated the game! But after the boys helped me deceive you this evening, so you'd find out you could bowl without me, I couldn't stay away! And you couldn't keep me away again!"

George put his arms around her, and kissed her right there, with the team cheering him on. Then he turned around with a big grin on his homely pan and let us in on a secret.

"Women!" he said. "I can't understand them!"

The End

Terminus

Post Card from Stuart Tynan
September 16, 1941

Dear Mr. Martin;
    Your assignment script Lesson #3 has been placed on the rounds of the markets. Keep your finger crossed and here's hoping.

Sincerely,
Stuart Tynan

Late Fall of 1941
From Stuart Tynan
Re: *Terminus*

Dear Mr. Martin;
    I have placed your lesson #3 on the complete rounds of each available market because I felt and still feel it follows every point set down in that lesson. I put it on the markets because I liked your story. I do not want you to be disappointed—I want you to feel that turning out NEW stories is now your job, and keep constantly in mind that

if one fails to click, then the next story you are working on IS THE ONE FOR YOU TO CONCENTRATE ON AND BELIEVE IN.

In a few words now that it had returned I am able to point out why this story failed to cross the line into the "sold" batch of stories. The climax contains your same end-story errors of 1) Lack of punch, 2) Lack of utter synchronization in its tie-up to the FIRST, SECOND, and THIRD paragraphs of the script—even though you have built this script upon my own personal formula erection of plot plan which has insulated more weak errors, but which has let your major weakness of climax tie-up slip through. Now then, KEEP MOVING ON TO NEW WORK. That this story failed to stick on one of the editorial desks is no indication that YOU, as a writer, failed to click—YOUR ABILITY is to be judged by myself and the scored of stories you are to turn out. You have taken long strides toward that goal for which we are both striving toward for you. You are on my list of writers we plan will come through. So stand by confidently on this or *any other* disappointment. In the long run you will have profited!

Sincerely Yours,
Stuart Tynan

E.S. Martin
1708 N. 8th St.
Terre Haute, Indiana
Lesson 3, Assignment 2
August 26, 1941

TERMINUS

By E.S. Martin

Excepting Helen, his wife, the one person he would least wish to see him here was Harry Adams. And as he crossed the lobby of the Seaside Resort Hotel with the cute little trick of a blond on his arm Ted Johnson looked up to see Harry Adams staring at him, mouth agape, and looking as if he was seeing a ghost. "Caught in the act," Ted thought.

Ted had been married to Helen less than two years. Harry Adams was the man Helen was going to marry until Ted came along with his smooth line and beat his time. Helen still saw a lot of Harry, having him and an extra girl in to dinner whenever she had a gang for cocktails or bridge. Now here was Harry at Seaside Resort staring at Ted and his companion, and Harry knew that Ted was supposed to be upstate on a weekend business trip. Ted would have to think fast.

He patted the blonde's hand and whispered "Excuse me, Babe. There's a man I'll have to talk to. Meet you in the coffee shop in a few minutes."

As Ted disengaged the blonde, Harry glanced nervously around the lobby and over his shoulder at the elevators, and then hurried across to Ted. "The bar isn't open yet. I'll buy you a Coke," Harry offered, voice tense and face pale. "I want to talk to you."

"Here comes a lecture," Ted thought, and with a shrug of his wide carefully tailored shoulders he let the stubbier Harry steer him into the drugstore and soda fountain opening off the corner of the lobby.

In the booth Harry sat on the edge of the seat and gripped the table with nervous excitement. He gulped a couple of times and then blurted "I don't see why you married Helen if you were going to cheat on her. She's too fine a girl to deserve that. This isn't the first time you've cheated on her and I don't suppose it will be the last. Why don't you give up this philandering and be true to her?"

Ted stared out the drug and novelty-cluttered window at the scattered Sunday morning strollers on the boardwalk. Could he convince Harry that he had finished his business upstate at two o'clock this morning and started right home rather than sleep in and fight the Sunday traffic later in the day? Could he convince him that he had stopped at Seaside Resort to rest and have a bite of breakfast, and that he had picked up the blonde just for her company while he ate and played on the beach for a couple of hours to freshen him up for the rest of the drive? He decided not.

Ted knew that Harry knew that he had done some plain and fancy stepping around before he married Helen. In fact, the little black address book that he had sentimentally tucked away where Helen wouldn't find it under the insurance papers in his desk drawer at home had been one of the most complete lists of available feminine pulchritude in town when he had quit using it.

Since his marriage Ted had been on a lot of weekend business trips. They had been strictly business trips and they were putting him ahead in the world, but he could see how Harry might suspect him of philandering, especially after seeing him here in the hotel with the blonde pick-up. He was sorry now for his momentary weakening in picking her up, and he wouldn't want Helen to hear about it. He really loved Helen. Helen, the beautiful. Helen, that Poe had in mind when he penned those classic lines "Helen, thy beauty is to me—". Helen who called him "lover," and meant more to him than all the casual blondes on earth. What was the best way of keeping Harry from carrying tales home to Helen of his momentary indiscretion?

Stanley Martin with daughter Nancy and her best friend Joy—he is obviously delighted to pose with the pretty ladies!

Ted leaned across the table. "Harry, you're right. I've been a fool. I do love Helen and I'm going back home and be true to her from now on. When I have to go on business trips I'll take her with me." Harry's jaw looked like it had come unhinged.

Ted pulled out his billfold and slipped a five in an envelope and thrust it in Harry's hand. "The blonde is waiting for me in the coffee shop. Will you hand her this and tell her I've been called back to town? Harry, you're a pal and I'll never forget your bringing me to my senses this way." He pushed himself up from the table. Harry still stared at him blankly.

Ted poked Harry with his thumb. "Don't think I mean it, huh? Well, just watch me from now on." He paid for the drinks and left Harry sitting in the booth.

The apartment was deserted. On the vanity was a note. "*I get lonesome when you are away on these business weekends, and you have so many of them. I'm going weekending myself. Be good. Helen.*"

Sunday in town and Helen away. Ted wandered through the apartment, lonesome, lost. He dropped in a chair, picked up a magazine, thumbed through the pages idly and cast it aside. Finally he scooted down in the chair and stared at the ceiling. He remembered the little black address book in his desk drawer. He hadn't even seen it for a year. He'd better get it out and destroy it before Helen ran on to it and she too suspected him of philandering.

Brisk with the thought of something to do, he went to his desk, pulled the drawer open and lifted out the insurance policies. There on top of the little book was a note. He stared at it for a minute and then picked it up and read, *"Dear Ted. You are a born woman chaser. I thought you'd reform when we married, but you haven't. I am going away and I'm not coming back unless you definitely give up your philandering and weekending. I'll read the "personals" column for a few days, and then I'm going to Reno. Goodbye now—Helen.*

Ted felt his world come to an abrupt end. He was suddenly desperately alone and the air of the apartment redolent with their happiness together was stifling. Where had Helen gotten this idea? Harry? Harry always had talked too much, and especially since Ted had wooed and won Helen right out from under his nose.

What was he going to do now? She would read the personals column. He found a pad and a pencil and stared at them abstractedly.

For an hour he wrote, crossed out, and started over. Then he stopped to frown at his handiwork. *"I have reformed. There will be no other women in my life. If you can forgive me, I am ready to prove that I am forever, Your Lover. Box XXX, Star-Telegram."* It sickened him, but if that's what she wanted, he'd do it. He pulled the telephone to him, finally found a clerk at the newspaper who would take his ad, and read it to her.

The next day at the office he couldn't keep his mind on his work. He cleared his desk an hour early and headed for the newspaper office to claim his letter. When the girl handed him a sheaf of letters two inches thick he shook his head. "There must be some mistake," he assured her. "There should be only one reply."

The girl ran through the stack. "These are all yours."

Dazedly he thrust the letters in his pocket and drove to the apartment where he dropped into his chair and thumbed through the miscellany of envelopes. None of them were in Helen's handwriting. Finally out of curiosity he opened one and then all of them. *"Darling, I knew you'd reform. I'm at Sis's. She has a phone now and the number is—." "Lover, I'm so happy that you've come to your senses. I'm in a little room at—."* And then one on pink perfumed paper, *"What does she have that I don't have? Before you go back to her why don't you come up and investigate?"*

He stacked them all on the arm of the chair. But where was Helen's letter? In the mailbox, of course. She'd write to the apartment. Why had he used the newspaper box, anyway? Yes, there it was, in the familiar lovable scrawl. Trembling, he opened it.

"Dear Ted, Harry tells me that you missed me by only a few minutes at the Seaside Resort Hotel. He was waiting for me in the lobby when he saw you and got you out of the way to avoid a scene. If we'd known you were going there we'd have gone somewhere else. Harry also tells me that you've promised to reform, but I know he's wrong. I put that note where I did so that I would know that if you found it and ran an ad, that you were going to be unfaithful and call one of the girls in your little book when you found my note. If you hadn't run the ad, I planned to come home in a few days, but after this weekend with Harry I'd have gone to Reno anyway. Goodbye now. Helen."

The note fluttered from his hand and he slumped in his chair. "The end of love," he thought. "The fate of the faithful." Then he spied the stack of letters on the arm of the chair.

"Now there's a bunch of girls that are willing to try it again," he thought, and reached for the stack. "Let's see, where's the one on the perfumed stationery?"

The End

Six Stories of John and Edith Osburn

Six Stories: The Other Woman
By E.S. Martin

Edith Osburn sang a merry little song as she pulled the ironing board from its little cabinet and set it upright. The house was cleaned till it shone, and everything was in order. Supper was on the stove, and the table was set. Now she had time to press John's suit.

She got the iron down from its shelf in the pantry and plugged it in at the wall outlet by the ironing board. She waited a moment and then felt of the bottom of the iron to see that it was heating. It was, so she went to the bedroom and took the suit off its hanger and carried it to the kitchen.

The iron was not hot enough as yet, so she went back to the bedroom and laid out a clean shirt, a new tie, a clean pair of socks and underwear. Then she went to the basement and lit the gas under the water heater. John would want a bath and clean clothing after his day at the office, to set him up for his evening's job of entertaining the visiting manager of one of the company's branch offices.

Edith was glad that John was getting out a little more than he used to. It was good for him. He had always worked too hard, but now that he was in the front office he was doing some of the Company's entertaining, at the company's expense, and it was doing him good. She wished that she could go with him sometimes, but she realized that it would not be good business for him to take her and let the company foot the bill. She was glad enough that he could go.

She dampened the pressing cloth under the tap and laid it carefully over a trouser leg. The iron sizzled as it touched the damp cloth, and a cloud of steam arose, smelling of good wool and ironing wax. She finished the trousers and hung them over the back of a chair. The vest took only a minute or two. She draped the coat over the board. There was a bulge over the inside pocket.

Edith was still singing her little song. She slipped her hand into the pocket and pulled out three envelopes. One was the gas bill, marked PAID. One was an insurance prospectus. The third one was a pink envelope, addressed in a woman's hand. She laid them on the table and turned back to the coat. She wasn't singing now. She ran the iron over the coat. Who could the pink envelope be from? It had an air of familiarity but she couldn't place it. It wasn't his mother's handwriting. Whose could it be?

She turned and surveyed the letter again. Maybe she shouldn't read it, but John wouldn't care. Hadn't he often told her that he had no secrets from her? She slipped the pink note-sheet from its envelope.

> "*:Tuesday*," she read. "*Darling Boy. The world is so beautiful this morning. Everything is different now. The sunshine is brighter and the birds sing a happier song than ever before. My heart is so filled with new happiness it almost chokes me.*
>
> *Last night when you held me in your arms and kissed me, I knew it was to be the happiest moment of my life. I had looked forward to that moment since the first time we met. I had hoped for it and been afraid you would never realize that we were created for each other. Now that there is no longer any uncertainty I am so happy I can scarcely keep from shouting my happiness to the world.*
>
> *I am looking forward to seeing you on Thursday evening. Until then all of my thoughts of every waking moment are yours. I love you.*
>
> *Your Sweetheart.*"

She looked at the heading of the letter again. Tuesday. So that was where John had been and what he had been doing on Monday evening when he had told her he was going to take a buyer to a show. And this was Thursday. He was going to see her again tonight, and he had said it was the manager of one of the out-of-town branches. Her heart swelled with pain and felt as though it would break. Her throat was choked and her eyes filled with tears. She stumbled to a chair and dropped her head in her arms on the kitchen table, the letter still clutched in her hand.

So this was the end of love. Four happy years of slaving and serving, and then some other girl got your man. She knew that it happened to other people, but she hadn't thought it would happen to them. She wouldn't believe it now if she didn't have the evidence in her hand. Tears came, and broken sobs shook her.

John was untrue. The thought rang through her head and pounded at her temples with a dull pain. John, whom she knew so well and loved so much had fallen for some other girl. She couldn't believe it, but it was true. She had lost him. He was going to see this other girl tonight, and he had lied to her, his own Edith, about it. Her head ached, and her whole body was filled with a dull pain.

She heard John come in and hang his hat in the hall closet. She hastily arranged her hair and dried her eyes. She wouldn't let him see that he had hurt her. She would act as if nothing had happened, and when he asked for his freedom, she would let him go. She was hurt too deeply to try to hold him. She got up listlessly and moved towards the ironing board. The life was all gone out of her.

"Hello, Honey," John said, as he came into the room. "Pressing my suit up nice so I'll look like a million dollars?"

He came around and kissed her. She let him, but she made no response. Her heart and her lips were cold. He glanced at the letter in her hand.

"Oh, I see you found that letter you wrote me the day after we were engaged. I've been keeping it down at the office, but I thought I'd better bring it home before it got lost. You can put it with *

* *The final page (or paragraph) of the story is missing, this was typed on brittle and yellowed pages that were falling apart. KHB*

E. Stanley Martin
681-1/2 Wabash Ave.
Terre Haute, Indiana
825 words
Usual Rate

Six Stories: Hash for Supper

By E. Stanley Martin

From the depths of the brown paper bag Edith Osburn produced a dozen medium sized potatoes and placed them in the white granite kettle. She placed the sack back on the shelf and carried the kettle out of the pantry and in to the kitchen sink.

As water cascaded merrily over the potatoes, Edith hummed a little tune and smiled happily to herself. The sun was shining in the west window and made a spot of gold of the yellow tulips in the center of the green kitchen table. Outdoors a robin was hopping from the emerald of the grass to the budding lilac bush along the fence and back again. Mr. Smith, next door, was diligently spading his garden patch. Youngsters were shouting and laughing somewhere down the street. A warm fresh breeze skipped through the open door and played at the crisp white curtains. It was spring.

Edith pulled her green stool up to the drain board of the sink. From the cabinet drawer she got her favorite black-handled peeling knife, and from the bottom of the cabinet, a green saucepan. Sitting on the stool, the kettle in her lap, she set to work carefully peeling the potatoes. Long thin shavings of peel gave way before her knife and dropped into the kettle. Then each remaining black speck was cut away, and after a thorough rinsing under the tap, the now white and naked potato was dropped into the saucepan. When they were all peeled, she drained the water from the kettle and carried it out to the garbage pail and emptied it.

Back in the kitchen she took the heavy iron skillet from its accustomed place on the bottom of the stove and put it on the biggest burner. Then the potatoes were rinsed again and sliced paper-thin into the skillet.

Now for the onion. John liked just enough onion in his hash. She hated to peel potatoes, she hated worse to peel onions, and she hated worst of all to make hash, but this was for John, poor boy, so she hummed another tune and dug an onion from its hiding place beneath the carrots in the vegetable basket. She peeled it in the sink. Then she sliced it into the potatoes, covered them with water, and turned on the fire under them.

John would be pleased with the hash, she knew, for it was his favorite dish. He hadn't had any for quite a while. He hadn't been eating much of anything lately, and he had looked bad as he started for work this morning. That's why she was making the hash. She didn't care much for it herself, but if it would jar John's jaded appetite she'd be happy. It was spring.

She stirred the hash from time to time with her big enameled spoon. When the potatoes began to cook up, she opened the can of corned beef and emptied it into the skillet. With the spoon she broke up the fibrous brown chunks and stirred them into the potatoes and onions. A pinch of salt ended the procedure, and the hash had only to cook a few minutes longer and it would be fit for the table of a king.

Edith glanced up at the clock. Ten minutes more and John would be walking in the door. She turned the fire low under the hash so it wouldn't scorch, and started setting the table.

She had just finished slicing the bread and setting out the butter when she heard John's step on the front porch. She snapped the burner off under the skillet and quickly emptied the hash into its appointed dish. Then she set the skillet back, ran her hand over her hair, and stood expectantly with her hands clasped behind her, a flush on her cheeks. The odor of hash filled the room. It smelled divine.

She heard him stop in the hall and put his hat in the closet. Then his step sounded again coming across the dining room.

"Hello, Hon," he greeted her.

He crossed to the door and closed it. Then he closed the window. He shivered and blew his nose. He snapped on the light and dropped into a chair. The room felt chilly. The curtains looked miserably dirty and gray in the lamplight. The tulips looked faded and old. The odor of hash was suddenly flat and sickening in the room.

"What's the matter, John?" The roses were gone from her cheeks. She, too, felt faded and old.

"Nothing much," he said. "Went to see the doctor today. Says I've been eating too much heavy food. Stomach's all wrong. Got to eat oranges and spinach and milk from now on. No bread or potatoes, and no meat."

"Oh, I'm sorry, John," she told him, and patted him absently on the shoulder. "I've got milk in the icebox, and I think there's a can of spinach in the pantry. I'll see."

She carried the dish of hash outside and carefully emptied it into the garbage pail.

The End

E. Stanley Martin
681-1/2 Wabash Ave.
Terre Haute, Indiana
1050 words
Usual Rate

Six Stories: A Loaf of Bread

By E Stanley Martin

John Osburn was whistling as he came up the front walk. He waved at Johnson pushing a mower over his lawn across the street, and he cast a cheery "hello" in the direction of Mr. Smith who was reading a newspaper on his front porch next door.

Everything was lovely outdoors. The trees were new green, and the Hibiscus bush was sporting a brand new blossom. The lawn was smooth shaven and the long afternoon shadows played across it. There were fresh curtains at the windows, and Edith had set the fern on the front step to air.

He took the front steps at a single bound, crossed the porch, and entered the hall, still whistling. He opened the closet door and tossed his hat at a hook.

"Hello, honey," he called in the general direction of the kitchen.

There was no response.

He closed the closet door and started whistling another tune. Through the living room he went. The clean curtains looked nice. Edith had changed the chairs about. Everything shined and smelled of furniture polish. The glass flowers on the mantel had a fresh look as if they had been washed. Good housekeeper, Edith. He wondered where she was.

He stuck his head in the bedroom door. Everything was neatly ordered and attractive, but she was not there. The dining room was empty of habitation, and the bathroom was snowy white but unoccupied. He tried the kitchen. The green table was set for supper, a vase of flowers on its center, but Edith's apron was hanging on its hook and she was not in the kitchen or in the pantry. He stuck his head out the back door. Drops of water sparkled on the grass where it had been freshly sprinkled, but Edith was nowhere to be seen.

He went back to the living room and turned on the radio. He was tired of whistling. He listened to a dialogue for four minutes, got disgusted and shut it off. Where was Edith?

Restlessly he went out and brought in the fern and put it in its wrought iron stand. He opened the paper, but it held nothing of interest. He cast it aside. What day was this? Oh, yes, Friday. She played bridge on Thursdays. She was always home on Fridays.

He was hungry. There would probably be something in the icebox. Back to the kitchen he went. Supper was on the table. Roast beef, mashed potatoes, gravy, sliced tomatoes and apple pie gave forth intriguing aromas. The gravy was steaming, and melted butter was running down the snowy hill of potatoes. Where could Edith be?

He'd wait for her. He'd eat a slice of bread and jam to keep from starving, and then he'd go out and sprinkle the front lawn or something till she came. He went to the icebox and found some butter and a jar of strawberry preserves. He set them out and went to the breadbox. It was empty. There was no bread on the table. Even the cracker box was empty. Well, he wasn't very hungry anyway. Where could she be? She was always home when he came in on Fridays, or at least when she was going to be away, she always called him at the office. What could be wrong?

He went back to the living room. The newspaper was on the floor where he's thrown it. The headlines leaped up at him. "KIDNAPPER AT WORK AGAIN".

Kidnapped. A picture of Edith, a black cloth wrapped 'round her head, being carried away by sinister masked men in a long black automobile popped into his mind. He picked up the paper. The dateline said Petersburg. That was a hundred miles away. He breathed a sigh of relief and threw the paper down again. But where was she?

Could she have gone out for some reason and been hit by an automobile and hurt or killed? Could some of her folks have taken sick and sent for her?

If they had, she would have left a note. He looked. There was no note on her writing desk, and none on the mantel. Maybe she had left a note on his pillow. He had read of people doing that. He dashed into the bedroom but his pillow was a bare expanse of white.

Back in the living room again, he sunk into a chair. Might as well face this thing calmly. Something had happened to her. What, he had no idea, but he couldn't do any good by dashing around like a chicken with its head off. She always carried identification. If she was hurt, the hospital would let him know. If she'd had to go to her folks in too big a hurry to leave word, she would wire him or call. Kidnapping was preposterous. Maybe she'd gone to one of the neighbors where someone was sick. If she had, she'd phone him.

It was getting dark outside. The house felt stuffy. The odor of furniture polish was obnoxious. He could scarcely breathe.

There was a step on the walk. At last—a messenger to let him know what had happened. His heart was in his throat. He left his chair so violently that it tipped over backwards.

At the door he came face to face with—Edith. Her cheeks were flushed and she was smiling. He stared at her.

"Hello, Johnnie," she greeted him. "Isn't it lovely out this evening? I discovered there wasn't any bread in the house when I had supper ready so I went after some. The weather was so nice I walked clear up to that Tristate Grocery at Thirteenth and Chestnut after it. Let's take a walk in the park after supper. We haven't for a long time, you know."

The flush of sunset was in the sky. Cars hooted happily as they scooted past the corner. He fumbled for a cigarette.

"All right, Honey," he said. "But let's go eat now. I'm starved."

The End

E. Stanley Martin
681-1/2 Wabash Avenue
Terre Haute, Indiana
975 Words
Usual Rate

Six Stories: Dirty Dishes

By E. Stanley Martin

Edith Osburn noisily collected the silverware from the table and dumped it in the sink. She saved a tablespoon and scraped the scraps from the dishes into the sink strainer with it. She stacked the dishes as loudly and recklessly as she could without endangering them, but John sat on in the living room reading his paper and paying her no heed.

When they were first married John had helped her with the dishes on occasion, but four years of so-called marital bliss had made him indifferent to her household tasks. Now he was content to sit reading the paper, section by section, and throwing the pieces around him on the floor as he finished with them in a way that would make the most work for her when she got ready to pick them up.

The plates and dishes were scraped and in the sink. The empty coffee cups were nested together. She reached for the saucers. The butt of John's cigarette was mashed in his saucer and there was a dirty and evil-smelling mess of ashes soaked in coffee at the bottom. It revolted her. No less than a hundred times she had asked him not to put his ashes and cigarettes in the saucers, but it seemed that no amount of talking would break him of the habit. She was convinced that he did it just because she asked him not to—that, and because he liked to make as much work for her as he could. She scraped the saucer angrily and slammed it in the sink. It broke. That was the third saucer out of her set, and it was John's fault that it had broken. He was always doing little things to aggravate her.

The dishes all in the sink, she got out the dishpan and plate rack. The plate rack she set on the drain-board. She turned up the fire under the tea kettle so that the water would be hot to scald the dishes with. Then she dumped a handful of soap chips in the pan and filled it with warm water from the tap. She knew that John could hear her but he went on reading his paper. He always said he was all in when she asked him to help, but she was all in too. She had ironed the clothes and washed the windows today. Well, let him read his paper. She was tired of asking him to help, and she was tired of having him around cluttering up the house. Some day she'd go away and leave him, and then she'd see how he got along without her. Maybe he'd appreciate her a little more then.

She washed the glasses and set them on the drain board. John might at least offer to help her. It wouldn't hurt him a bit. She washed the plates and set them in the rack. There was a good show on at the Lyric. She'd like to see it but it wouldn't do any good to ask John to go. He was always too tired, and he didn't like movies. That's what he said, but she knew he was ashamed to be seen on the street with her. He was out all day seeing good looking women, while she stayed at home and worked, and then when she wanted to go somewhere in the evening he sat and read the paper and let her do the work. It wasn't fair. She slammed the other saucer into the dishpan and it broke. John continued reading his paper.

Rebellion was in her heart. She wasn't going to stand for it. Tomorrow she'd pack up her things and go to her sister's. Her sister had been wanting her to come for a long time, and now she'd do it. She had some money in her purse, and she'd go and let John read his paper all he wanted to. He could stack the dishes in the sink and leave them 'till there wasn't a clean one in the house. Then she supposed he'd go to a restaurant and eat. That's just the way he'd do things.

She washed the silverware and stood it in the little cup in the end of the plate rack. Now for the pans and the skillet. She saved the skillet for last. She hated to wash skillets, especially gravy skillets.

John cast the last section of the paper aside and pulled his feet up and propped them on the davenport table. She'd told him more times than she could remember not to do that. She was almost tempted to throw the skillet at him.

She dumped the skillet into the dish water and started scrubbing at it viciously with the pot scraper. The tea kettle boiled over and put out the gas burning under it. She turned to shut off the gas and her wet hand slipped on the white porcelain handle and she burned it against the hot tea kettle. Tears of exasperation were in her eyes. She'd go tonight. Just as soon as she finished washing the skillet and drying the dishes, she'd pack her bag and go.

As she dumped the dish water, scalded the dishes, and reached for the dish towel, John pulled his feet down and started for the kitchen.

He slipped his arms around her in spite of her protests, and pressed his cheek against hers.

"Listen, honey," he said. "There's a good show on over at the Lyric. You give me the dish cloth and I'll dry the dishes while you go get dressed, and we'll go. Put on that green dress. When you wear that I think you're the prettiest girl I ever knew."

She looked at him sidewise. "I'll do the dishes John. You're tired. It won't take a minute longer."

He captured the dish towel. "You do as I say, honey. That extra minute will give me extra time to parade you around and show how proud I am of you. Now, scoot."

She scooted.

The End

E. Stanley Martin
681-1/2 Wabash Avenue
Terre haute, Indiana
990 words
Usual Rate

Six Stories: Buttons

By E. Stanley Martin

John Osburn looked at his watch. Seven fifty-two. He was up early. How long, he wondered, would it take him to get over the habit of getting up at seven-thirty and being at the office by eight-thirty?

He had been promoted to the front office and he was not supposed to show up until nine. That gave his secretary time to have his mail opened up, sorted, and ready for his consideration when he arrived.

He liked his new job. It had more responsibilities, but it paid more money. Just day before yesterday he had handed Edith his month's paycheck and it had been bigger by twenty dollars than the one before. The pleased look in her eyes had gratified him. Maybe now he could have a clean shirt every day. That was the height of his ambition.

He looked at the shirt spread over the back of the chair. Edith had laid it out for him yesterday morning, and as he eyed it critically he saw that the collar and cuffs were a little soiled. Edith only put out a clean shirt for him every other morning, and this wasn't one. He wanted a clean shirt and he wondered where Edith kept them. He eyed the chest of drawers speculatively, then he pulled open the bottom drawer. No, that wasn't it. He pulled open the drawer above. Yes, there was a shirt, right on top—a white shirt, neatly ironed and folded.

John took the shirt out, unfolded it, and approved it with his eyes. A clean white shirt every day. He was coming on in the world. He slipped his right arm into a sleeve, then his left arm into the other sleeve. The cool broadcloth felt good. He pulled the shirt close and fit himself into it. He pulled the collar snug around the neck and started to button it. There wasn't any button.

He ran his finger down the row of buttons. There were only three an the entire shirt-front. He looked at the cuffs. Neither had buttons. He noticed that there was a rip in one sleeve. Darn it. Wasn't Edith supposed to keep his shirts in shape? Well, he'd try another. He took the shirt off and tossed it on the chair.

From the drawer he took another shirt. He unfolded it and spread it out across the bed. There was a button on the collar but no other buttons down the front. One cuff had a button but the collar was frayed, and there was a rip in the back. Edith had work to do instead of playing bridge in the afternoons. He could hear her getting breakfast ready in the kitchen. She'd hear about this. He wanted a clean shirt.

He reached into the drawer and took out the rest of the shirts. There were four of them. The top one was heavy white linen. Where did it come from? He unfolded it. It was entirely buttonless, although it seemed to be in fairly good condition. He looked at the size marked in the collar. Size 15. That was half a size too small, but where had it come from? Oh, yes. That was the shirt he'd worn when he was married. It was four years old and more. He could well afford to retire that one.

Not a one of the shirts was in a fit condition to wear, although they were all clean, and carefully ironed and folded away. He wanted a clean shirt but there seemed not to be any. Edith was too darned careless about these things. His blood pressure was mounting. He wondered how many more things he had that needed attention. Edith was going to catch hell about this. Twenty dollars extra pay two days ago, and he'd bet his next paycheck she hadn't even bought buttons to fix his shirts. She was always buying a new hat, or new curtains for the dining room, or something, but never anything *he* needed. Well, he'd tell her about it, and in no uncertain terms.

He dived into the drawer in a burst of fury. He could hear Edith merrily singing as she banged breakfast around on the stove. His cheeks flushed and there was a glint in his eye.

Triumphantly he dug out three undershirts and four pairs of shorts that needed attention. He piled them on top of the shirts. Further delving brought to light fourteen pairs of socks, neatly tucked together in sets of two, and every one of them with holes in the heels or toes, or both. Most of them he didn't remember ever having worn. No wonder he always had to growl about clean socks. The stack of accusing evidence was growing.

A pair of linen gold knickers with a break in the back seam completed the contents of the drawer. There they were, all of his clothes, and not a thing in the bunch he could wear. Damnation. He could hear Edith in the kitchen setting the breakfast table.

A dangerous look in his eye, he grabbed the stack of clothes and headed for the kitchen. Edith looked up as he came in.

"Look here," he said.

She looked. "Oh, John," she said. "I'm glad you got that stuff out. None of it's fit to wear and I want to send it to the Charity Club. You don't need any of it any more, because I got you ten new shirts yesterday, and half a dozen suits of underwear and some socks. They're in the top drawer. Put that stuff in that chair over there and go get a shirt on. Breakfast's ready."

He put it on the chair and went after a shirt.

The End

E. Stanley Martin
681-1/2 Wabash Avenue
Terre haute, Indiana
1050 words
Usual rate

Six Stories: A Shave

By E. Stanley Martin

The kitchen floor felt sticky to John Osburn's feet as he stalked to the gas range. Rain was blowing against the window. The morning sky outside was dirty and gray. The battered clock on the kitchen cabinet said seven-thirty.

He swore to himself as he pressed the pilot light and the long yellow fingers of flame reached over to the burners under the double boiler filled with rice, and the tea kettle filled with water for his morning shave, and lit the gas under them with a faint "plop".

He hated rainy mornings. He hated to get up and light the fire under the breakfast on the stove. He hated to shave. Shaving was his particular obsession.

While he waited impatiently for the water to heat, he went back into the bedroom, pulled on his trousers, and his socks and shoes. Then he went into the bathroom and scrubbed his teeth in an impotent fury of waiting. After rinsing the washbowl, he ran into it two cupfuls of water—just enough to be about right when he added the hot water.

Back to the kitchen he went then, to see if the water was hot enough. It wasn't quite, but he turned off the fire under it and stalked back to the bathroom with the tea kettle. He poured water into the basin. A little splashed onto the back of his hand, and he swore again, although the water was hardly hot enough to burn him.

From the medicine cabinet he took his shaving brush, and after dipping it in the water, squeezed half an inch of shaving cream onto the end of it. Then he slammed the cabinet door shut and eyed himself in the mirror front as he smeared the cream across his beard and started working up a lather. Two vertical wrinkles of a frown stood guard on his forehead between his eyes. His eyes were squinted, and they glared at him from the mirror. Damn nuisance, shaving. Do it every morning, and what good does it do? All to do over again the next morning.

Now the lather was satisfactory. He opened the cabinet door and reached for his razor. Damn. The razor was dirty. Dried lather and hair clung to it. He eyed it malevolently. Just as he thought, Edith had used it to shave under her arms and had forgotten to clean it. He'd told her about that before. After four years of married life she should know better. This was his last blade, too.

He'd had about enough of Edith, he thought. Every morning she lay in bed peacefully snoring while he got up and started breakfast, shaved, and got ready for work. At the last minute she'd hop out, slip on a robe, wash in the kitchen sink, and then bawl him out for not being ready for breakfast. She didn't have to shave in the morning. Once a month she used his razor. And then she didn't clean it. Had she no sense at all?

He rinsed the razor, took it apart, and stropped the blade on the heel of his hand. The blade was rusty from standing in the razor. It would pull at his beard. He was angry—angry enough to chew up the blade and eat it—and hungry enough, too. Wasn't Edith ever going to get up and fix breakfast? He could hear her snoring.

Finally he got the razor back together. Now the lather had dried on his face until the little foam-like bubbles flew around him like snow when he breathed. He wet the brush and went to work again. The lather worked up to his satisfaction, he dipped the razor in the water and went maliciously to hacking at the beard along the left side of his jaw. The razor pulled, and in his exasperation he let it slip a little sideways, cutting a gash in his cheek. He swore volubly and sulphurously while he rinsed the cut and applied a piece of paper to it.

He heard the bedsprings groan as Edith sat up and put on her bedroom slippers. As he finished the other jaw and started on his chin—those close-set stubborn whiskers that always defied him—he heard her in the kitchen noisily washing her hands.

The lather was dry on his chin, so there was nothing to do but wet the shaving brush and work it up again. He could hear Edith taking the rice off the stove as he proceeded. She would be calling breakfast before he finished shaving if he didn't hurry. The razor slipped and nicked his chin as he pulled the last stubborn whisker.

This was too much. This was the end. Two cuts in one morning, and it was Edith's fault. As soon as he could rinse his face he'd put on his shirt and vest and coat and leave the house. He'd do it coldly and without any display of feeling. He became dramatically calm at the thought. He wouldn't stand for all this heinous behavior any longer. He'd go away and not come back. Edith could have the place. She could use his razor and leave it dirty, and she could lie in bed 'till noon if she wanted to. He was through.

He rinsed his face and slapped on some lotion that bit into his scarred jaw and made him wince, while at the same time it invigorated him. Breakfast must be almost ready. But he'd eat out this morning—and all other mornings.

He dabbed at his face with the towel. Then he ran a comb through his hair, and started for the bedroom. He slipped into a clean shirt that Edith had thoughtfully laid out for him, and tied his tie before the mirror of her dressing table. As he slipped into his vest and coat, Edith called from the kitchen.

"Breakfast's ready, John. Are you about dressed?" She sounded mighty sweet this morning. The rice smelled good. Rice was his favorite breakfast food.

He felt of his jaw reflectively with one hand as he buttoned his vest with the other. He was hungry as a bear, and his jaw felt lots better. A ray of sunshine brushed the clouds aside and peeped in the window. The rain was over. He'd have to get new razor blades today. After all, Edith was a pretty good sport.

"Coming right away, Honey," he called. "Dish up the rice."

The End

Mabel and Stanley Martin in 1961, Photo by Martin

Chapter 9

Wild West Adventure

For the purpose of associative memory, I have always linked Gramps Martin's birth with the historic San Francisco Earthquake[27], with Gramps' birth in August and the quake in April of 1906, respectively. Many modern day genealogists are finding that the connection between local and world social history and their own studied progenitors, along with a look at personal stories, letters and photographs, brings a welcome warmth to family histories.

At the turn of the century the Intercontinental Railroad[28] had been completed a mere 30-plus years before, at Promontory Point, Utah. Stanley Martin's hometown of Terre Haute, Indiana, was a hub of railroad activity during his childhood. In addition, throughout his childhood the horse-drawn carriages and streetcars that previously dotted the main streets of the city were being systematically replaced by the noisier and faster automobiles. Industry and transportation systems encouraged a new kind of speed and mobility in the nation, and between his early freight-hopping to the west coast, his early service in the U.S. Army, and his interstate travels as an itinerant photographer, Stanley established his sense of wanderlust as a young man.

Stanley's pioneering spirit of adventure was sparked by authors like Leonard Clark (The Rivers Ran East[29]—a favorite!), Mark Twain, and the poet Robert Service. With his identity rooted in the Hoosier heritage, he also loved the poet James Whitcomb Riley, and the author Gene Stratton Porter[30], whose name he gave to my mother, Nancy Gene Martin Harper. Many books and periodicals of the times reflected a nostalgic popularity for the days of the frontier, and the "old west". The original traveling Wild West Show with Buffalo Bill Cody would have been every child's dream during those early years of the twentieth century. Hollywood was an up and coming power, and western themed movies were common. Add to this a compelling top current event item: John Collier[31], who eventually became Commissioner of Indian Affairs (1933-1945), was instigating and promoting American Indian Reform to repeal the flawed and outdated Dawes Act of 1887 and replace it with reforms intended to support and protect the beauty and integrity Collier had experienced in his connection with the Pueblo Indians in New Mexico as well as subsequent tribes he studied. His studies and publications as well as the resulting legislation known as the Meriam Report[32] of 1928, inspired a new interest in Native Americans, both politically and in the entertainment world.

The Wild West collection of stories in Chapter Nine shows not only Gramps' interest in the history of the old western frontier, but his alignment with and interest in the Native American Indians in particular. Contemporary political correctness aside, his respect and appreciation for a way of life he could only read about and imagine are apparent in his series titled *Wilderness Incident*. I flash on a memory that my mother had before me, of the traditional visit to Charlie Eagleplume's trading post in Estes Park, Colorado, whenever we were visiting cousins or traveling through. In 1960, at the young age of four, on a cross country trip to visit relatives and research genealogy, Gramps and Gram allowed me to choose a sweet little Indian doll at Charlie Eagleplume's, with long black braids and sparkling eyes and beautifully fringed soft leather clothes and moccasins. The real treasure, of course, was the way we, as visitors, were treated as old friends by Charlie and any others who happened to be in the shop. Though Charlie passed on in the early 90's, I don't think I would miss another visit to Eagleplume's, given the opportunity. Just another warm "Gramps" memory . . .

Buffalo Horn

(story opener)
By E. Stanley Martin
October 2, 1956

Even in this gathering of his peers, the war chiefs of the tribe, Buffalo Horn was an imposing figure. When he rose to speak he unfolded himself to his full six foot height with deliberate dignity, the knowledgeful black eyes in the angular face calmly surveying the gathering.

The white scar across the tawny cheek, from mouth to ear, seemed to lift one side of his face in a smile, although the other was stern, with firm purpose.

The black braids were covered by an ornately beaded and colorfully feathered headdress, trailing feathers nearly to the ground behind him, each feather marking a coup, or feat of valor.

His buckskin shirt was decorated with porcupine quills in an intricate design, and his moccasins were colorfully beaded, evidence of the handiwork of Morning Star, his squaw.

Broad shoulders back, head erect, left hand holding the calumet at waist level, his deep vibrant voice, when he spoke, belied his more than fifty years of active, often violent, living.

Edward Malone

By E. Stanley Martin

As the buckboard topped the last of the rolling hills on the road from town, Elizabeth Johnson pulled the horses up to let them catch their breath. Behind her, she knew, the road undulated down through the buffalo grass and sagebrush to the cluster of houses, false-fronted stores, and saloons, and the tiny red brick church where she and the children had just attended Sunday School. But she was looking ahead into the cozy valley—their valley—hers and Bob's—waiting impatiently for the dust that had drifted past them to settle so she could see and admire and be reassured by the little cluster of buildings that was home.

The white-washed ranch house, the barn and the shed came into focus in the late afternoon sunlight. Again she felt the swell of pride in her troubled heart. Then she saw the pinto standing by the corral fence. Her chin lifted. Her eyes brightened. A faint flush showed on her cheeks. *If she only dared hope—*

"Mama! Didn't David slay Goliath with a sling-shot?" It was Ted, sitting on the other end of the seat demanding an answer, and by the tone of his voice she realized that he had repeated the question at least once.

"Ted, are you and Mary arguing again?" Elizabeth could feel Mary's black curls shaking in negation against her arm.

"I'm not arguing Mama," Mary said. "Just Ted. He said David killed Goliath with a sling-shot and I told him Daddy said he killed him with a rock."

"Yeah!" Ted retorted. "A rock in a sling-shot! Mr. Brown said so in Sunday school."

Elizabeth held the reins in one hand and reached the other to pull the children towards her in a hug. "I'm glad you paid attention to the Sunday school lesson. David killed Goliath with a rock in a sling, but it wasn't the kind of sling-shot that little boys use. When Daddy gets back he can show you."

I wish there was a David to slay Bob's Goliath, she thought.

"When will Daddy be back, Mama?" They asked the question a dozen times a day.

"In two or three days. The conference is over today. We'd better hurry along home now and get the horses bedded down before dark." She shook out the lines and clucked at the horses.

The horses trotted ahead of the dust into the valley. The lowering sun put a green glow on the willows and cottonwoods bordering the creek beyond the corral. The whitewashed clapboards of the house stood out in bold relief against the plowed pasture behind it. Cattle in small groups drifted down towards water.

Ted leaned across Mary to tug at Elizabeth's sleeve. "There's somebody there, mama!"

"So I see."

"Who is it?"

"We'll see when we get there." Being a mother and a minister's wife imposed certain restrictions as to veracity which kept her always on her guard as to the truthfulness of the statements she made.

As the buckboard jostled out of the trail ruts towards the ranch yard a tall man rose from the chopping block by the shed. As Elizabeth pulled up he reached one gloved hand for the bridle of the near horse and removed his flat-crowned wide-brimmed hat with the other.

She watched him intently. It had been ten years since she had seen him last, but except that the lines of his face seemed to be chiseled a bit more sharply, he appeared no older. The wide shoulders and lean hips still moved with the same easy rhythm. The gun belt that angled across his black shirt and trousers under the buckskin jacket, and the holster tied to his right thigh with a rawhide thong might well be the same he had been wearing when she saw him last. Her hands trembled as she handed the lines to Ted, gathered her skirts, and stepped down.

"Howdy, Mrs. Johnson. It's a pleasure to see you again." The firm mouth barely smiled, but the blue eyes in the tanned leather of his face were relaxed and friendly. She thought there might be a touch of irony when he said "Mrs. Johnson."

"It is our pleasure, Mr. Malone. Have you been waiting long?"

"Just rode in, ma'am," he told her, but she noticed that his saddle was atop the corral fence, and by the dust marks she judged that the pinto was either mighty restless or had been tied to the fence for some time.

"I'm sorry Bob isn't at home. He'd be happy to see you. You haven't met our children. This is Mary, our baby, and this is Ted, our eight year old range boss."

Mary had clambered down and now hid behind her mother's duster. Ted jumped down and shoved his hand forward awkwardly.

"Howdy, Mr. Malone. Can you plug half dollars with that six gun? I oncet saw a man with his holster tied thataway who could plug half dollars every time someone threw one up."

"Ted, you unhitch the horses and put hay down for them right away!"

Ted glanced at his mother quickly, said "yes, ma'am," and led the horses towards the barn.

Elizabeth, seeing the amused look in Malone's eyes, realized that she had spoken too sharply to Ted. She slipped her hand under Mary's arm affectionately. "Honey, do you suppose you could stir up the fire and start warming up some coffee for Mr. Malone?"

"Sure, Mama," and she went scampering for the kitchen, her petticoats rustling.

"Slip on an apron first," her mother called after her.

With the children out of hearing for the moment, Elizabeth felt her knees trembling under her skirts. "Shall we go sit on the steps?" She tried to turn on a smile, but she knew that she didn't quite make it.

His fingers touched her elbow lightly as they moved across to the front veranda. She had forgotten how courteous he had always been in the presence of ladies; that he was, first of all, a gentleman at heart.

She unpinned her hat, slipped off her gloves and laid them on the porch floor. She ran her hands across her hair, straightened her skirts, sat upright on the step and placed her hands firmly in her lap.

"Mind if I smoke?" he asked, as he hunkered on his heels where he could watch her face.

"Not at all."

She watched him as he rolled and lighted a quirly. He inhaled deeply. She saw his shirt tauten with his breathing.

"Ted, I'm glad you're here," she said. "I can call you Ted, can't I? You know our Ted is named after you."

"I guessed as much."

"I hesitated to send for you, but I knew Bob wouldn't. I didn't know anyone else I could call on. I couldn't just sit here. I suppose you're wondering why I sent for you."

He looked at her quizzically, little curls of smoke twisting up around his face. "There is only one reason you would send for me," he said flatly. "Trouble! Bad trouble!"

"Then you know of it?"

"About your trouble? No." His mouth set in a wry smile. "But it would have to be bad trouble for you, a minister's wife, to send for the likes of me. Especially since there are people who know I once asked you to marry me."

Her cheeks flushed crimson. She nervously twisted the gold band on her ring finger.

"You made the right choice," he said, and there was a sadness in his voice. "Tell me about your trouble."

"It's a man named Piaute Stover. You may have heard of him. After you left Carson Wells, he and two of his cronies held up the bank there about ten years ago. They killed the teller and a rancher who had come in to make a payment on his loan. Bob was still marshal there. He had been out of town and rode in just as they came out of the bank. He killed the two fellows with Stover and put a bullet in Stover's left shoulder. Stover was left-handed. When they tried him he only got ten years because he had friends on the jury."

Ted interrupted her. "Stover is out now? Is that it?"

"He's in town and asking for Bob."

"And where's Bob?"

"He is at the regional conference at Wallace. He's been gone ten days but he'll be back Tuesday or Wednesday. And Ted, I'm afraid. I've prayed, and I've fasted, but I'm still afraid."

"Does Bob know that Stover is in town?"

"No. Stover came into town the day after Bob left."

"And what do the people in town say?"

"A few of the men got together and called on Stover. Asked him to leave town. He just laughed at them. There's nothing they can do, really, until he starts something, and then it will be too late."

"What will Bob do when he hears about it?"

"He'll hunt up Stover and invite him to come to church on Sunday."

"Will he use persuasion?" Ted patted the holster on his thigh.

"He hasn't worn a gun for ten years. He doesn't even own one, and wouldn't use it if he did. It wasn't a month after Stover went to prison that Bob went back east to finish college. When he was ordained he came back to take up his ministry here. It's a poor charge and he has to ranch to make a go of things, but he loves his work and he says the Lord will take care of him."

"He hasn't gone daffy on religion has he?"

"Oh no—he calls himself a working preacher. He helps folks with their crops and stock, and gets a good word in for the Lord while he's doing it. They all show up for church on Sunday, too."

"What sort of man is this Stover?"

"Wide and squat with a sag to his left shoulder. Bushy hair, turning gray. Dark face with squinchy eyes and a scar on the left side of his chin.

"Is he heeled?"

"He has a forty-five strapped to his right leg, and the holster is oily. Mr. Brown, one of our Sunday school teachers, says that Stover can outdraw anyone in these parts. Says he hears that Stover spent his whole ten years in prison practicing drawing with his right hand and keeping his muscles in shape."

"Mama, the coffee's hot, and I warmed up the beans," Mary called from the doorway.

"Thank you dear. You're a sweet child."

Elizabeth saw young Ted coming up from the corral through the dusk. She could see him slapping his hand to his thigh and jerking it up in the motion of drawing a gun. She shuddered.

Elizabeth rose and picked up her hat and gloves. "Shall we eat a bite? You must be starved."

"Thank you," Malone said, and followed her in.

As they entered the kitchen where Mary had lit the lamp and set it in the middle of the table, young Ted came bouncing in the back door.

"Oh boy! Supper! And am I starved!"

"Did I see you practicing a fast draw just now?" Malone asked him.

Ted grinned and blushed. "Yeah, and I'm fast, too. See!" He slapped at his thigh and started to jerk his hand up. The barrel of Malone's Colt rapped him smartly on the wrist before his hand had more than cleared his leg.

Elizabeth caught her breath and her hand flew to her breast. Ted grabbed his right wrist with his left hand and looked up at Malone wide-eyed. Tears were welling up.

"I'm sorry, Ted," Malone said matter-of-factly. "I had to do that for your own good. You said you were fast, but I could have put two bullets in you before you cleared leather. I just wanted to show you that no matter how fast you think you are with a gun, there's always somebody faster. Now listen to me! Don't ever carry a gun or practice with one. There is no room for gunmen in this country any more. It's civilized now, and your Dad is preaching peace and brotherly love. Practice what he preaches, and forget about guns. Did I hurt you?"

Ted tossed his head. "nope. But gosh, that was fast, How'd you do it?"

"I wish I had never learned," Malone said. "If I hadn't I might have some nice lady like your mother for a wife now. Let's eat; I'm hungry too."

After two plates of beans, with home baked bread, two cups of coffee, and a generous helping of cake, Malone rolled and lighted a quirly and leaned back in his chair.

"That was a very nice supper, Mrs. Johnson. That cake was the best I've had in many a day."

"Thank you," she said. "I'm sorry we didn't have more."

"How far is it to town?"

"About six miles. Won't you stay the night? There's hay in the barn and we have extra blankets."

"No, thank you. I have my bedroll, but I want to get on into town."

"Will you be around town a few days? Bob will be sorry if he doesn't get to see you."

"Probably not. I don't like to stay in one place long enough for word to get around. There's always someone wanting to see if I'm as fast as they've heard. So I just keep riding."

"Did you know my Daddy when he was marshal?" Ted asked.

Elizabeth caught her breath. "Why, Ted! Where on earth did you hear about that?"

"Shucks, everybody knows it. Mr. Brown says Daddy was a good marshal. Said he shot three bad men."

"Yes, your Dad was a good marshal. One of the best," Malone said. "As a matter of fact he saved my life once."

Elizabeth's brows arched up. "I didn't know that. I knew that you and he were friends of course. Was that why?"

"Bob got a job at the ranch where I was riding when he first came west. We rode together two years. Then he got a job as deputy marshal. I was honeying a little blonde town gal. A half-breed that was sweet on her put out word that if I wasn't out of town by sundown he'd come looking for me. I didn't scare easy. Right after sundown I started down the middle of the street, and pretty soon I saw the half-breed coming towards me.

We weren't close enough for shooting in the fading light, so I kept on walking. Just as I came even with the hotel somebody fired a shot right behind me. Then somebody let out a screech over by the hotel. But I couldn't look to see what was going on. I had to keep my eye on the breed. About then he turned sort of green, and all of a sudden he took off up an alley, running and dodging.

I put a couple of bullets at his heels to keep him going. Then I turned around to see what the ruckus was. There was Bob, heading into the hotel. In a minute he was back with one of the breed's cronies that had a hole in his hand. The way I got the story, Bob had been walking up the sidewalk not far behind me to see that I got a square deal. He spotted this fellow poking a rifle out of the hotel window, aimed at me, ready to shoot me the minute I started to draw. He was one of the two Bob shot at Carson Wells. That half-breed has never forgiven me—or Bob, either,—for that night."

"That must have been before I met Bob. Would I know the half-breed?"

"He was a mangy Piaute by the name of Stover. Always thought I'd like to do something for Bob sometime to repay that favor. Well, I have to ride. Thanks again for the nice supper."

He chucked Mary under the chin. "Keep up the good housework. You'll make some lucky fellow a good wife one of these days."

He held his hand out to Ted. "Is it a deal, partner? No guns?"

"It's a deal," Ted said, and shook hands awkwardly.

Elizabeth followed him out to the corral in the starshine. "What are you going to do, Ted?"

He slipped the saddle into place and tightened the cinch. "I'm going to ride into town and take care of some unfinished business."

"You're going in to hunt up Stover. I hoped you would when I sent for you, but now I wish I hadn't sent for you. It's wrong, Ted. The Bible says 'Thou shalt not kill!'"

"But there are times when you have to."

"Suppose Stover is as fast as they say?"

"Then they'll bury us both in boot hill. I've stood up to a lot of fast men in my time, and I don't think the man lives who can stop me before I put at least one bullet in him."

"And if you kill him and walk away, what then?"

"Then I'm going to mount up and ride west. As far as I can go. Some place where no one knows me. Then I'll sell my horse and my gun and get a job of work and try to live like other people. I've worn a gun too long. The country has grown up until there's no place for men like me any more. Tell Bob I'm sorry I missed him. Tell him 'hello' for me—and 'goodbye'. And don't tell him you sent for me."

He lifted easily into the saddle in one seemingly effortless motion and rode off into the night.

She watched the solid bulk of him blocking out the stars in a diminishing profile, heading west, until the tears blurred her vision.

"Good-bye Ted," she whispered. "Good luck—and thanks."

Then, as she turned towards the house, as an afterthought: "And thank you, Lord, for men like Ted Malone."

THE END

Wilderness Incident, a collection

Big Snake

by
E. Stanley Martin

To my thinking there is naught more shameful than our treatment of the Indians. Always we have moved in upon their lands, killed their game, despoiled their forests and pushed them away from our settlements.

The Jamestown Colony was our first inroad, and Captain John Smith would have paid with his life had it not been for that fair princess, Pocahontas. And after sparing his life, what happened? The colony grew and prospered, and by the very dint of their greater number and superior arms, they pushed the Indians back from their plantations.

At Plymouth Colony, where my own grandsires landed, we did the same. The Indians brought us corn and beans, and showed us how to trap the alewives in the river in the spring so that we could plant a fish in each hill of corn. But we needed their land, so we pushed them back, and as more of our people came, we pushed farther and faster. When the Indians fought back to protect their own we called them heathen redskins and piously put the fear of God in them by shooting them on sight.

Penn, for all his treaties and protection, couldn't keep his Quakers from clearing the fields and shooting the game that was the Indians' livelihood. True, there was not so much bloodshed, but the effect was the same. Now there is scarcely a tribe left east of Pitt's town.

To my way of thinking the French have done better by our red brothers than we have. In the first place, the French have not set up the same kind of settlements that we have. They have not been eager to have big farms and plantations as we have. They have traded with the Indians, and lived with them. They have not moved into the Indian country in force, slaughtering as they came. They have moved in singly or in pairs, making friends as they came. Many of them have married into the tribes. They are respected by the Indians and have become a part of the Indian way of life. In the settlements the ladies make a hullabaloo about marrying "squaws", as they put it. I for one cannot hold with them. Many an Indian maid have I seen that would make a man a better wife than some blonde harlot from Piccadilly, which is what the Jamestown boys settled for.

It is true that I have fought Indians myself, to my shame. When Mad Anthony Wayne was recruiting for his foray to settle the Miami's I thought it was my duty to go along. But when I was scouting at Fallen Timbers and got an arrow in my brisket, that was the luckiest thing that ever happened to me. I crawled into a thicket to escape the prying eyes of the savages, but after a while I fevered and went out of my mind. I must have wandered quite a ways from the shape my uniform was in, and finally I stumbled right into a village full of women and children and old men. And did they scalp me? No!

As you can see, I still have my hair. Even though our men were shooting their braves down, they took me in, pulled my arrow, brewed poultices for the wound, fed me broth and nursed me back to life. When the war party came back and they began counting their dead, there was some muttering about putting me to the stake. By then I was back in my right mind, but was too weak to stand. I thought about crawling out of the tipi and into the woods before some hothead could talk up a following. I had quietly lifted up the side of the tipi with that thought in mind, but what I saw put the thought out of my mind.

There was a naked little Indian boy just old enough to toddle tottering my way, and there, between me and the boy was a four foot copperhead coiled and just ready to strike. I think the baby wanted the snake for a pet. He was cooing and reaching out his hand. Two more steps and the snake would sink his fangs into the outstretched hand.

I had to do something, and I didn't have anything to do it with. So I just gave a big lurch and grabbed that snake just below his head and hung on for dear life. I must have scared the baby, because he yelled. A squaw came running, and when she saw me you never heard such a commotion in your life. Indians came from all directions. They ganged up on that snake, uncoiled him from around my arm and took off his head with a tomahawk. Then I passed out again.

Well, when I came to, I thought I was really in for it. I was all bedded down on furs in a big tipi, and what must have been all of the braves in the tribe were standing around grunting and talking, fit to be tied. When they saw I had my eyes open they all turned their attention to me. The biggest one said something to me, but I couldn't make it out so I just shook my head. Then he pulled another Indian up from the back of the crowd and said something to him. This brave turned to me and said, "Chief say, you save him boy. You be him brother. He call you Big Snake."

Well it all boiled down to the simple fact that the Indian boy had been the Chief's son, and I was a hero. I went through the blood brother ceremony with the chief, and since that time I have never offered harm to an Indian.

In due time, when I was able to travel, and had learned some of the language, I explained to the chief that I would have to go back to the regiment so that I would not be accused of being a deserter, but I assured him that as soon as I could I would be back to live with his people. And as soon as I was discharged I married your mother and brought her back here with me, that being a condition of our marriage.

It has been a happy time, but because of the way our people have always treated the Indians I am afraid it is about over. The tribes to the east keep moving past us to the westward, because the palefaces keep crowding in upon them. It is a shameful thing, but for all my thinking I cannot think how to change it. I have a feeling that it must be destiny.

Tom and Red Hawk

By
E. Stanley Martin

Tom moved rapidly and silently down the familiar trail to the Kickapoo village, through the darkness. He hoped that the village dogs would not awaken and herald his coming.

As he was nearing the village a sudden commotion startled him, and he slid behind the nearest tree. He sighed with relief as he realized that a deer had jumped at his approach and streaked across the village clearing. In the wake of his passing, all of the village dogs gave voice in hot pursuit.

Tom looked up at the stars for a few minutes as he waited for the sound of the dogs to dwindle in the distance. Then he moved forward again, now crouched low and feeling the ground with each moccasin toe before placing his weight on it, lest some snapping twig reveal his presence. At the edge of the clearing he turned and moved directly to the side of the second lodge.

Tom lowered the long rifle gently to the ground. Then he slipped the powder horn and shot pouch from his shoulders and deposited them by the rifle. Then he dropped to his hands and knees and stretched prone on the ground.

Tom's fingers slid noiselessly along the edge of the tipi and lifted gently. Then head first, he inched under the wall. Half into the lodge he held his breath as a restless sleeper turned on his palette. After a minute he let his breath escape silently and continued his inching until he was entirely within the lodge.

The air was heavy with the smell of Indian bodies and the odors peculiar to Indian lodges. He could hear the sounds of deep breathing from various parts of the room. At first he thought the lodge was totally dark except for the light of one lonely star through the smoke-hole. Then he caught the tiny spark of banked embers in the fire hole.

Having located the fire hole, he was able to orient himself. He had been in the lodge before and knew that the palette of Red hawk should be only an arms length to his right. He raised to his hands and knees and began to crawl towards the sound of Red hawk's deep breathing.

Suddenly he recoiled as if bitten by a copperhead. His hand touched a foot at the same instant his head had bumped some fleshy object where nothing should be. At that moment a vagrant breeze stirred the door of the tipi and blew into wavering flame the embers in the fire hole. Tom looked up to see Buffalo Horn towering over him, tomahawk upraised.

Tom's heart was pounding in his throat, and for a second he lacked the power to move. Then as he caught a glint of recognition in the beady black eyes, he pulled his awkward boyish frame to its full five feet eleven inches and put on the full dignity of his sixteen years. If he was to die in the lodge of his friend he would at least be a credit to his race.

"Buffalo Horn up early," he stated as matter-of-factly as he could, but in spite of himself his voice cracked a little.

He saw the brave move his foot sideways and push a wisp of straw and a faggot of kindling onto the embers. Little tongues of flame began to cast wavering shadows on the sides of the tipi.

Tom, watching the upraised tomahawk in fascination, saw out of the corner of his eye a movement on Red hawk's pallet and in a moment Red Hawk was standing by his father.

"Good morning, Red Hawk," Tom said. "Are you ready to go hunting?"

Red Hawk looked at the upraised tomahawk in the hand of his father, and then at Tom. "What happen?" he asked.

It began to be apparent to Tom that he was not going to die instantly. He took a deep breath and pointed to the side of the lodge where he had entered.

"I thought it would be fun to sneak in and wake you in your bed, like a Kickapoo," he said. "But the mighty hunter, Buffalo Horn, was not caught sleeping like a squaw."

Buffalo Horn's chest swelled a little and the tomahawk dropped to his side. He turned to his son and muttered a few words, and Red hawk responded quickly. Buffalo Horn shrugged and turned away.

Glancing around the room Tom saw the gleaming black eyes of Red Hawk's mother, and of his two sisters peeping over the edge of their robes. He felt a flush on his face.

"Ready?" he said to Red Hawk.

Red Hawk nodded, slipped on his moccasins, picked up his bow and quiver of arrows and followed Tom through the door.

Once outside, Tom slipped around to the side of the lodge and retrieved his rifle, powder horn, and shot pouch. Then he and Red hawk struck out towards the faint flush in the eastern sky that announced that it would be dawn in half an hour.

The Attack

by
E. Stanley Martin

For all his youth and vigor, Tom felt his heart pounding a little as he trudged the last few steps up to the top of Lookout Point. He lowered the butt of the long rifle to the ground and leaned on it as he paused to look out over the valley beyond, bright with new green and spotted with the white of dogwood and the pink blush of haw.

Although it was a little farther to come by way of the point instead of following the creek trail, he always came home from his hunting trips this way for a few minutes of rest as he admired the panorama before him. His eyes swung to the far right and followed the sweep of the river down to the little clearing opposite him and about two miles across the valley where he would see the wisp of smoke from the kitchen fire.

But as he found the clearing with his eyes they suddenly narrowed to slits. He dropped the turkey and brace of rabbits he was carrying and brought his hand up to shade his eyes from the afternoon sun. He stiffened at what he saw. Not the wisp of smoke from the chimney that he had expected but billows of smoke from the cabin site.

The cabin was a-fire! The rifle swung up under his arm and he started to run down the slope, his game forgotten behind him. Then he saw the other column of smoke to the left where the Jones cabin stood and he stopped abruptly to scan the rest of the valley. Seven columns of smoke marked the site of every cabin in the valley. Indians! His heart sank within him. So the peaceful Oubache's had finally grown tired of being crowded out, and had burned out the settlement.

His eyes swung to the far left where the little Oubache village stood at the lower bend of the river. But there again he saw smoke. Not peaceful smokes, or ceremonial fires, but the smoke of destruction. Then it must be that a marauding tribe of Hurons or Miamis were raiding the settlements.

At that thought he crouched suddenly, his rifle at the ready. Pulling his powder horn and shot pouch into handier positions he slipped silently into the nearest covering of brush and began gliding from cover to cover, his eyes scanning every tree and bush and catching every movement.

As he neared the clearing he turned and made a complete circle around the five acre patch. The sun was westering and the shadows were growing deeper. Carefully he scanned each bush and tree and patch of shadow but saw nothing strange or out of place in this, his little world.

At the alder thicket he dropped to his hands and knees and carefully inched his way forward to the edge of the clearing. His heart sank at what he saw. Where the cabin had stood was now only a pile of glowing embers. The little barn was a heap of ashes. Beyond he could see Bessie, the cow, and the yearling heifer lying with arrows protruding.

His heart was pounding in his throat and he gripped his outthrust rifle grimly. What of Mom and Dad and Sis? What had happened to them? Had they been captured or killed? He had heard many stories of Indian torture but he had thought that was all long ago, for in all his sixteen years he had not heard of a single Indian raid in this frontier.

His eyes caught sight of a mound on the far side of the clearing. In the growing dusk he could not identify it at the distance, so he backed quietly into the woods, half circled the clearing, and crawled to the edge again.

There was enough light left to identify the object and it was as if something died within him. It was his father lying on his back, one hand grasping the shaft of an arrow protruding from his stomach. But there was something else wrong—his hair. Then Tom realized that there wasn't any hair. Just a patch of blood, clotting, and a myriad of flies.

Suddenly he wanted to rush forward and pull the deadly arrow from his father's body, fit it to a bow, and kill an Indian. Kill all Indians. He knew how to handle a bow and arrow for he had often visited the Oubache village and had many friends among the young braves. He had learned well their lore. Then he remembered that they, too, had been massacred. And all the neighbors. He felt suddenly alone, terribly alone, and young, and he wanted to cry, for all his sixteen years.

This was his father,—big, strong, powerful, patient, peace-loving and God-fearing, felled by an Indian arrow. His father, who had resigned his commission and put away his uniform because he could not stomach the endless slaughter of the Indians. His father, who had moved freely among the Indians as preacher, teacher, and friend.

A kaleidoscope of pictures flashed through Tom's mind. His father, tall and powerful, bending over a sick Indian baby in its mother's arms, gently seeking the cause of its illness. His father on Sunday preaching to the Indians—first a verse in English and then in sign language—bringing them both the Word of God and the language of the white man. "Our troubles with the Indians result partly from a lack of understanding," his father had told someone. "When we speak the same language we will understand each other better."

His father had been patient in the face of bigotry. He could recall his father facing Brick Jones, the blacksmith, when he had wanted to gather a party together to exterminate "those pesky, thievin' redskins" in the neighboring village because of some depredation in his garden patch. "The Bible says 'Thou shalt not kill', and 'Love thy neighbor as thyself'," his father had said. "You would not begrudge one of us a few vegetables from your garden. The Indians get just as hungry. 'Do unto others as you would have them do unto you'. Don't forget the venison they brought us when we were starving."

Tom recalled the day when his mother was in the garden picking beans and his father had stepped into the cabin doorway just as Tom had reached his hand into the cookie jar. "Son," his father had said. "The Lord is watching you, even when no one else is watching. So before you take anything that is not yours, ask the Lord if you are deserving. Of course a cookie isn't a very big thing to bother the Lord with, so in this case you could ask your mother, if you think you are deserving." He had done without the cookie.

"The Lord works in mysterious ways, His wonders to perform," he could remember his father quoting. This was a mysterious way, he thought, for the Lord to act, killing his father by the hand of the very Indians his father was trying to help.

Wilderness Incident

by
E. Stanley Martin

Tom stopped short, suddenly frozen into immobility.

How many times had he halted thus at some strange sound or movement since he had eluded his Indian pursuers five days ago? He had lost count. And each time it had been for some natural phenomenon—a startled deer, an indignant skunk, or n alarmed sentinel crow. But even so, vigilance was the price of life in this wilderness, he knew.

So suddenly had he come to a halt that one moccasined foot, toe down, Indian fashion, remained suspended six inches off the ground. He lowered it with infinite caution, feeling along the ground for a twig-free footing before resting his weight on it. Now only his eyes, slitted to keep as much of the whites from showing as possible, moved in the deep-tanned, angular boyish face. His glance darted from tree, to bush, to river, and back again.

Something was amiss and for the moment he did not know what it was. Some sound, some movement had warned him that all was not as it should be. His quick survey disclosed nothing to alarm him. He started another visual sweep of the heavily wooded and deeply shaded riverbank, this time carefully scrutinizing each tree and bush and deadfall. His ears seemed to point forward in their eagerness to pick up any alien sound.

He saw May-apples and yellow dogtooth violets in bloom. He saw elms, oaks and sycamores in bright new green leaf. He heard a cardinal splitting its throat in an ecstasy of song. Other birds chirped and fluttered busily on the ground and in the trees. Somewhere down the river below the bend a woodpecker hammered on a hollow limb. From up the river drifted the faraway sound of a man singing—

Singing! That was it! That was the foreign sound in this uninhabited wilderness! Tom frowned at his stupidity. Then a wry little smile tugged at his lips and he began to relax. But he stiffened again, and this time he had spotted the location of the movement that had caught his eye the first time.

Tom concentrated his attention on the clump of willows between the elm and the red oak on the riverbank. One branch of the willows had moved when there was no breeze to stir the others. For what seemed like many minutes he stared but could see nothing except the trees and the flowers and the wide river beyond. The willow branch did not stir again.

His ears continued to register the distant sound of singing, increasing now in volume. He could recognize the tune, *Yankee Doodle*, in a lusty if not melodious voice. He couldn't quite catch the words yet, muffled as they were by the distance and the trees.

From the corner of his eye he noted a movement in the sunshine on the blue of the river upstream. He turned his eyes in time to catch a glimpse of a raft, a little tent amidships, floating down the river, a tall young man at the sweep. Now he knew the source of the singing. He turned his eyes back toward the willows. An Indian was standing there! His heart throbbed at his throat and he stared in amazement at the buckskin clad brave, standing there bringing a rifle to bear on the raft. He had not been there an instant before!

Tom puzzled a bit and then guessed what had happened. The Indian standing yonder must have been rowing close to the bank of the river in a canoe and had either heard or seen the approaching raft. He had pulled to the bank under the overhanging willows and lifted his canoe up and under the leafy canopy. That would be when the branch had moved. Then he had crept up to the point of vantage where he now stood. Here he could see but not be seen by the man on the raft. His intention was obvious. He was going to shoot the unsuspecting fellow singing so lustily on the river.

Tom knew that the raft was still too far away for a shot to have effect, and he thought it was too far out in the stream to be in any great danger in any case. He again sought to catch sight of the raft through the screening leaves. He saw with dismay that the current was carrying the clumsy thing inshore. I fact it was already so close inshore that Tom could see only the upper half of the fellow, the rest being hidden by the bank. It would pass quite close to the bank where the Indian stood before sweeping out and around the bend below. Why didn't the fool stay out in the middle of the river out of the reach of arrows and bullets?

Tom knew that he dared not call out to the riverman to warn him of his peril. Slowly, reluctantly, he brought up his rifle, glanced at the priming, then across at the brave following the movement of the raft with his rifle. Tom hesitated to put the gun to his shoulder.

"Thou shalt not kill," Tom's father had quoted from the Good Book. "Indians are people the same as you and me," he had said. "They are entitled to live their lives the way they want." Tom considered the possibility of creeping quietly away.

Then into his mind flashed that nightmare of grisly mental images that kept torturing him. Those scenes of gruesome carnage and utter devastation that he and Red Hawk, his Kickapoo friend, had come upon when they had returned home after a hunting trip; Tom's father dead and scalped in the clearing, an Indian arrow through his gut. The cabin reduced to smoking ruins, the scorched bones of his mother and sister visible in the glowing embers. The horrible thud and dying gasp of Red Hawk when an arrow ripped through his heart as he was helping Tom dig a grave for his father. Then Tom's headlong flight, with silent, naked, horribly painted savages in hot pursuit. That he had escaped at all was tribute to Red hawk's many patient lessons in woodcraft, aided by the closing in of darkness.

Tom shuddered at the memories. Possibly this Indian before him had been one of the marauders, although that was not likely, he reminded himself, since he was now five days and more than two hundred miles west of those gruesome scenes. Maybe that is the Indian's way of life, Tom thought—killing and being killed. In any case it was up to him to do something and quickly.

Tom shouldered his rifle and drew a careful bead on the buckskin clad back. Shooting a man in the back was even more abhorrent to him than the killing itself. He held his sights steady and gently increased the pressure on the trigger.

He saw the jerk of the shoulder from the impact of his bullet. He saw too the puff of smoke from the Indian's weapon, fired at almost the exact instant Tom's bullet hit him. The sound of the two shots blended into one and shattered the tranquility of the forest, echoing and re-echoing from the river.

Tom dropped the butt of his rifle to the ground, spilled powder from the horn into his palm, dumped it into the barrel and followed it with patch and ball and rammed them home with quick strokes of the rammer. He divided his attention between the loading and the Indian crumpling to the ground. The Indian was still twitching convulsively as Tom swung the gun up, put a pinch of powder in the pan and shook it into place. He was now ready again to sell his life dearly if the Indian had friends nearby.

Standing motionless and almost invisible in his leafy cover, Tom realized that he was trembling. This was the first time that he had killed a human being, and he felt deeply saddened, even as pride in his marksmanship reminded him that one shot had been sufficient.

Still watching alertly, Tom caught another glimpse of the raft through the screening trees as it swung out into the stream again before going around the bend. Except for the little tent, the raft was empty! There was no sign of life aboard!

So his killing of the Indian had been futile! The Indian's bullet, too, had found its mark. Now Tom paled and doubled over suddenly. He retched and vomited violently.

After a time he straightened up, wiped his mouth with the back of his hand, looked quickly around to see if he had been detected. He knew it was time to move after all that noise. He wanted to run—to put as much distance as possible between himself and this evidence of his wicked handiwork. But he forced himself to stalk silently through the underbrush and to stand and stare down at the dead Indian.

Tom was glad the man had fallen face down so the staring eyes could not reproach him. Blood stained the back of the buckskin jacket. By the feathers in the scalp lock Tom took the man to be some sort of chief, obviously a young one. Without turning the man over he could only guess at the tribe, Peoria, possibly, although he was now west of the Peories, he thought.

Tom looked away, his face bloodless under the tan, a terrible emptiness in him. He was only sixteen. He was alone in a hostile wilderness. Saint Louis must be quite a ways down the Mississippi. Tears were in his eyes, and he dashed them away angrily. He shrugged his powder horn and his bullet pouch into more comfortable positions and headed downstream.

He lengthened his stride as he continued his interrupted journey, again moving swiftly and silently through the woods along the river. His eyes returned to their ceaseless scanning of the dense growth through which he was moving and his ears were again attuned to pick up any discordant note in the now resuming melody of sound about him.

But in spite of his endless vigilance, he was completely without warning when a huge figure hurtled from behind a twisted old sycamore and strong hands clutched his throat. His air was shut off instantly. His mouth popped open but no sound came forth. His attacker was shaking him violently and he could see nothing, try as he might.

Instinctively he jerked his rifle up with both hands and pushed it suddenly with all of his strength against his attacker's chest. At the same time he jerked his right knee up purposefully, seeking his opponent's groin, and his foot shot back to hook over the man's leg.

As suddenly as he had been attacked, he was free. His assailant was writhing on the ground at his feet. Tom got his first look at the man. This was not an Indian as he had thought, but a tall young white man, barefoot, shirtless, and in homespun breeches, soaking wet. Probably the young man off of the raft, Tom thought with a start, although he could not be sure.

Now the fellow was squirming onto his side, twisting Tom's right leg between both of his own, obviously with the intent of throwing Tom to the ground. Tom felt himself toppling and saw huge hands clutching eagerly towards him. He brought the butt of his rifle in a swinging arc against the mop of yellow hair below him and heard a resounding whomp as it hit. The twisting legs relaxed and the young man lay still upon the ground.

Tom scrambled up, looked at the priming in his gun, and put a pinch of powder in the pan. Then he stared down at the tow-headed giant. Six foot two or three, Tom guessed, and wide and muscular. Maybe twenty years old. Relaxed as he was, with his mouth half open, he didn't look to be a bad sort.

Tom was tempted to stomp him, beat him mercilessly to a pulp for his unprovoked attack. But of course he couldn't. He hadn't been raised that way. But why had he attacked without warning or provocation?

The rising and falling of the chest told Tom that the man was only stunned and would soon recover. He moved back a few paces to a driftwood log lodged against a tree. He perched himself upon it, leaned back against the tree, and laid his rifle across his thigh, the muzzle aimed at his molester.

A glance up through the dense canopy of leaves at the sun told Tom it was nearly noon. He reached in his pocket for a handful of the roots he had grubbed out of the ground that morning. Roots that Red Hawk had taught him how to find in that far off happy time.

So it was he was sitting, munching on a root, when the prone figure emitted a groan, blinked and struggled to a sitting position, one hand moving up to rub the bruised head.

"Hurt a mite?" Tom drawled.

The blond head jerked up. Remembrance flooded the blue eyes at the sight of Tom. The giant tensed and started to spring up, a malevolent scowl on his face, a growl deep in his throat. Tom's hand dropped to the trigger of his rifle.

At sight of the rifle barrel aimed right between his eyes the fellow sagged back, but the scowl remained.

"What you got agin me?" he asked.

Tom's eyes widened. "I was about to ask the same of you," he retorted.

"You shot at me, didn't you?" It was more a statement than a question. "And now you're a-sittin' there aimin' to finish the job."

Realization of the reason for the man's anger began to dawn on Tom, but the fellow sure had his facts wrong.

"If I was indenting to kill you," Tom said, "You'd be dead. And as for me shooting at you, I generally hit what I shoot at."

"You hit me right enough," the fellow growled. "But you'd best aim a little better this time or I'll rip you apart for wolf bait." He pulled up the soggy pants leg with the holes in it and gingerly felt of the red welt across the right calf.

Tom saw the blue eyes searching the ground for a missile within reach. His hand steadied on the stock of his rifle.

"Take it easy, fellow," he warned. "I can shoot you before you move an inch. For your information, I did not shoot you, and I'm not about to shoot you if you just cool off a little."

Disbelief was on the scowling face. "Then who did shoot me?" As the fellow asked this question, his eyes burning into Tom's, his right hand snaked out, grasped the egg-size rock he had spotted, and flung it with terrific force at Tom's head.

Tom had seen the thought in the man's eyes and ducked his head to let the rock bounce off of the tree behind him. He held his fire. He had no cause to kill the man if he'd only simmer down and let him explain.

Tom knew what was eating on the fellow. He had been going down the river minding his own business and someone had shot at him from the bank. When he had gotten to shore and started up the river to see who was doing the shooting, there was Tom carrying a rifle. Tom guessed he couldn't blame him for being mad. But he could listen to reason. Tom had already told him that he hadn't shot at him, but apparently the fool still didn't believe it.

Tom slid carefully down from his perch, his eyes and his rifle steady on the man. It was time to put him straight on a few things.

"I'm getting right put out at you," he said. "Now turn over easy, get up and start walking up the river. I want to show you something."

The big fellow shrugged and rolled over deliberately. He hitched himself cautiously upright and started walking, careful where he put his bare feet. Once he half turned his head to see if Tom was still there, so silently was he following.

"I'm right behind you," Tom assured him. "And my finger is still on the trigger. Just head a little to the left where that big red oak stands just beyond the elm."

When he reached the place the fellow stopped.

"Now what?" he asked.

Tom stared, disbelieving, at the spot where the dead Indian had been lying. The body was gone! But that could not be! He had looked at the body. He knew the man was dead. But where was the body?

Again Tom felt a sudden emptiness. His heart was pounding in his throat. He was scared.

Tom's voice took on a sudden urgency. He whispered in a voice barely audible to the shirtless man in front of him. "L-l-look Mister," he whispered through chattering teeth. "I don't want to scare you, but when I left here a little bit ago there was a dead Indian right there by that tree. I shot him and he shot you. Now his body's gone and that only means one thing. There's more Indians around. Where's your gun?"

The fellow half turned. "A likely story," he sneered. Then he saw that Tom was no longer aiming the gun at him. He saw the anxious look on his face. He looked at the ground where Tom was staring and saw the pool of drying blood and the marks that showed where something heavy had been dragged down the bank.

The fellow's expression changed suddenly, and now he was as intent as Tom. "My gun's in the river," he whispered. "Lost it when I went overboard."

"The Indian had a rifle," Tom said. "It must have fallen here in the weeds. If we had it . . . ." He began searching among the weeds.

For all Tom knew there might be a hundred Indians in the woods around them. He could feel his back muscles tensing in anticipation of an arrow through his short ribs. He searched desperately for the gun, and he knew the big fellow was searching too. So intent was he on the search that he jumped when the fellow laid an urgent hand on his shoulder.

"Look!" the fellow whispered, and pointed up the river.

There, close in against the bank not far beyond them, moving erratically upstream, was an Indian dugout canoe. In the stern, clumsily trying to row, was a squaw. Just in front of her huddled a black haired child about two years old. Dumped in the front of the craft was the buckskin clad body of the dead Indian. The rifle lay atop the body.

Tom quit worrying about Indians in the woods around them as he stared at the canoe, but his heart became a leaden weight in his stomach. Full knowledge of the enormity of what he had done descended upon him and he sagged with the weight of it.

Since he was big enough to toddle he had lived among Indians. He knew their customs and their ways of thinking. Seeing the squaw and the child, he knew of a certainty that the chief, who had so lately stood here, his rifle aimed at the raft, would not have fired unless the boatman had tried to land. The brave had only stood in readiness to protect his child and squaw in case the paleface offered harm. He knew full well that a brave traveling with his family never attacked unless crowded into it.

As Tom watched, the canoe was caught in an eddy and swung towards the middle fo the river. He held his breath as the squaw paddled desperately to swing the craft back inshore. Finally she succeeded in heading the bow upstream again, but she was making very little progress against the river.

"She'll never make it," Tom thought. "Too much weight in the front of the canoe to handle it with one oar that way. If she gets caught in the current it will turn her over. Squaws are no good in a canoe anyway, except at a front oar with a brave at the back oar."

It was his fault that she was out there. He would have to help her. He turned to the young man beside him.

The big fellow was eyeing Tom ruefully and half holding out a big hand. "I see I was wrong again," he said. "Looks like you said the truth and saved my life. Thanks."

Tom met the fellow's eyes squarely, but he did not take the extended hand. His face showed the torment of his thoughts.

"I have done a terrible thing," he said. "When you were coming down the river, the brave stood here with his rifle aimed at you. I thought he was going to shoot you. I didn't know he had his family with him, or I would have known he wouldn't fire unless you tried to land. He didn't fire at you until my bullet hit him. I murdered him. Now his wife and baby are out there in that canoe and if I don't get them ashore it's going to upset and drown them." He turned and was gone.

"Wait!" the fellow said. Then he struck out after Tom's disappearing figure.

Tom moved far enough back from the bank to put a screen of bushes and trees between himself and the canoe. Then he headed upstream, almost running but making not a sound. Behind him he heard the big fellow crashing through the brush, following him. He hoped the squaw would not hear him above the sound of the splashing of the oar.

Tom knew that to bring the canoe safely ashore he would have to take the woman by surprise. Otherwise she would head out into the current and the craft would surely capsize.

He ran until he was certain that he was beyond the dugout, and then wormed his way back to the river bank behind a clump of willows. Just below him the squaw worked frantically at the oar. The clumsy craft wobbled not fifteen feet out in the river.

Tom stood his rifle against a tree, shucked off his shirt, bullet pouch, and powder horn and dropped them by the gun. Then at just the proper moment he crouched and sprang in a long arc into the water so that he would come up at the stern of the canoe just behind the squaw. The coldness of the water took him by surprise and he gasped as his head popped out.

As he shook the water out of his eyes and reached his hand for the rough hewn stern he saw the oar descending, jabbing at his head. He jerked his head aside, but the oar hit his shoulder a glancing blow and he winced. Quickly he ducked under the canoe and popped his head up on the other side.

"Friend," he said urgently in the Kickapoo language.

The similarity of the word in the various Algonquin dialects was such that she recognized it, he saw, as she hesitated an instant. Then she jabbed the oar at his head again. The fierce hatred burning in her eyes told him that she had been watching from the willows when he had stopped to look at her dead husband, and she knew him for the killer. Probably the only reason she had not attacked him then was because she had been holding her hand over the child's mouth to keep him from whimpering.

This time he ducked under the canoe, caught the jabbing oar, and jerked it from her grasp. Then he treaded water just out of her reach, smiled at her engagingly and repeated, "Friend," and held up one hand in the two finger sign for friends.

Doubt slowly replaced the hatred in her eyes. She reached one hand forward to comfort the whimpering child, her eyes boring into Tom's. Finally she whispered "Friend?" tentatively in a dialect strange to Tom.

Again Tom smiled and said "Friend," and made the sign. Then he pointed to the river bank and offered her the oar. Half disbelieving, she took the oar and paddled as he swam and pushed the dugout towards the little stretch of sandy beach below the bank.

As he scrambled out of the water to pull the bow up onto the sand, Tom caught sight of the big fellow above them on the bank. He had Tom's rifle and he was aiming it at the Indian woman.

"Don't!" Tom shouted, and jumped in front of the woman and child, facing the big fellow and the gun.

The fellow grinned and dropped the butt of the rifle to the ground. "Just playing safe in case she changed her mind and tried to use the paddle on you again," he said. "After all, she's an Injun and I never did trust Injuns."

"Well, put up the gun and help me beach the canoe," Tom suggested.

He turned back to the canoe, smiled into the beady black eyes of the boy and lifted him out onto the bank. Then he steadied the canoe while the woman stepped out.

She was slender and young, Tom saw. Scarcely more than a girl. Her black braids glistened from careful grooming. Her deerskin dress was handsomely worked with porcupine quills and beadwork.

The big fellow took hold of the bow of the canoe on one side and Tom on the other, and between them they tugged the thing up onto the sand out of the water. Tom turned his head to avoid looking at the dead Indian in the bottom of the craft.

Tom straightened from his effort and turned to the big fellow. "Thanks," he said. "I'm Tom Wilson. I'm sorry for the trouble I've caused you and the woman." He put out his hand and the big fellow took it in his own.

"Jack Nielson here," he said. "You did what you thought was needful. I'm sorry I jumped you, but you can see why I did. No harm done, either, except for the Injun and my gun. That gun there sure looks like a good one." He was eying the gun in the canoe longingly. Then he turned his eyes back to Tom. "What do we do now?"

"The boy's hungry," Tom said. "We'd best find something to eat. Then if I can remember enough sign language we can see about getting the young woman and her child to wherever they were going."

"I can't rustle much grub without a gun," Jack protested.

"I know," Tom told him. "I'd rather have a bow and arrow myself. A gun's too noisy. But I guess we'll have to make do with what we have."

The young Indian woman had been standing on the sand, her face expressionless, watching the two intently. One hand absently patted the black hair of the round-bellied boy whimpering and clinging to her leg. Now she stepped to the canoe and rummaged among the camp gear and other plunder. When she rose and turned she handed a bow and quiver of arrows to Tom. To Jack she handed the rifle and a beaded deerskin pouch.

"I give," she said, and turned back to the canoe. Now she came up with a small smoke-blackened pot, half filled it with water from the river, and started climbing up the steep bank.

Tom stared after her in amazement. Evidently she understood English, and spoke it some. That would make it easier to find out where she wanted to go.

"Well how do you like that?" Jack asked, fondling the rifle. "How do you say 'Thanks' in Injun?"

"You don't say thanks," Tom told him. "You give them something in return, or you do something for them. You rustle up wood for a fire and I'll look for some game to put in the pot."

Tom picked up the Indian boy, climbed the bank, and strode to the tree where he had left his rifle. He set the boy down and slipped into his shirt. Then he rummaged in his shot pouch and found a little package wrapped in oiled deerskin. This he unwrapped and handed the cake of maple sugar in it to the Indian boy. The little fellow popped it into his mouth and sucked on it eagerly. Tom picked up the bow and quiver and disappeared into the woods.

Ten minutes later he was back, two rabbits in one hand, a bunch of wild onions in the other. He had already slit the bellies of the rabbits and gutted them. He handed them to the woman and she began skinning them in readiness for the pot. Tom turned to where Jack was gathering a huge pile of brush.

"We don't want a bonfire," he said quietly. "Just a smokeless cooking fire." He selected a few sticks the right size and arranged them in a circle like the rays of the sun. With his knife he furred a dry branch and stuck it in the center. Then he put a pinch of gunpowder on it, struck a spark with his flint and steel, and in a few minutes had a good cooking blaze going. Tom poked two forked sticks into the ground, one on either side of the blaze, and placed a stout green limb across them on which he suspended the pot.

"That's a handy way to build a fire," Jack said. "Different from cabin cooking."

"And no smoke to tell the Indians where you are," Tom pointed out. "Think you can whittle some spoons?"

"Never did," Jack told him. "I'll try."

Tom turned to the woman, who was now dropping the pieces of rabbit into the pot. Tom cut the onions into short lengths and dropped them in with the rabbit. Then he rummaged in his shot pouch again, found an elderberry stem, pulled the wooden peg from the end of it and shook salt into the stew.

"You speak English?" Tom asked the woman.

"Some," she said. She dipped her hands into the sand and rubbed them briskly to get rid of the blood from the rabbits. Then she brushed them clean and picked up the boy, who was whimpering again.

"Where did you learn?" Tom asked.

"I am daughter of chief and squaw of chief," she replied. Tom saw a cloud of pain cross her eyes for a moment. Then she continued.

"When I small we catch paleface. Keep in chief's lodge. They teach me speak English."

"They?" Tom asked. "How many?"

"Two girls," she told him. "After while they get sickness like the people. They die."

Tom nodded. He knew that when she said "The People" she referred to her tribe.

"Where were you going?" he asked, and motioned upriver.

"Home," she said. "He go," nodding towards the bank below which the canoe rested, "to meeting of chiefs three sleeps down river. I go with to visit. We come back two sleeps."

"Then you live upriver? How far?" he asked.

"Not far. Maybe half-sleep," she said.

"Say, Tom," Jack interrupted. "How do you whittle a spoon?"

Tom looked at the piece of wood Jack had been whittling, and saw that he had been working on a full round piece without much success. Tom selected a branch of about the right size, broke it to length, and then split it with his knife. "First the bowl," he said, as he shaped it. "Then the handle. There, how's that?" and he handed Jack a neatly fashioned spoon.

"That looks easy," Jack said. "I'll try it that way."

Tom walked to the edge of the bank, looked down at the canoe critically and then turned back to the woman.

"That canoe isn't big enough for all of us. Can we bury the chief here? Then we can take you home."

"Bury? You mean in hole in ground?" Tom thought she was going to cry. He nodded in the affirmative.

"No! No!" she said. "Not bury. We wrap chief in blanket and put in tree. Then I take boy and walk."

"But we can take you in the canoe," he protested.

"No!!" She shook her head. "Leave canoe here. We go! You stay! You kill chief. Warriors kill you. Is not right but is way of the people."

"But I did not *want* to kill the chief," he said. "And if I had known you were with him I would have known there was no need to kill him. That was a mistake."

"But warriors no know. They kill you. We eat now. We put chief in tree. Then I go."

Tom nodded reluctantly. "Maybe it's better that way, but I don't feel right about it." He took the spoon he had whittled and stirred the stew, blew on the broth and tasted it.

"Stew's ready," Tom said. "How are the spoons?"

Jack proudly exhibited two crude but serviceable implements.

"Those are fine," Tom assured him. "Here, we'll set the pot off the fire and dip in. The meat won't be too well cooked, but we can eat it if your teeth are good."

Tom took the pot from the fire and set it upon the ground in front of the woman, now sitting cross-legged, the boy in her lap. Then he and jack sat down, cross-legged, on either side. The woman took one of the proffered spoons, dipped in, and blew on the soup to cool it for the boy. Tom and jack followed suit and sipped at the hot stew warily.

"After we eat, will you help wrap the chief and put him in a tree?" Tom asked Jack.

"I heard you talkin' about it. How do you do it, and what's the idea?" Jack asked.

"It's an old Indian custom. They bury their dead in trees. We wrap the chief in his blanket with his trinkets. Then we hoist him up into a tree and tie him on a limb and leave him."

"I'll help," Jack said. "What now?"

Tom had turned his head towards the woods suddenly. Now he motioned with his hand at jack for silence. Jack could hear nothing but the medley of bird songs and the call of a Bob-White.

Tom turned back to look at the woman. She too was listening, and peering into the woods. "My brother," she said. "He chief also. Don't tell him," and she nodded towards the bank beyond which lay the canoe. Then she pursed her lips and made the call of the quail.

Out of the half-gloom of the woods emerged a tall young brave in buckskins, carrying a hunting bow, and behind him a younger, slighter lad.

Tom stood and faced the young chief, raising his hand in the peace sign. Jack stood, but because he didn't know what to do, he did nothing.

As the stalwart young chief raised his hand in solemn greeting and then folded his arms to stand before the woman, Tom noted the similarity between them. He was taller and perhaps three or four years older, but the family resemblance was plain.

Tom could feel his heart pounding slowly in his throat again. It looked like they were trapped for sure this time. Wait until the woman told her brother about her dead husband. The best they could expect would be a quick arrow in the heart. The worst would be slow torture and death at the hands of the whole tribe. Tom glanced longingly out of the corner of his eye at his rifle and pouch against the tree. Even the bow and arrows a dozen feet away on the ground where he had laid them would be better than nothing. How had he let them get in a fix like this? The younger Indian had stopped behind the chief and was looking the two white men up and down.

The woman spoke to the chief. "My brother. I am glad to see you."

Tom's heart skipped a beat. She spoke in English. That meant she wanted them to hear and understand.

"Me glad see you," the chief intoned slowly, as if in a strange language. "Where you chief?"

"My chief have trouble. He dead. These paleface help me." She motioned towards Tom and Jack.

The chief was silent for so long Tom's heart began pounding again. Then he said, "Me hear shot."

Tom's heart sank. Here it comes, he thought. He held his breath, waiting for her answer. She pointed at Tom. "He shoot rabbit for cook. We hungry."

Tom began to breathe again, but with an effort kept his face expressionless.

"Good!" the chief grunted.

"You go to village now?" she asked. Her brother nodded his assent.

"We go with you," she said, "Paleface go south."

"Bring to village," the chief protested. "Big feast for them. We give presents for help you."

"No," she said. "I give presents already. They go other way in hurry."

Tom took a deep breath. He hoped his voice would sound natural. "You will go home with the chief then? In that case we will get on down the river."

She turned to him. "Yes. Go in peace." He thought he saw tears in her eyes, and by the tone of her voice he knew that she wanted them to go quickly.

Tom raised his arm again in the peace sign. "Goodbye," he said, and then barely loud enough for her to hear, "Thank you."

He turned, and with a nod at Jack, picked up the bow and arrows and his rifle and strode into the brush downriver. Jack paused only long enough to pick up the Indian rifle and pouch, and followed. As soon as they were safely out of hearing of the Indians, Tom whispered "come on," and struck out at a faster pace for the raft.

When they reached the place of their earlier encounter Tom turned to Jack. "Where's your raft?"

"Just below," Jack said.

"Well, let's get aboard and out in the river before those braves figure out that I shot the chief," Tom said.

In a few minutes they were safely aboard, Jack at the seep, and the raft was moving with the current out into the middle of the stream. Tom and Jack both anxiously watched the river bank behind them, but no hostile movement was to be seen. Jack heaved a sigh of relief.

"There's something I want to know," he said finally. "How'd you know that wasn't a Bob-White whistling?"

"That's easy," Tom told him. "The Bob-White is a prairie bird. He doesn't whistle in the woods like that."

Jack nodded. Then he asked "Where you headed?"

"Saint Louis," Tom told him. "Since the Indians killed my folks five days ago on the Wabash I haven't any home and I thought I might find something to do there."

Jack stared at him in round-eyed amazement. "And you still like Injuns! I was prentice to a miller upriver. I was twenty-one last week, and I left because I didn't like him. I'm headed for Saint Louis too, looking for a job. Want to ride down with me?"

Tom looked at the immensity of flowing water around them. "Any choice?" he laughed, and offered his hand to Jack, who took the slim hand in his own big paw.

"Saint Louis, here we come," he said.

The End.

Setting for a Story

(prelude to a sequel)
By
E. Stanley Martin

Dozens of boats of all descriptions were tied up at the edge of the river or pulled up onto the muddy bank. Shirtless and barefoot Negroes struggled and slipped up the slope, backs bent under the weight of the boxes and bales they were toting from a keelboat to the warehouse above.

Indian braves in buckskins, Indian squaws in blankets and glittering trinkets, and an occasional brave clad only in breach-clout stood watching the unloading, strolled idly about, or staggered from a saloon door towards one of the tipis set up willy-nilly between the store and the houses, wherever space offered.

French merchants in satin jackets moved purposefully along the boardwalks. Creole boatmen laughed, yelled or sang lustily according to their stage of inebriation as they worked among the boats or roistered from saloon to saloon. Two men in muddy buckskins trudged slowly up the hill away from the town, each prodding and roundly cursing a heavily loaded pack mule. A team of well-groomed roans harnessed to a closed carriage came to a prancing halt in front of one of the few stores with a painted façade.

The mid-morning sun sent the last of the rain clouds scurrying into the East and smiled down on the bustling confusion. It sparkled on the jewels dripping from the bright green leaves of the trees crowding to the edge of the bluff behind the town. It danced in the mud puddles along La Rue Principale, and reflected from the glass windows of the stately homes of the traders.

The gentle breeze following the rain was laden with the fragrance of wood smoke, the ammoniac odor of stable manure and the reek of untanned pelts in the warehouses. It also carried the ring of an anvil, the clatter of hooves, and a myriad of voices—gay, earnest, or labored—in French, Spanish, Portuguese, the gutturals of the plains tribes, and the occasional down-east twang of a Yankee.

This was the Village Under the Hill, the French Capital of the Mississippi country—Saint Louis!

Thank you for walking along with Gramps and me through the last century or so. He was a fascinating man of many talents and interests, and I have come to know him so much better through these stories and memories. I hope you have too.

Granddaughter Kristin Joy Harper on Gramps' lap, Pleasant Hill, CA, 1966

Endnotes

1   Tim and Dawn Patterson ministry, Campus Crusade for Christ 1-888-278-7233, *www.ccci.org*, staff #0038976; or direct at <TPatterson@eamail.net>

2   Image 3—Gramps directs little "Kristy" at Christmas, 1959.

3   Image 4—Gramps and Kristy decorate Christmas Cookies, 1968

4   Kristy and Gramps in a thoughtful mood, 1968

5   Throughout Chapter 2, italics are used to identify Stanley Martin as the speaker, whether from his autobiography or from his letters to family members.

6   http//Corozal.com

7   Image 15 is Gramps (Stanley) feeding the turkey leg to little Kristy Harper in the high chair, 1957

8   Image 16 is Mabel and Stanley Martin, showing good recovery several months after the 1957 auto accident that broke Mabel's neck.

9   Image 17 is the Martin Farms, No 7th St, Terre Haute, IN. Looking northeast, Ella Martin with Ray, Willard is up ahead. John J Martin/Eliza Wood Martin home is in the center; Frank James Martin house is further back. Abt 1905, Photo by Martin.

10   www.chicagohs.org/history/century.html

11   Image 18 is Gramps heading up one of many family Scrabble games—a favorite for all of the Martins.

12   Image 19 is four generations—Nancy Martin Harper and her dad Stanley Martin, Ella (Hockett) Martin and Nancy's son Robbie Harper

13   *http://docsouth.unc.edu/southlit/chesnut/menu.html* (A Diary From Dixie, by Mary Boykin Miller Chestnut)

14   http://www.annefrank.com/ (Website dedicated to Anne Frank and her history)

15   The Volstead Act was the Prohibition Act of 1919; this comment refers to the Prohibition years.

16   Gandy-dancer refers to railroad maintenance workers, a slang term. www.gandydancer.com

17   *http://en.wikipedia.org/wiki/Jack_Woodford* Jack Woodford was a pulp fiction writer, and more to the point, wrote an expose on the publishing industry, titled *Trial and Error*.

18 http://*www.archives.gov/national-archives-experience/charters/constitution_amendments* for Eighteenth amendment text.

19 Image 25 shows the polished professional and conservative look of Stanley Martin, ready for work. Photo by Martin

20 Robert ("Bob") Harmeson was owner of the Grand Garage, Santa Rosa

21 *http://www.tfaoi.com/aa/4aa/4aa340.htm*—Article on Hometown Terre Haute: Photography from the Martin Studios

22 *http://images.indianahistory.org*—The Indiana Historical Society holds a large collection of Martin photos and negatives, donated by Kenneth Martin after his retirement in 1976.

23 *http://www.monmouth.army.mil/historian*—When brother Willard taught at the Signal School in the early twenties, they did not yet have photographic lab facilities; however, these were added when Stanley was stationed there in 1926.

24 http://en.wikiquote.org/wiki/Benjamin_Franklin

25 Image 39 is Frank James Martin. A Photo by Martin, Stanley's daughter Nancy says that "Uncle Willard captioned this photo *Keeper of the Shop*, a sobriquet fondly given to him by the family".

26 Image 35 is the wedding photo of Stanley and Mabel Martin, taken in 1932, Photo by Martin Studios

27 *http://earthquake.usgs.gov/regional/nca/1906/18april/index.php* http://www.eyewitnesstohistory.com/sfeq.htm

28 *http://www.linecamp.com/museums/americanwest/western_clubs/transcontinental_railroad/transcontinental_railroad.html* http://www.sfmuseum.org/hist1/rail.html

29 *http://www.travelerstales.com/catalog/riverseast/intro.html*

30 http://www.indianahistory.org/pop_hist/people/gs_porter.html

31 http://historymatters.gmu.edu/d/5058/ Shares a 1938 text reflecting John Collier's work, Report of the Secretary of the Interior

32 *http://www.skc.edu/netbook/09-IRA.htm* Meriam Report outline, 1928 http://www.digitalhistory.uh.edu/native_voices/voices_display.cfm?id=93

Printed in the United States
101673LV00004B/344/A